COMMUNITIES AT A CROSSROADS

MATERIAL SEMIOTICS FOR ONLINE SOCIABILITY IN THE FADE OF CYBERCULTURE

ANNALISA PELIZZA

Theory on Demand #28
Communities at a Crossroads: Material Semiotics for Online Sociability in the Fade of Cyberculture
Annalisa Pelizza

Cover design: Katja van Stiphout
Design and EPUB development: Kelly Mostert

Published by the Institute of Network Cultures, Amsterdam, 2018

ISBN: 978-94-92302-25-0

Contact
Institute of Network Cultures
Phone: +3120 5951865
Email: info@networkcultures.org
Web: http://www.networkcultures.org

CONTENTS

FOREWORD TO THE 2018 EDITION

This book was written between 2007 and 2009 as part of my Ph.D. promotion.[1] At that time the reasons for not publishing it outnumbered the motives to follow up. First, by the time this book was finalized, the 2008 financial crisis was ravaging Europe. Some of the research centers with which I collaborated in conducting this research were discontinued in the same weeks in which I was laying down the conclusions. In such a scenario, this book was more likely to mark the end point of my research endeavours — as that of many others, rather than its beginning. Even when publishers started to approach me, I preferred not to indulge in what at that moment appeared as pointless vanity.

Second, at that time I was probably not fully aware of the importance of keeping a memory of the present. Being myself involved in some digital communitarian initiatives, conducting research was a way to reflect upon our collective grassroots practices in a moment when they were mimicked by commercial services run by multinational corporations. The attempt to figure out in what ways our practices and infrastructures were different from the emerging services prevailed over the thrust to historicize.

Last but definitely not least, as a young researcher, I was caught in the modesty of the witness. As Haraway has recalled, in order for modesty to be visible, the modest witness must be invisible.[2] It took me some years, several readings, and many meaningful relationships to realize that modesty and invisibility are a luxury that women cannot afford. I wish to thank Joy Clancy, Stefania Milan, Nelly Oudshoorn, Lissa Roberts - and more recently Evelyn Ruppert, Lucy Suchman and Sally Wyatt - for having nurtured this awareness. I am also deeply grateful to Geert Lovink, Miriam Rasch and the staff at the *Institute of Network Cultures* in Amsterdam for having expressed their enthusiasm in making this work visible.

So, why have I made up my mind and decided to publish this book almost ten years after its first release for academic purposes? A few factors led me to overcome my reticence. First, in January 2017 I read a *Wired* article titled 'How Silicon Valley Utopianism Brought You the Dystopian Trump Presidency'.[3] The main argument of this article – i.e., that Donald Trump came to power by cleverly harnessing cyberculture's libertarian myths and social media – was almost embarrassing. *Wired* was indeed admitting that populism had been boosted by social media and underpinned by libertarian credos. That *Wired* was admitting it was noteworthy. One could say that nowadays no one can avoid being populist, for the reason that cultural traits introduced by libertarian cyberculture are not recognized anymore in their historically situated genesis. They have become universal and *Wired* has had a major role in such universalization. Only an archaeology can return anarco-individualism, suspicion of institutions,

---

1   A. Pelizza, *Tracing Back Communities: An Analysis of Ars Electronica's Digital Communities archive from an ANT perspective.* Ph.D. thesis, University of Milan-Bicocca, 2009.

2   D. Haraway, *Modest_witness@Second_Millenium. FemaleMan_meets_ Onco_Mouse™: Feminism and technoscience*, New York: Routledge, 1997.

3   J. Tanz, 'How Silicon Valley Utopianism Brought You the Dystopian Trump Presidency', *Wired*, 20 January 2017, https://www.wired.com/2017/01/silicon-valley-utopianism-brought-dystopian-trump-presidency/?mbid=nl_12217_p3&CNDID=.

and techno-localism to their historical context, and thus trim their universalistic reach. To some extent, this book constitutes an archaeology. A double archaeology. I will soon return to this point.

Second, the *Cambridge Analytica* scandal is only starting to reveal the subtle mechanisms of manipulation allowed by social media platforms. For those who participated in the early 2000s critical internet studies wave, these revelations can hardly come as a surprise. Very early social media abdicated to their communitarian, peer-oriented roots, and reproduced the intermediated broadcasting model. It is thus worthwhile to recall — as this book does in its first part — the genesis of the Web 2.0 ideology in a period in which internet cultures were confused by the Dotcom burst and new business models were lagging behind.

This point brings me to the third reason for publishing this book now. The book is thought for those who have not lived the early days of the Web 2.0 hype, a cohort that has now reached the age of higher education. These are primarily Generation Z students and those who are interested in how the internet looked like before *Facebook* and *YouTube*. My students at a technical university in Northern Europe, for example, know about the mailing list culture of the 1990s. They also know about art and communitarian experiments in the same period. However, they know less about how utopian roots turned into ideologies that eventually brought on the commercialization of the internet, its geographical closure, and its securization. While the goal of this book is not nostalgic, it suggests that things could have been otherwise.

In 2018, a book written between 2007 and 2009 can be read under the lens of a double archaeology. On one hand, the 2009 edition encompassed both hegemonic and minor early digital experiences. From the here-and-now of 2009, it looked back to the genesis of network cultures in the 1980s and 1990s. In the second part, it compared those early discourses and practices to (at that time) current communitarian developments. On the other hand, this 2018 edition adds a second perspective. From the 2018-now, it looks back ten years, before Snowden, when Lawrence Lessig was committed to foster the Creative Commons, and when a book such as Goldsmith and Wu's *Who Controls the Internet* could cause a stir.[4] That was a time when peer-to-peer networks still challenged centralization attempts by big players. Many of those networks are analysed in this book. Some of them have ceased to exist for various reasons, some others are still active today.

This double temporality allows diving into digital communalism at different depths. The reader could approach it from the present tense indicating the 2009 now, and follow communitarian accounts as they unfold. Alternatively, she can retain a 2018 point of view and trace back current developments to that period of profound internet transformations. On a close look, these two attitudes may be respectively compared to Silver's descriptive and analytical stage of internet studies.[5] It is in order to keep this double archaeological lens that the manuscript

---

4   J. Goldsmith and T. Wu, *Who Controls the Internet?: Illusions of a Borderless World*, New York: Oxford University Press, 2006.

5   D. Silver, 'Looking Backwards, Looking Forwards: Cyberculture Studies, 1990-2000', in D. Gaunlett (ed.) *Web Studies*, London: Arnold Publishers, 2000.

has undergone mostly stylistic and linguistic modifications in its 2018 edition, with method-ological and epistemological chapters being shrunk for readability's sake. Data and cases are those from the original 2009 manuscript. When a note was added in 2018 in the light of major developments, this is clearly marked.

Communities at a Crossroads returns a multi-faceted picture of internet sociability between the two centuries. Almost one thousand digital communities are analysed here through their own words and rationales, as well as by focusing on the degrees of access and participation that their software architectures allowed. What emerges is a composite landscape made of non-profit and commercial, grassroots and institutional, deterministic and open efforts to articulate the tension between technology and society. Above all, this rather encompassing study of digital sociability shows that in the 2000s stabilization and innovation dynamics materialized in similar ways in textual and software artefacts. Today, one could say that this study anticipated the 'material turn' in Technology Studies, without opposing it to discursive accounts, but seeing them as complementary.

Annalisa Pelizza

Amsterdam/Sydney, August 2018

To my family, in whichever odd geometry it materializes

ACKNOWLEDGEMENTS

As the ANT teaches, showing gratefulness to all those who contributed to the course of action that led to this work could turn into a short summary of the pages that follow.

I thank Elisa Ribaudo, Carmela Torelli, Valerio Minetti, and Davide Diamantini at the 'Quality of Life in the Information Society' QUA_SI Ph.D Program, University of Milan-Bicocca. Guido Martinotti, my promoter, prodded my stamina in a risky but clever way. Tommaso Venturini was a study partner not only in Milan, but since our undergraduate studies at the University of Bologna. His lucid (and ludic) suggestions on handling large qualitative data sets were a moment of nimbleness amidst many doubts.

At the Emilia-Romagna government - where I used to work during the last edits of this endeavour - I am grateful to Silvia Pagnotta, Francesca Paron e Giancarlo 'Ambrogio' Vitali for understanding the needs and anxieties of a doctoral student. Thanks also to Giovanni Grazia for his suggestions on pc emulators for Mac OS.

I wish to thank Neil Hartley and the Leximancer staff at the University of Queensland for providing me with a full trial release of their software for research purposes. In 2006 Anne Balsamo (University of Southern California) and David Theo Goldberg (University of California at Irvine) accepted and facilitated my participation in the Seminar in Experimental Critical Theory: 'technoSpheres: FutureS of Thinking' at the Human Research Institute, University of California at Irvine. This was an amazing possibility to enlarge the scope of my research, and I hope these pages bring forward traces of that experience. Thanks also to the Annenberg School Center for the Digital Future, University of Southern California, for having provided me with a copy of their 2007 'Digital Future Report'.

I am grateful to Tatiana Bazzichelli and Antonio Caronia for their interest in this research, which brought about my involvement in the AHA mailing list. Within this network I had an early opportunity to publicly discuss the theoretical foundations of this work. I would also like to thank the global Transmission.cc network for having welcomed me - a non-techie - at their spring 2006 workshop, and for the food (for thought and for the belly) I was fed with at that event. Thanks to Agnese Trocchi, Andrew Lowenthal, and Andy Nicholson. A huge credit goes to the Telestreet network, and Orfeo TV in particular, where I developed my early reflections and doubts, which have found (partial) answers in this work.

I am particularly indebted to Ars Electronica and the Boltzmann Institute Media.Art.Research. in Linz for the interest they have shown towards this research since its inception. Notably, I wish to thank Gabriela Blome, Dieter Daniels, Katja Kwastek, Bianca Petscher, and Gerfried Stocker. The warmest gratitude goes to Andreas Hirsch and Ingrid Fischer-Schreiber, design-ers and coordinators of the Digital Communities competition, for their unique capability to conjugate professionality and friendship.

Those who will be patient enough to reach the end of this work will learn that the degree of heterogeneity of actors is an evaluation criterion for textual accounts. These acknowledgements should thus be a good text. There are long networks that have few opportunities to strengthen, and yet they are present, especially when made of women. In this work there is something by Roberta Buiani, Monica Fagioli, Ilenia Rosteghin, and Sara Zambotti. I would also like to thank Daniela Panosetti for her willingness to engage in scientific discussions, even in a field that is not her own cup of tea, and Francesco Mazzuchelli, for the precious support with 'computer science diplomacy'.

Finally, my gratefulness goes to the shorter networks. To Cesarina, Gino, Giuseppe, and Mercedes, for waiting for me. To Michela, who was there at the right moment and in the right way. To Giorgia, for her power in facing challenges that have the sole merit of having relegated mine to placid cabotage. To Ciro, with whom I have crossed these prairies for the second time. To Antonio e Anna, for having escorted me until this point with their great energy and entrepreneurship. To that assemblage of actual and potential elements that could be labeled 'I', for having kneaded the contributions of many with the yeast of curiosity.

Linz/Milan, February 2009

INTRODUCTION

'Digital Communities', a Shifting Subject

'To what extent is talking of communal ties on the internet meaningful today?' At the turn of the 21st century this question resonates with many who had taken part in the early waves of TCP/IP-mediated grassroots cultures.[1] With the 2000's 'Dotcom burst', the War on Terror and its privacy intrusions, and the emergence of the 'Web 2.0' wave, spontaneous online aggregations find themselves at a crossroads. This book investigates the conditions under which, since the early 2000s, it has been possible to re-launch a discourse on online digital sociability, despite increasing trends in commercialization, securization, and territorialization. Far from being ill-timed, investigating online communities today is strategic. Indeed, after the Dotcom burst and the aftermath of 9/11, on one hand, and the explosive renaissance of digital participation with social networking applications, on the other, the culture of digital communitarians[2] seems to have either lost autonomy in favour of giant internet companies and governments or been popularized and absorbed into the 'Web 2.0' hype.[3] [4]

The experiences that marked the birth and development of digital communitarian cultures until the end of 1990s have been extensively mapped by historical, cultural, and media literature. From cold-war academic research with its cybernetic decentralized logics, to early civic networks pursuing the democratization of information technology; from counter-culture's communitarian legacy, to virtual life on the *WELL*; from 1970s' and 1980s' early Bulletin Board Systems (BBS), to Free and Libre Open Source Software (FLOSS) communities based on reputation capital; from net art's focus on the aesthetic of interaction and underground lists like *Nettime*, to the encounter of media artists with the global movement for social justice which saw the emergence of *Indymedia*: these diverse experiences have partly overlapped and contributed elements to the communitarian cultures which crystallized by mid 1990s.

What came after the first internet bubble has received less systematic scholarly attention. This was partly due to diverse sectors and actors appropriating the landscape of digital sociability in the first decade of the 21st century, so that its boundaries became less clearly identifiable.

---

1   As mentioned in the Foreword, the research underpinning this book was conducted on a data set created in the period 2004-2007. Ethnographic observation and participation in digital media groups, mailing lists, and online networks started however much earlier, in 2001. With the exception of the Foreword – written for the 2018 Edition, throughout the book the present tense refers to the period 2007-2009.

2   With 'communitarian', 'communalism' and 'communitarianism' I do not refer to those political philosophies whose most influential exponents are Alasdair MacIntyre, Michael Sandel, Charles Taylor, and Michael Walzer, quoted by D. Bell, 'Communitarianism', in E. N. Zalta (ed.) *The Stanford Encyclopedia of Philosophy*, Stanford CA: Stanford University, 2016, https://plato.stanford.edu/archives/sum2016/entries/communitarianism/. Differently, I use these terms in their most mundane meaning of 'related to community', the goal of this work being to ask actors themselves what they mean by it.

3   Goldsmith and Wu, *Who Controls the Internet?*

4   H. Jenkins, *Convergence Culture: Where Old and New Media Collide*, New York-London: New York University Press, 2006.

While 'online communities' disappeared from the digital culture's agenda, articles about 'social networking sites' colonized high-tech magazines' columns; 'communities of practice' constituted the backbone of corporate knowledge management policies; and internet marketers invoked use of 'Web 2.0' platforms as strategic components of business strategies.

To understand the origins of a shift that has transformed the online communitarian landscape for good, this book begins by recognizing that the anarchic prairie of the internet has turned into a battlefield. Nowadays it is well acknowledged that many of the utopias that underpinned the 'digital revolution' have revealed their naivety, if not complicity with the established order.[5] The book shows some signs of this shift that have become undoubtedly visible in this first decade of the new century, when libertarian cyberculture that had nurtured a virtual communitarian utopia of peer networks – as means for the empowerment of individuals, strengthening of democracy, and achievement of social justice – has come to a crossroads. In the last years, free internet communitarian culture had to face three major threats: massive commercial expansion of internet companies; increasingly strict laws on intellectual property; and the proliferation of 'dataveillance' technologies related to the 'War on Terror'.[6]

By the end of 2000s, disenchantment about the use of information and communication technologies (ICTs) for collaborative production of knowledge was shared by many. According to *Nettime*'s moderator Felix Stalder, 'by now it is clear that something more than simple collaboration is needed in order to create community'.[7] According to Stalder, the aim of collaboration has shifted from community-making towards purpose-specific projects. Such conviction is shared by activist and artistic networks that reflect on state-of-the-art forms of digital aggregation. They are trying to re-focus the scope of online communities, while at the same time questioning the innovative potential of social networking platforms.[8]

The Crisis of Foundational Myths

Between late 1990s and mid-2000s, three main techno-libertarian myths had to face counter-evidence. These myths were based on the cybernetic vision of information technology as the source of a second industrial revolution that bore the promise of emancipation for the citizenry. First, in spite of declarations of cyberspace independence, it turned out that geography matters, and that the libertarian credo of an intrinsically ungovernable internet was an illusion. In 2006, Stanford's researchers Goldsmith and Wu depicted a more and more controlled and

---

5   F. Turner, *From Counterculture to Cyberculture: Stewart Brand, the Whole Earth Network, and the Rise of Digital Utopianism*, Chicago and London: The University of Chicago Press, 2006.
6   C. Formenti, 'Composizione di classe, tecnologie di rete e post-democrazia', in A. Di Corinto (ed.) *L'innovazione necessaria*, Milano: RGB – Area 51, 2005.
7   Interview with Stalder in T. Bazzichelli, 'Stalder: il Futuro delle Digital Communities', *Digimag*, 14 May 2006.
8   M. Fuster i Morell, 'The new web communities and political culture', in VV.AA., *Networked Politics: Rethinking Political Organization in an Age of Movements and Networks*, Seminar Networked Politics, Berlin, June 2007, https://www.scribd.com/document/118788762/Networked-Politics-Rethinking-political-organization-in-an-age-of-movements-and-networks.

territorialized internet. The 'Balkanization of the Net'[9] was the result of cooperation between governments and global internet companies, officially fostering freedom of networking. As a consequence, one of the pillars of cyberculture – i.e., the possibility that the virtual and the brick-and-mortar domains could be kept separate – began to crumble.

The second libertarian myth, that had to face the new climax of early 2000s, was the that of the emergence of a creative class: a new social class whose roots would lie at the convergence of cultural values prompted by the social actors that had led the digital revolution, on one side, and internet entrepreneurs' vision, on the other. The lifestyle and economic weight of such a class was expected to influence the global market as well as political systems. However, the Dotcom burst ratified the failure of the 'Fifth State'.[10] Even if the net economy did eventually recover from the burst, the coalition between knowledge workers and internet companies – that in the meanwhile had become giant corporations – never did.

The third myth that had to face a self-reflexive stage concerned the creation of digital commons. The digital commons, it was believed, would empower disadvantaged individuals against governmental authorities and business interests. However, while the openness of digital architecture – of code, practices, and standards – was a *condicio sine qua non* for the existence of the early internet, the question of how a digital commons-driven economy should or could distribute resources and wealth has long been a matter of dispute. The rapid diffusion of social behaviours and commercial services subsumed under the heading 'Web 2.0' is a perfect example. With commercial multi-user platforms and user-generated content, the rationale behind independent communities focusing on collaborative knowledge production seemed to have come to large-scale realization thanks to the corporate facilities provided by *YouTube*, *MySpace*, *Flickr*, and *Yahoo!*. However, as Lovink has pointed out, while the 'ideology of the free' has been pushing millions of people to contribute with their content to Web 2.0 platforms, there is a endemic lack of models fostering a distributed and decentralized internet economy.[11] No consistent distribution of resources corresponds to the 'cult of the amateur'[12].

These arguments will be further discussed in chapters 1-3. For the time being, we can anticipate that they highlight a set of contradictions between recent developments and key characteristics that had originally marked the growth of the online community paradigm, and of the internet as a whole. The Dotcom burst, the territorialization of the net, and the advent of Web 2.0, in particular, brought to light fractures in communitarian internet cultures. These fractures have been pointed to by scholars from diverse disciplines, who indeed wondered about the enduring possibility of communitarian ties on the internet.

---

9   Goldsmith and Wu, *Who Controls the Internet?*
10   Formenti, 'Composizione di classe, tecnologie di rete e post-democrazia'.
11   G. Lovink, *Zero Comments*, New York: Routledge, 2007.
12   Lovink, *Zero Comments*.

Scholars' Reactions to the Crisis of the Digital Communitarian Culture

By introducing 'network individualism', Manuel Castells and Barry Wellman have called into question the possibility of identifying communitarian relationships online. According to Wellman, portability, ubiquitous computing, and globalized connectivity fostered the movement from place-to-place aggregations to person-to-person networks. As a consequence, communities are not to be found in bounded groups anymore, but rather in loose networks.[13] Similarly, in Castells' 'space of flows' the individual is the hub of different kinds of flows that move from the place to the subject and vice versa.[14]

Rather than advocating for macro models, humanities on their side have produced meta-reflections aiming at putting order among the multiple souls of digital communitarian culture. Sociologist of culture Patrice Flichy, for example, called into question the existence of a homogeneous internet communitarian culture. He identified three principal imaginaries related to amateurs experimenting with information technology: initiatives linked with counter-culture and the hippie movement; hackers interested in technical virtuosity; and ICT community projects originated by civil society.[15] Differently, historian Fred Turner has traced the cultural origins of the U.S. cyberculture movement to the early days of the Free Speech movement. By focusing on spokespersons like Kevin Kelly, Stewart Brand, and the *Wired Magazine*, Turner has shown that over the years the libertarian, anarchist *digerati* culture has turned into open support for neo-conservative political positions, like Newt Gingrich's Contract with America.[16] As a consequence, those scholars who are more optimistic about the renaissance of digital ties based on commonality can be so only on condition that communitarian efforts get rid of libertarian ideology. Notably, media theorists Geert Lovink and Ned Rossiter have re-examined the notion of virtual communities as 'organized networks' and 'osmotic interfaces' that reflect society while anticipating new forms of social interaction.[17]

A Non-essentialist Perspective for Diluted Communities

According to many analysts, the crisis of foundational myths suggests that cyberculture utopias are facing the counter-evidence of both a more and more controlled and territorialized internet and of a newly new economy based on the exploitation of informal cognitive labour.

---

13   B. Wellman, 'Physical place and cyberplace: The rise of personalized networking', *International Journal of Urban and Regional Research* 25.2 (2001): 227-252.

14   M. Castells, *The Rise of The Network Society, Volume I: The Information Age*, Oxford: Blackwell, 1996; *Internet Galaxy*, Oxford: Oxford University Press, 2001; 'Space of Flows, Space of Places: Materials for a Theory of Urbanism in the Information Age', in S.Graham (ed.) *The Cybercities Reader*, London: Routledge, 2004.

15   P. Flichy, *L'imaginaire d'Internet*, Paris: La Découverte, 2001, see section 1.2.1 in this book.

16   Turner, From Counterculture to Cyberculture.

17   G. Lovink and N. Rossiter, 'Dawn of the Organised Networks', *Fibreculture Journal* 5.29 (2005), http://five.fibreculturejournal.org/fcj-029-dawn-of-the-organised-networks/. Note to the 2018 Edition: this early insight was further developed in G. Lovink and N. Rossiter, *Organization after Social Media*, Colchester / New York / Port Watson: Minor Compositions, 2018.

This seems to have consequences for online communalism. First, at stake is the correlation between access to digital networks and empowerment of individuals and communities. As we will see in chapter 1, such correlation lies at the core of the digital communitarian paradigm. However, with the rise of social networking services acting as intermediaries, the immediate character of this correlation cannot be taken for granted anymore. That uploading personal information on a digital platform, participating in e-democracy focus groups or keeping a personal blog would necessarily empower individuals and communities indeed needs demonstration.

Second, with the above crisis, the communitarian paradigm has acquired a paradoxical character. While this first decade of the 21st century is witnessing the diffusion of the virtual *gemeinschaft* well beyond *digerati* niches, counterculture or civil society experiments, this proliferation entails an ontological 'dilution'. It is by no means clear whether there exist ties that are specific enough to be labelled 'communitarian', and that could make up a special type of relationship. 'Community' seems to be diluted everywhere and yet it is difficult to describe what it is supposed to be made of. While communitarian ties enabled by digital platforms are more and more invoked, the internet is revealing itself as a more bureaucratic, controlled, and profit-oriented domain than ever.

As a consequence, scholars and commentators have argued that when the cyberculture paradigm – together with its actors and technical platforms – shows its limits, other players are likely to appropriate 'online communities' as techno-social assemblages made of specific ideologies, interaction models, values, rules, and technical protocols. Drawing on similar evidence but avoiding swift conclusions, this book suggests that such developments can constitute an opportunity to answer a still open question by means of empirical analysis: under what conditions is it possible to conceptualize online sociability in the first decade of the 21st century?

By avoiding macro accounts and linear evolutionary perspectives, the book answers this question by investigating theories of actions that have underpinned the development of techno-social assemblages for online collaboration after the fade of the 'golden age' of digital communities. It privileges the analysis of probably the largest archive on digital communities worldwide, and in doing so it returns a multi-faceted picture of contemporary sociability online. This outcome, however, requires a radical epistemological turn and well-thought empirical methods. In particular, it needs an anti-essentialist approach that frees the communitarian perspective from some of the constraints that pulled it into the blind alley anticipated above, further described in chapters 1-3.

In order to introduce such an approach, it should be recalled that the conceptualization of community lies at the very heart of the social sciences. It has been of crucial importance in identifying the types of society brought about by modernity. The evolutionist distinction between *gemeinschaft* and *gesellschaft* by Ferdinand Tönnies, for instance, marked the dichotomy between a pre-modern form of human organization based on emotional will

(*Wesenwille*) and a modern society based on rational will (*Kürwille*).[18] An opposition between pre-modern group solidarity vs. individual inclusion into a modern organizational structure was conveyed also by Émile Durkheim's notion of mechanical vs. organic solidarity.[19] Such a binary distinction between a supportive community and an evolution towards individualized networks persists also in contemporary references to 'community'.[20] Here, the term 'community' indicates social assemblages whose elements are maintained together by strong, solidarity-based ties, as opposed to weak, individual-based ties. In other words, 'community' is a 'substance' that differentiates a specific type of social aggregate from other types.

Following this tradition, studies on digital communities have often concentrated on the extent to which online collaboration could be conceived of as a 'real' community, rather than a simple transaction. Durability over time, regularity of the rhythm of interaction, presence of one or few shared interests were used as indicators to distinguish 'successful' communities from other types of looser social aggregates.[21] These approaches acknowledged as genuine online communities only those groups featuring *a priori* established characteristics like emotional investment, sense of belonging, active engagement, durability over time, and face-to-face encounters.

From an epistemological viewpoint, social research methodologists label this epistemic strategy 'intensive classification'.[22] Intensive classification proceeds by articulating the characteristics an item must manifest in order to be classified as a concept. As in Plato's cave, once an abstract 'Form' (*Idea*) of online community is established, only cases of online collaboration matching those criteria can be considered as its occurrences. Latour calls this classification method 'ostensive', and highlights its inadequacy to account for change:

---

18   F. Tönnies, *Gemeinschaft und Gesellschaft,* Leipzig: Buske, 8th edition 1935. English translation by C. P. Loomis, *Community and Society,* Mineola, N.Y.: Dover Publications, 2002.
19   É. Durkheim, *De la division du travail social,* Paris: PUF, 8th edition 1967. English translation by G. Simpson, *On the Division of Labour in Society,* New York: The MacMillan Company, 1933.
20   U. Beck, *The Reinvention of Politics: Rethinking Modernity in the Global Social Order,* London: Polity Press, 1996;
     Castells, *The Rise of the Network Society; The Power of Identity; The End of the Millennium;*
     A. Giddens, *Modernity and Self-Identity: Self and Society in the Late Modern Age,* London: Polity Press, 1991;
     Wellman, 'Physical place and cyberplace', see section 3.1 in this book.
21   G.S. Jones, *Cybersociety 2.0: Revisiting Computer-Mediated Communication and Community,* Thousand Oaks, Cal.: Sage Publications, 1998;
     A.J. Kim, *Community Building on the Web: Secret Strategies for Successful Online Communities,* London: Addison Wesley, 2000;
     M. Smith, *Voices from the WELL: The Logic of the Virtual Commons,* Unpublished Dissertation, University of California Los Angeles Los Angeles, 1992, https://dlc.dlib.indiana.edu/dlc/bitstream/handle/10535/4363/Voices_from_the_WELL.pdf?sequence=1&isAllowed=y.
     M. Smith and P. Kollock, *Communities in Cyberspace,* New York: Routledge, 1999;
     M. Taylor, *The Possibility of Cooperation,* Cambridge: Cambridge University Press, 1987.
22   G. Gasperoni, and A. Marradi. 'Metodo e tecniche nelle scienze sociali', in *Enciclopedia delle Scienze Sociali,* vol. v, Roma: Istituto della Enciclopedia Italiana, 1996.

[t]he problem with any ostensive definition of the social is that no extra effort seems necessary to maintain the groups in existence [...]. The great benefit of a performative definition, on the other hand, is just the opposite: it draws attention to the means necessary to ceaselessly upkeep the groups.[23]

Ostensive definition does not fit unstable social groups. This is particularly true of online communities. Despite their ostensive efforts, early authors agreed that online assemblages were transient aggregations where durability, stability, and order were exceptions.[24] Even when the social assemblage reached a sort of self-consciousness as a community, it was somewhat impossible to trace clear delimitations between the inner and the outer social space. In the WELL, for example, more than 80 per cent of the subscribers where lurkers: ephemeral participants rarely intervening in discussions.[25] This fleeting character of digital communities has only been accentuated by the above-mentioned proliferation of digital sociability in diverse domains, which contributed to its 'opacity', a resistance to being 'grasped'.

If internet instability is the norm, then the presence of communitarian ties needs to be demonstrated each time anew and cannot be simply postulated. Are there homogeneous ties that are peculiar to a substance labelled 'community'? Does the traditional distinction between *gemeinschaft* and *gesellschaft* retain its meaning? What is difficult – if not impossible – when researching online forms of aggregation is exactly individuating a closed list of features that are specific to communitarian digital assemblages.

In order to address this conundrum, the book proceeds in a different way than earlier studies. It does not aim to distinguish 'genuine communities' from 'simple transactions', nor does it postulate specifically 'communitarian' types of relationship. It does not set any specific social aggregate or theory as a starting point. For example, it does not begin with setting 'networks' rather than 'groups' as the best social assemblage to start with, nor does it take 'social networking sites' as the brand new machinery for social capital production. Rather, it asks involved actors themselves what they mean by 'digital community'.

---

23   B. Latour, *Reassembling the Social. An Introduction to Actor-Network-Theory*, Oxford: Oxford University Press, 2005, p. 35.
24   Smith, *Voices from the WELL*.
25   H. Rheingold, *The Virtual Community: Homesteading on the Electronic Frontier*, Reading, Mass.: Addison-Wesley, 1993 (2000);
     J. Nielsen, 'The 90-9-1 Rule for Participation Inequality in Social Media and Online Communities', *Nielsen Norman Group Newsletter*, 9 October 2006, http://www.useit.com/alertbox/participation_inequality.html.

In other words, in this book I prefer to adopt a 'Wittgensteinian'[26] epistemic approach in which a concept is defined *a posteriori*, as the result of clustering together occurrences seen as similar. This 'extensive classification'.[27] corresponds to Latour's performative definition. Concepts are empirically defined through recognition of objects as members of a cluster: 'they are made by the various ways and manners in which they are said to exist'.[28] Since they need to be constantly kept up by group-making efforts, digital communities cannot be the object of an ostensive definition, but only of a performative one: '[t]he object of an ostensive definition remains there, whatever happens to the index of the onlooker. But the object of a performative definition vanishes when it is no longer performed'.[29] Research dealing with the transient nature of online sociability thus needs to focus on how heterogeneous entities are woven together, and the means whereby they are kept assembled, instead of postulating the substance of community.

This anti-essentialist approach avoids defining beforehand what communitarian ties are supposed to be. Rather, it suggests to start from the observation of different, conflicting selections. To do so, the research summarized in this book adopts a bottom-up method that asks social actors themselves which theories of action supported their forms of online communality.

For this reason, this book is not written in the specialized meta-language of specific disciplines, but rather strives to adopt a language based on lay words.[30] Indeed, any preliminary classification based on the type of technology used, the type of social ties created or the shared interests and commons would get stuck in the necessity to define those types in advance, thus postulating concepts derived from other researchers, other disciplines, or from the market-driven digital hype.[31] Paradoxically, if we want to keep our feet on the solid ground of science, we cannot rely on other concepts but those provided by social actors themselves.

---

26 I wish to thank Prof. Dieter Daniels for the suggestion of this label during my talk at the 'Community vs Institution' panel organized by the Boltzmann Institute Media.Art.Research at the *re:place* conference in Berlin, 14-18 November 2007. One can find an echo of this way of proceeding in Wittgenstein's language games. In 1933 the philosopher introduced language games to his students as a technique aimed to address one of the major philosophical puzzles, namely the tendency to make questions about general substantives – 'what is knowledge, space, numbers, etc.?' – and to answer them by naming a substance. Wittgenstein substituted Platonic Form by 'family resemblance': 'we tend to think that there must be something shared by, for instance, all games, and that this common property justifies the application of the general substantive "game" to all the games, while, on the contrary, games constitute a family whose members display family resemblances. Inside a family, some members share the same nose, some others the same eyebrow, some others the same gait. These resemblances combine and intertwine'. L. Wittgenstein, *The Blue and Brown Books*, Oxford: Blackwell, 1975, pp. 26-27. Author's revised translation. Italic in the text.
27 Gasperoni and Marradi, 'Metodo e tecniche nelle scienze sociali'.
28 Latour, *Reassembling the* Social, p. 34.
29 Latour, *Reassembling the Social*, p. 37.
30 Notably, the terms 'digital', 'virtual', 'cyber' and 'online' community are used as synonymous. Similarly, we use the terms 'group', 'assemblage', 'aggregate' in their most plain meaning indicating a whole composed of heterogeneous elements.
31 The fluctuating meanings associated with the popular, market-driven label 'Web 2.0' is an excellent example of this.

Ars Electronica's Digital Communities Competition as Space of Controversy

Driven by an interest in recent transformations of digital communalism, and adopting an anti-essentialist epistemic approach, this book aims to investigate the communitarian potential of digital techno-social assemblages in the first decade of the 21st century, as it is accounted for by those actors who are directly involved. Notably, it inquiries how actors themselves account for the relationship between access to information technologies and societal empowerment, a relationship that lies at the core of the digital communitarian paradigm.

To do so, the second part of the book analyses theories of empowerment that have underpinned the development of computer-mediated sociability in 2000s. It draws upon research conducted between 2004 and 2009 on probably the largest digital communities archive worldwide. Cases are provided by the applications submitted to the world's leading competition on digital culture, the *Prix Ars Electronica* in Linz, Austria.

Initiated in 1979, the *Ars Electronica Festival for Art, Technology and Society* (www.aec. at) was the forerunner of 1980s' festivals on art and new media technologies, like *VIPER International Festival for Film Video and New Media* (Basel), *Imagina* (Montecarlo), *ISEA International Symposium on Electronic Art* (worldwide), *Multimediale* (Karlsruhe), *Next Five Minutes* (Amsterdam), *DEAF Dutch Electronic Art Festival* (Rotterdam), *Transmediale* (Berlin). As Bazzichelli has recalled, these events characterized the emergent phase of an electronic culture that was meant to fill the gap between humanistic and techno-scientific forms of knowledge.[32] In mid 1980s, engineers and computer scientists started to collaborate with architects, musicians, and visual artists on electronic art projects that required multi-faceted skills and know-how from both the technological and the humanities domains.

The *Prix Ars Electronica*, 'competition for CyberArts', was established in 1987 as an international forum for artistic creativity and innovation in the digital realm. The first edition included three categories. Over the years categories have expanded, to reach eight categories in 2007. Since the early days, an accurate selection of the jury members among the top experts in each category, the largest prize pursued worldwide in this domain, and pervasive media coverage characterized the *Prix* as a leading international competition in the field of digital media art.

Thanks to its yearly pace, its international scope and its leading position in the digital media art domain, nowadays the *Prix* retains one of the largest archives of media art from the last 30 years. Long-term archiving characterizes its treatment of participant projects. Textual and visual materials of all winning works since the competition's inception, as well as information on the winning artists and jury members, are collected in the open *Prix* archive. Furthermore, a closed database gathers all applications submitted over the years in all categories, including non-winning entries. This database represents an extremely rich resource to map the evolution of digital culture. As such, it is used as a data source for the empirical analyses conducted in the second part of the book.

---

32   Bazzichelli, *Networking*.

Established in 2004, the Prix's *Digital Community* competition is meant to focus on the socio-political potential of digital networked systems. It aims to acknowledge important achievements by online communities, especially in the fields of social software, ubiquitous computing, mobile communications, peer-to-peer production, and net.art. It acknowledges innovations impacting human coexistence, bridging the geographical, economic, political or gender-based digital divide, sustaining cultural diversity and the freedom of artistic expression, enhancing accessibility of technological infrastructures. As the call for entries affirms, 'the "Digital Communities" category is open to political, social, cultural and artistic projects, initiatives, groups, and scenes from all over the world utilizing digital technology to better society and assume social responsibility'.[33] The competiton is open to non-profit projects developed by governments, businesses, and civil society organizations.

The designers of the new category dedicated to online communities explicitly referred to four leading paradigms of early 2000s: the counterculture legacy, the renaissance of political activism in the form of the Global Movement for Social Justice, the popularization of the web, and the wide diffusion of collaborative patterns of organization.[34]

Despite this initial categorization, the cases analysed here have not been *a priori* labelled as occurrences of digital communities by the researcher. Rather, they have been identified as such by several expert actors. First, projects participating in the competition have been *said* to be occurrences of digital communities by the project representatives who submitted their application, or by the International Advisory Board who proposed some of the entries. Second, they have been *acknowledged* as such by the independent international jury who excluded those projects that did not fulfil the requirements. Projects which passed all these stages thus *became* digital communities, and are analysed and discussed in the second part of this book.

Methodologically, the Prix Ars Electronica's *Digital Communities* competition is seen as a peculiar form of controversy dealing with the acknowledgement of the most innovative practices of online collaboration and sociability. Controversies are ideal methodological entry points whereby it is possible to penetrate the inner workings of science and technology before they get crystallized into a black box. Situations where techno-social ties are indeed made visible and graspable are those where meaning emerges from comparison and 'polemic structures':[35] meetings, trials, and plans in science labs, distance in time or space, breakdowns and fractures, but also fiction, archives, and museum collections.[36] Prix Ars Electronica's *Digital Communities* competition thus constitutes an arena wherein the black box of techno-social assemblages is re-opened, contrasting meanings are made explicit, and the most innovative

---

33   Prix Ars Electronica (2004), *Call for Digital Communities application.* http://www.aec.at/prix_categories_
       en.php?cat=Digital%20Communities accessed 30 October 2008.
34   Andreas Hirsch, initiator of the competition, personal e-mail exchange with the author, 21 October 2007.
35   A. J. Greimas and J. Courtés, *Sémiotique. Dictionnaire raisonné de la théorie du langage*, Paris:
       Hachette, 1979. 'Polemic' define polemic structure as the dualistic principle (subject/anti-subject) on
       which any human activity is based. As they can be also contractual (agreement, cooperation, etc.) and
       not only hostile (blackmail, provocation, open struggle, etc), polemic structures lie at the core of any
       form of narration.
36   These situations are numbered in Latour, *Reassembling the* Social, pp. 79-82.

ones are selected by an internationally renowned board of experts.

Notably, the *Digital Communities* competition can be associated with a form of controversy in three respects. First, contests constitute a primeval form of polemic structure, an arena where meaning emerges from comparison between different projects. Projects struggle in order to be recognized as successful digital communities. Second, like controversies, competitions present some recurring elements like a spokesperson, anti-groups, limes, and accounts.[37] The *Digital Communities* contest is the place where online networks achieve representation: it constitutes the moment in an unstable process of social innovation when spokespersons must emerge and – together with them – self-representations, identity, and opponents. In other words, online assemblages are caught in the moment in which they struggle to crystallize into the form of 'digital community'. Third, to grasp controversies one needs accounts: agencies and actors are made visible into accounts. In this analysis I have been using as accounts the traces left behind by group-makers: the applications submitted from 2004 to 2007 by participants for the purpose of an award. Since the applications are produced in the moment when online assemblages fix the instant and take a picture of themselves, they represent accounts about what participants conceive of as digital communities.

Quali-quantitative Methods

Given the epistemological considerations anticipated above, in order to answer the overarching question addressed in this book (i.e., under what conditions is it possible to conceptualize online sociability in the first decade of the 21st century?), the Prix Ars Elextronica data set was analysed by focusing on how actors speaking for online communities describe the theories of actions underpinning techno-social collaboration. Three sets of sub-questions were identified to operationalize the main question for analytical purposes.

The first sub-question asked community spokespersons what they mean by 'online community'. To do so, concept profiling methods were adopted to explore the semantic elements *explicitly* associated with the notion of 'online community' in the submissions to Prix Ars Electronica. In chapter 4, the resulting semantic configuration was then compared to those of the early subcultures recalled in chapter 1. Furthermore, Wellman's well-established distinction between communities as bounded groups vs. loose networks was tested.[38] Chapter 4 thus attempts to provide a definition of online/digital community, as established by communities' spokespersons. It shows which paths have been abandoned in the first decade of the 21st century with respect to the original cyberculture: cybernetic discourse and its reliance on technology as a neutral organizational agency and the immaterial gift as a way to maintain communities as social homeostats. All in all, it shows that new framings in the 2000s have taken the place of the old 'online community', which do not necessarily distinguish between bounded groups and loose networks.

---

37   Latour, *Reassembling the Social*, pp. 52-58.
38   Wellman, 'Physical place and cyberplace'.

While the first sub-question analysed how online communities are *explicitly* profiled, the second did it *implicitly*. It indeed identified the most recurring and central topics, and narratives addressed in the data set. Here, no prior concepts were profiled *a priori* – not even 'online community'. Rather, as discussed in the previous sections, submission to a competition for 'digital communities' was conceived of as a performative act defining what this kind of techno-social assemblage is supposed to be. My aim here was identifying the matters of concern emerging from the whole data set, and related narratives. To do so, I extracted some concepts and narratives through quali-quantitative analysis supported by co-occurrence patterns. As discussed in chapter 5, those narratives only partially overlap with the discourses prompted by early cybercultures. Even when they do – like in the case of creative labour, public art, and social software – they articulate originally simplistic oppositions in more elaborated accounts of the peculiar mediation exerted by techno-social assemblages.

Finally, in order to map the different theories of action underpinning the digital communities participating in the competition, the third set of questions analysed the expected relationship between societal outcomes and role of technological artefacts, as it was laid down by communities' spokespersons. In order to do so, I conducted narrative analyses of fewer cases. By focusing on the artefacts whereby groups are assembled, chapter 6 describes the theories of action underpinning the rationale of prize-winning techno-social assemblages self-labelled as digital/online communities, and proposes a typology. Chapter 7 expands this typology by focusing on a different type of materiality, and looks at the possibilities of access provided for on the project's website.

The book argues that in order to conceptualize online sociability in the first decade of the 21st century, it is necessary to get over the foundational distinction between *gemeinschaft* and *gesellschaft*. It is only when the foundations of 21st century's social theory are put into discussion – notably the demise of sociability and commitment in modern technological societies – that it is possible to grasp and theorize contemporary techno-social assemblages. In particular, such a move allows accounting for the performative role of (digital and analogue) artefacts in upkeeping communalist efforts.

In order to achieve this evidence, qualitative and quantitative analytical methods were developed. The choice of the techniques for data analysis had indeed to take into account two main constraints. First, the high number of applications made the Ars Electronica archive unsuitable for purely qualitative analysis. Original submissions for the period 2004-2007 amounted to 1411. Out of these, 920 participating projects and related applications resulted after excluding blank applications and submissions discharged by the International Advisory Board and the jury as non-representatives of digital communities. I tackled the problem by planning two distinct analytical moments. The first took into account the whole data set (N cases) and used mixed quali-quantitative techniques provided by textual co-occurrence analysis and Boolean analysis software applications, while the second concentrated on a selected number of case studies (n cases), using narrative analysis techniques.

As to the second constraint, I needed to avoid *a priori* postulating analytical categories. In line with a non-essentialist, bottom-up approach, no hidden forces nor actors could be assumed in advance. As a consequence, when analysing the whole data set (N cases) I chose to use relational analysis, a method based on measuring how often concepts occur close together within the text. Concepts co-occurrence turned out helpful in addressing my main episte-mological concern: that *a priori* categories impose the reality of the investigator, rather than measuring the categories used by the authors of the text themselves. By using relational analysis, 'relevant categories' were defined as those that are most frequent *and* co-variate the most with other high-frequency words recurring in the text.[39]

More details about this software-embedded definition of relevancy – and the diverse ways in which software was set to answer different questions – are discussed in chapters 4 and 5. For the time being, it suffices to highlight the coherence and consistency of techniques for data collection and analysis with epistemological choices, as outlined in Table 1.

Epistemological assumptions	Choice of the sample	Technique of data collection	Technique of data analysis
Performative classification of digital communities (DC): DC definition is the result of clustering together objects said to be occur-rences of the concept. Acknowledgement as dis-tributed enuciative action	Objects of study are the projects participating in Ars Electronica's compe-tition. They are said and acknowledged as DCs by different social actors: the projects authors + Prix Ars Electronica's International Advisory Board + indepen-dent jury	Submissions exported from online archive as txt file with ASCII codification	Quali-quantitative (for N cases) and qualitative (for n cases) analysis of sub-missions

---

39   R.P. Weber, *Basic Content Analysis*, Newbury Park, CA: Sage Publications, 1990.

Epistemological assumptions	Choice of the sample	Technique of data collection	Technique of data analysis
Study of controversies 1) Meaning emerges from comparison and/or polemic structures. 2) Controversies and agency are made visible into accounts	1) Prix Ars Electronica competition as a form of controversy, a situation where meaning emerges from comparison between different projects struggling to be defined as successful DC. 2) Use of archived submission forms as accounts: meaning emerges also from distance in time	Navigation of DCs' websites	Profile analysis of websites

Table 1: Resume: from epistemological assumptions to techniques of data collection and analysis.

Structure of the Book

This book is composed of two main parts. Drawing on offline literature and online sources, including mailing lists and email interviews, the first part recalls the heterogeneous origins of digital sociability. Even if diachronic comparison lies at the core of chapters 1-3, this book doesn't intend to provide a comprehensive historical reconstruction of early online forms of communalism. A systematic history would deserve a research work in itself, and consistent attempts in this direction are numerous. More modestly, the first part aims to return the complexity and heterogeneity of cybercultures (in the plural!) before the 2000s crisis. Chapter 1 addresses the legacies of libertarian, civic, artistic, and activist utopias inherited by digital communitarian culture. Chapter 2 throws light on its aporiai, concerning both socio-economic developments and the politics of information. Chapter 3 discusses the arguments of those authors who have addressed the question on whether it is possible to talk of communitarian ties online today. After having discussed some of the ideologies linked to the societal potential of ICT, a few hypotheses on the current condition of digital communities in 2000s are sketched.

The second part engages in empirical analyses of contemporary forms of digital communities, and compares them with the literature discussed in the first part. Chapter 4 provides a first definition of 'online community' by explicitly exploring the elements associated with it in the applications submitted to Prix Ars Electronica's Digital Communities competition. It also verifies a hypothetical counter-argument to Wellman's thesis on weak ties by conducting co-occurrence analysis.

Chapter 5 identifies some relevant topics and narratives emerging from the whole data set and compares them with those prompted by early cybercultures. Continuing with a purely qualitative method, chapter 6 conducts a narrative analysis of the prize-winning projects. After a detailed description of all the projects that won a first or second prize from 2004 to 2007, it draws a map of the different techno-social theories of action underpinning those projects. Finally, chapter 7 suggests a system of classification for digital communities based on two diverse forms of materiality, while chapter 8 draws conclusions and proposes further directions of analysis.

1. UNFOLDING CULTURES

This chapter reviews some of the experiences that marked the birth and development of digital communitarian culture, as they have been recalled by scholars as well as protagonists themselves. It highlights some of their cultural features, and reviews a few categorizations developed to bring order into highly dispersed and multi-faceted experiences. Notably, this chapter suggests that many – although not all – of the 'memes' that characterize the culture of the so called 'digital communitarians' are rooted in the U.S. cybercultural, libertarian paradigm. However, when it comes to explaining how digital communities are maintained and reproduced, that paradigm falls short of convincing explanations, and anti-essentialist, materialist perspectives have to be mobilized.

1.1 At the Beginning There was (Allegedly) the WELL

Since long before the popularization of the web in mid 1990s, community-making has been a significant driving force for the development of the internet. Group-making efforts may not be separated from the infrastructural development of the Net. From *Usenet* to early *Computer Hobbyist BBS*, from *Fidonet* to *Free-Net*, during the 1970s and 1980s, hackers, university developers, and simple amateurs pursued the utopia of a bottom-up digital infrastructure where technical applications went hand-in-hand with group formation.[1]

However, common knowledge usually refers the first appearance of the term 'virtual community' to Howard Rheingold's homonymous book describing affiliations arising from practices of computer-mediated communication.[2] The book aimed to introduce cyberspace to outsiders, as well as to enlighten stereotypes associated with early adopters' subcultures. It described social relations established through the *World Earth 'Lectronic Link* (WELL) and other computer-mediated communication systems (CMC) from the 1980s.[3] As some observers have pointed out, in so doing the book performatively unveiled the link between the 1960s' counterculture and the cyber age.[4]

In the early 1990s, the WELL – a San-Francisco-Bay-Area-based BBS started by Stewart Brand and Lawrence Brilliant in 1985 – involved eight thousand people in 'online conferencing'. The system ran on a Unix-based software called *PicoSpan* and was hosted on a

---

1   M. Benedikt (ed.) *Cyberspace: First Steps*, Cambridge, Mass.: MIT Press, 1991;
    W. Christensen and R. Suess, 'Hobbyist Computerized Bulletin Boards', *Byte*, November issue, 1978;
    T. Jennings et al., 'Fidonet History and Operation', 08 February 1985, http://www.rxn.com/~net282/
    fidonet.jennings.history.1.txt;
    M. Strangelove, 'Free-Nets: community computing systems and the rise of the electronic citizen', *Online
    Access* 8, (Spring, 1994).
2   Rheingold, *The Virtual Community*.
3   Actually Rheingold's book takes into consideration also other kinds of 'virtual communities', like MUDs,
    IRC channels, Usenet and mailing lists. However, since I am interested in his unmediated account
    as a direct participant, I take into account his direct experience as a WELLite, a member of the WELL
    community. Other types of online groups will be considered later on in this section.
4   Turner, *From Counterculture to Cyberculture*.

computer located in the offices of the *Whole Earth Software Review*. Users had to dial in with a modem, log in, call up a list of wide-ranging conference labels and select the preferred topic to post on or start their own.

Actually, the WELL was a resonant case among the many forms of social uses of telecommunication systems developed between late 1970s and 1980s. Nonetheless, even today the cybernetic version of the *Whole Earth Catalog* is widely recognized as one of the primary experiences that contributed to the intellectual and organizational context that influenced emergent internet communitarian culture. As Fred Turner recalls, 'in its membership and its governance, the WELL carried forward a set of ideals, management strategies, and interpersonal networks first formulated in and around the *Whole Earth Catalog* [...] by counterculturalists, hackers and journalists'.[5] [6] In order to review the experiences that marked the birth and development of the digital communitarian culture, I therefore start from Rheingold's approach to computer-mediated sociability.

As a first-person account by a native informant, *The Virtual Community* aimed to introduce cyberspace to wider segments of society, to inform them about its role in political liberties and to throw light on stereotypes associated with early adopters' subcultures. While conceptually resonating cyberculture's distinction between life online and 'real life', virtual *persona*, and bounded body,[7] Rheingold's description reveals the effort to show the social thickness of the digital domain:

> people in virtual communities use words on screen to exchange pleasantries and argue, engage in intellectual discourse, conduct commerce, exchange knowledge, share emotional support, make plans, brainstorm, gossip, feud, fall in love, find friends and lose them, play games, flirt, create a little high art and a lot of idle talk. People in virtual communities do just about everything people do in real life, but we leave our bodies behind. You can't kiss anybody and nobody can punch you in the nose, but a lot can happen without those boundaries. To the millions who have been drawn into it, the richness and vitality of computer-linked cultures is attractive, even addictive.[8]

---

5   Turner in part explains the WELL's impact on public perceptions of networked computing as due to the editorial policy that granted free accounts on the system to journalists and editors for the *New York Times*, *The San Francisco Chronicle*, *Time*, *Rolling Stone*, the *Wall Street Journal*, among others, see Turner, *From Counterculture to Cyberculture* p. 143. For an in depth study of the social dynamics taking place in the WELL, see Smith, *Voices from the WELL*.

6   Turner, From Counterculture to Cyberculture, p.141.

7   For a classical example of the binary distinction between virtual and physical domains see J. P. Barlow 'A Declaration of the Independence of Cyberspace', 1996, http://homes.eff.org/~barlow/Declaration-Final.html. For a cultural history account on how cybernetics led to the dismissal of human body in the information age, see K. Hayles, *How We Become Posthuman*, Chicago: University of Chicago Press, 1999.

8   Rheingold, *The Virtual Community*, pp. xvii-xviii. Author's emphasis.

In Rheingold's words one can notice the endeavour to clarify to outsiders the social practices that come about in a domain perceived as murky. The author seems to be conscious of the stereotypes of those unaware of the assorted cultural forms that had developed in the computer networks over the previous ten years:

> many people are alarmed by the very idea of a virtual community, fearing that it is another step in the wrong direction, substituting more technological ersatz for yet another natural resource or human freedom. These critics often voice their sadness at what people have been reduced to doing in a civilization that worships technology, decrying the circumstances that lead some people into such pathetically disconnected lives that they prefer to find their companions on the other side of a computer screen.[9]

In this excerpt, Rheingold rhetorically (and critically) echoes U.S. middle class' suspicion towards artificial life and cold war's dystopias on thinking machines. 'Ersatz', for instance, is an oft-recurring word in Philip Dick's novels.[10]

In order to familiarize the broad public with online behaviours, the author suggests a parallel between the North-American neighbourhood-community tradition[11] and the culture of early adopters of CMC systems. Computer-mediated social groups could thus represent an instance of that 'third place' – besides the living space and the workplace – of informal public life where people gather for conviviality:

perhaps cyberspace is one of the informal public places where people can rebuild the aspects of community that were lost when the malt shop became a mall. [...] The feeling of logging into the WELL for just a minute or two, dozens of times a day, is very similar to the feeling of peeking into the café, the pub, the common room, to see who's there, and whether you want to stay around for a chat.[12]

Echoing the foundational distinction between *gemeinschaft* and *gesellschaft*, individual solidarity and institutional bureaucracy, traditional village and modern city, Rheingold introduces the metaphor of digital communities evolving into bigger concentrations, as small towns of few inhabitants grow into metropolises. Differently from real life, however, in metropolitan cyberspace the values rooted in the essence of human beings will keep having a crucial role, they will not be replaced by mechanical rationality:

---

9   Rheingold, *The Virtual Community*, p. 8.
10   P. K. Dick, *The Simulacra*, New York: Ace Books, 1964.
11   I cannot account here for the vast North-American sociological and urban planning literature dealing with territorial communities and sense of belonging. A classic reference author for this literature is J. Jacobs, *The Death and Life of Great American Cities*, New York: Random House, 1961. Rheingold himself quotes R. Oldenburg, *The Great Good Place: Cafes, Coffee Shops, Community Centers, Beauty Parlors, General Stores, Bars, Hangouts, and How They Get You through the Day*, New York: Paragon House, 1991. Section 3.1 will tackle sociological approaches that criticize the (somewhat mythological) association between local assemblages and sense of community.
12   Rheingold, *The Virtual Community*, p. 11.

some knowledge of how people in a small virtual community behave will help prevent vertigo and give you tools for comparison when we zoom out to the larger metropolitan areas of cyberspace. Some aspects of life in a small community have to be abandoned when you move to an online metropolis; the fundamentals of human nature, however, always scale up. [13]

For Rheingold, online affiliation does not only offer the possibility to expand individuals' social capital nor does it only enable weak ties: it can also provide a strong sense of belonging and communion among individuals who had never met face to face. This is inherent in Rheingold's definition of virtual communities as 'social aggregations that emerge from the Net when enough people carry on those public discussions long enough, with sufficient human feeling, to form webs of personal relationships in cyberspace'.[14] [15]Indeed, his account often remarks the emotional support WELLites used to assure to members (or members' relatives) in difficult conditions:

> sitting in front of our computers with our hearts racing and tears in our eyes, in Tokyo and Sacramento and Austin, we read about Lillie's croup, her tracheostomy, the days and nights at Massachusetts General Hospital, and now the vigil over Lillie's breathing and the watchful attention to the mechanical apparatus that kept her alive. It went on for days. Weeks. Lillie recovered, and relieved our anxieties about her vocal capabilities after all that time with a hole in her throat by saying the most extraordinary things, duly reported online by Jay.[16]

In other words, for Rheingold, communitarian ties are a specific, qualitatively characterized type of social relationship, distinct from other relationships. His key purpose is to demonstrate that similar, supposedly genuine ties can also develop online.

The depiction of supportive, informed, self-organized citizens, as opposed to political and economic institutional powers, is deep-seated in *The Virtual Community*.[17] Not only does the author foresee the 'pitfall that political and economic powers seize, censor, meter and finally

---

13   Rheingold, *The Virtual Community*, p. xxxii.
14   The ambiguity of this definition is manifest. One could wonder what Rheingold means by 'human feeling' or which amount of time or persons constitutes 'enough'. Actually, the main direction of scientific research on virtual communities has tackled exactly the measurement of 'communitarian potential', authenticity of online sociability as compared to face-to-face relations, and the elements that transform an aggregation of individuals into a 'genuine community'. In the Introduction, I have already mentioned some of the limitations of this essentialist perspective. For examples of sociological literature dealing with the features of 'successful communities' versus informal aggregates or 'pseudocommunities' (not only online), see P. Bartle, *The Sociology of Communities*, Victoria, Canada: Camosun Imaging, 2005; Jones, *Cybersociety 2.0*; L. Paccagnella, *La comunicazione al computer: Sociologia delle reti telematiche*, Bologna: Il Mulino, 2000; Smith and Kollock, *Communities in Cyberspace*; M. Taylor, *The Possibility of Cooperation*, Cambridge: Cambridge University Press, 1987.
15   Rheingold, *The Virtual Community*, p. xx.
16   Rheingold, *The Virtual Community*, p. 4.
17   Rheingold, *The Virtual Community*.

sell back the Net'[18] to the real creators, the grassroots communities. He also fosters the role of citizens in deciding how public funds should be applied to the development of the net. A clear opposition between two cultures of initiators of the net is at stake in Rheingold's pages. On one hand, there are the NDRC-funded top-down, 'high-tech, top-secret doings that led to ARPANET'; on the other hand, there are the anarchic, transparent, bottom-up uses of CMC that grew explosively and almost 'biologically' led to BBSs and Usenet.[19]

More than a political concern, however, this opposition can be explained in terms of diverse organizational paradigms. Rheingold and the WELL core team were suspicious of hierarchically organized institutions.[20] As Saxenian has pointed out, decentralized collaboration, and informal, non-hierarchical labour relations were the unifying element of Silicon Valley hi-tech industry's culture.[21] That same computer industry assured employment to many WELL members working in the San Francisco Bay Area as self-entrepreneurs, software developers, consultants, journalists, researchers. Rapidly, the WELL became the favourite online place for a remarkable variety of experts, thus offering access to information and social relations that could eventually lead to job opportunities.

From a broader perspective, as scholars have argued[22] mid-1980s saw hierarchical industries reorganize themselves as project-oriented networks. According to Turner, for people like Rheingold the new organizational paradigm found its roots in technocentric patterns of management that merged the 1960s' New Communalists rhetoric of non-hierarchical forms of cooperation with the cybernetic paradigm of decentralized control.[23] The centrality of cybernetic principles for the emergent network culture is evident in Rheingold's own words describing virtual communities as self-regulating biotechnological experiments:

> although spatial imagery and a sense of place help convey the experience of dwelling in a virtual community, biological imagery is often more appropriate to describe the way cyberculture changes. In terms of the way the whole system is propagating and evolving, think of cyberspace as a social petri dish, the Net as the agar medium, and virtual communities, in all their diversity, as the colonies of microorganisms that grow in petri dishes. Each of the small colonies of microorganisms--the communities on the Net--is a social experiment that nobody planned but that is happening nevertheless.[24]

---

18   Rheingold, *The Virtual Community*, p. xix.
19   Rheingold, *The Virtual Community*, p. xxiii.
20   In this regard, Rheingold quotes Sara Kiesler's research on how e-mail systems changed hierarchical barriers and standard operating procedures in organizations. See S. Kiesler, *'The Hidden Message in Computer Networks'*, Harvard Business Review 64.1 (1986): 46-58.
21   A. Saxenian, *Regional Advantage: Culture and Competition in Silicon Valley and Route 128*, Cambridge, Mass.: Harvard University Press, 1994.
22   See, for instance, D. Harvey, *The Condition of Postmodernity: An Enquiry into the Origins of Cultural Change*, Oxford: Blackwell, 1989; S. Lash and J. Urry, *The End of Organized Capitalism*, Madison: University of Wisconsin Press, 1987.
23   Turner, *From Counterculture to Cyberculture*.
24   Rheingold, *The Virtual Community*, p. xx.

He asserts that not only virtual communities are self-sustaining systems, but that – following the biological metaphor – they are also *inevitable* forms of collective life: 'whenever CMC technology becomes available to people anywhere, they inevitably build virtual communities with it, just as microorganisms inevitably create colonies'.[25]

Rheingold's understanding of computer-mediated communities reveals its debt to cybernetics from a further perspective, as well. Recalling the efforts made by cold war research to design a communication-command-control network that could survive a nuclear attack,[26] the author takes part in the popular belief that the net cannot be controlled: 'information can take so many routes that the Net is almost immortally flexible'.[27]

We shall see in the next chapter how this myth, among others associated with cyberculture, had to face empirical counter-evidence. Yet for the time being, I wish to highlight the cultural threads linking the emergence of the digital community paradigm with North-American techno-libertarianism, my main concern being the identification of some distinguishing characteristics of the cultures wherein the notion of digital community has arisen.

Rheingold's notion of community is debtor in many respects to the anarchic, libertarian cyberculture expressed – among others – by the *World Earth Catalog*, *Wired*, *Salon* magazine, and the *Electronic Frontier Foundation*. Proximity can be traced at least in five respects. First, Rheingold's distinction between online activities and real life echoes the *Electronic Frontier Foundation*'s effort to introduce in the judicial sphere the notion of cyberspace as separated from the brick-and-mortar world dominated by nation-states. Founded by John Perry Barlow, Mitch Kapor, and John Gilmore, since its inception the EFF[28] has mainly focused on legal campaigns devoted to protect cyberspace from government control, by extending the interpretation of the Constitution's First Amendment on free speech to the internet. One of the Foundation's major successes was the rejection by the Supreme Court of the 'Communications Decency Act' that dealt with the protection of children from online exposure to pornography. The Court acknowledged that the Act's provisions were unconstitutional abridgements of the First Amendment's right to free speech. The decision was sensational, as it prevented the Congress from extending its control over the internet. In the long haul, it was seen as backing EFF-advocated separation between 'real world' and 'virtual life'.[29]

The closeness between the early digital communitarian culture and the U.S. spirit of the frontier reveals why cyberspace has been seen as the place where not only individual liberties, but also communitarian self-government could be pursued out of government control. It is

25 Rheingold, *The Virtual Community*, p. xx.
26 Actually many authors, among whom there is Manuel Castells cited above, have endorsed this account. See K. Hafner and M. Lyon, *Where Wizards Stay Up Late: The Origins of The Internet*, New York: Simon & Schuster, 1996.
27 Rheingold, *The Virtual Community*, p. xxii.
28 For the analysis of the EFF's submission to Ars Electronica's competition, see section 6.3.
29 John Paul Stevens, "Opinion of the Court, Reno v. American Civil Liberties Union," Cornell University Law School Legal Information Institute: Supreme Court Collection, June 26, 1997, https://www.law.cornell.edu/supremecourt/text/521/844.

therefore not by accident that the reference to the 'electronic frontier' appears in Rheingold's work subtitle.[30] As Turner has argued:

> on the WELL, such terms kept alive a New Communalist vision of sociability and at the same time facilitated the integration of new forms of social and economic exchange into the lives of WELL members. Ultimately, thanks to the work of the many journalists on the system, and particularly the writings of Howard Rheingold and John Perry Barlow, *virtual community* and *electronic frontier* became key frames through which Americans would seek to understand the nature of the emerging public Internet.[31]

In other words, the WELL acted as a bridge that linked the 1960s' communalist culture with the emerging cyberculture paradigm fostering networked forms of productive organization and labour.

Second, the spatial metaphor depicting the WELL as a little town inhabited by peers finds its roots in U.S. local community tradition. As we have seen, Rheingold's social assemblage enabled by computer networks finds its communitarian dimension in the relatively small scale and in the sense of solidarity among peers. As sociologist Stanley Aronowitz has noticed, these two aspects are also present in the cultural legacy of the New Left of the 1960s-70s. According to Aronowitz, the New Left fostered principles like localism, individual empowerment, distrust in professional expertise, and direct commitment of individual citizens to political affairs. These same principles, in turn, came from the Jeffersonian ideal of a democratic system based on locally self-governed townships whose decisions were taken during public open assemblies. Similarly – Aronowitz argues – direct involvement and commonality among peers can be traced to forms of self-governance enacted by computer-mediated social networks.[32]

Against Aronowitz's argument, the parallelism between the New Left's localism and the notion of cybercommunity is indirectly put under criticism by Turner.[33] Even if he acknowledges the re-emergence of a strong sense of community in the 1960s, Turner argues that the communitarian tradition that ended up into the virtual community paradigm of the WELL was that of the New Communalists and of the back-to-the-earth movement exemplified by the *World Earth Catalog*. Even if common knowledge considers the New Left and the New Communalists as part of the same countercultural movement – Turner argues – the youth of the 1960s developed two overlapping but distinct social movements. While the New Left grew out of the struggles for civil rights and turned to political action and open protest against the Vietnam war, the New Communalists found their inspiration in a wide variety of cultural expressions like Beat poetry, eastern philosophies, action-painting, rock music, and psychedelic trips. This second wing focused on issues of consciousness and interpersonal harmony as means whereby to build alternative, egalitarian communities. Between 1965 and 1972 several thou-

---

30   The book's complete title being, 'The Virtual Community: Homesteading on the Electronic Frontier'.
31   Turner, *From Counterculture to Cyberculture*, p. 142.
32   S. Aronowitz, *Post-Work. Per la fine del lavoro senza fine*, Roma: DeriveApprodi, 2006.
33   Turner, *From Counterculture to Cyberculture*.

sand communes were established throughout the U.S., thus setting a sort of 'rural frontier' that should mark the way to 'a new nation, a land of small, egalitarian communities linked to one another by a network of shared belief'.[34]

Whatever the origin, be it an actual or analytical distinction, both the U.S. New Left and the New Communalist traditions shared an attachment to localism which remained a reference for digital communitarianism. This is true even when – like in the WELL – it is used as a metaphor for networked, immaterial proximity.

Third, Rheingold's understanding of two conflicting cultures of creators of the net, summarized by top-down ARPANET and bottom-up Usenet, echoes counterculture's rejection of 1950s' 'closed-world's.[35] At the same time, the culture expressed by WELL's members actually has many points in common with cold-war military-academic research. These two worlds share the cybernetic utopia of a techno-scientific anarchism oriented to downsize the power of institutional actors in order to hand autonomy back to individuals. As Mattelart has recalled,[36] in his 1948 work *Cybernetics: or Control and Communication in the Animal and the Machine*, Norbert Wiener postulated information as the source of a 'second industrial revolution' bearing the promise of emancipation for the citizenry. To realize this utopia, however, information should be allowed to flow free of any obstacle set up by those institutions that control media and whose aim is the accumulation of power and wealth. Not very differently from Rheingold's warnings against political and economic powers seizing the net, Wiener was concerned with the tendency of the market to commodify information as well as with the government appara-ratus' temptation to subdue science to military ends.

Fourth and strictly related to this point, another element that emerged among cold-war aca-demic think tanks and spread through counterculture and later communitarian cyberculture is the distrust towards forms of leadership that do not derive from reputation capital. Goldsmith and Wu describe the decision-making models of 1950s' committees of computer scientists as based on 'rough consensus' reached among expert peers, rather than on hierarchical positions developed elsewhere. Similarly, it is well-known how in digital and hacker com-munities, in particular, leadership is based almost exclusively on reputation built inside the digital domain.[37] [38]

Formenti suggests that anti-intellectualism, refusing educational degrees, and bureaucratic rationality as benchmarks of leadership echoes North-American suspicion towards expert

34   Turner, *From Counterculture to* Cyberculture, p. 33.
35   S.J. Whitfield, *The Culture of the Cold War*, Baltimore: John Hopkins University Press, 1996.
36   'In cybernetic thinking, causality is circular. Intelligence does not radiate from a central decision-making position at the top, where information converges and from which decisions are disseminated through a hierarchy of agents, but rather involves an organization or system of decentralized, interactive control.', A. Mattelart, *Histoire de la société de l'information*, Paris: La Découverte, 2001, p. 51.
37   Castells, *Internet Galaxy*; G. F. Lanzara and M. Morner, 'Artifacts rule! How Organizing Happens in Open Source Software Projects', in B. Czarniawska, and T.Hernes (eds) *Actor Network Theory and Organizing*, Copenhagen: Liber, 2005. I will address this aspect in more depth in the next section.
38   Goldsmith and Wu, *Who Controls the Internet?*

knowledge.[39] This aspect is related to the above mentioned decentralized organizational paradigm: in technological and scientific domains, reputation capital related to knowledge of specific issues has replaced forms of interpersonal power derived from class belonging or political affiliation, simply because they were not valuable in project-oriented networks.[40]

The fifth source of proximity between Rheingold's understanding of virtual community and the anarchic, libertarian cyberculture of the 1980s concerns the resources that are co-created by a virtual community. Rheingold identifies two kinds of resources: community for community's sake and information. The WELL is both a source of emotions and an information-seeking device bringing value to his professional life. By putting together a sense of common identity and professional knowledge, the digital community acts as an information gatekeeper:

> since so many members of virtual communities are workers whose professional standing is based on what they know, virtual communities can be practical instruments. If you need specific information or an expert opinion or a pointer to a resource, a virtual community is like a living encyclopedia. Virtual communities can help their members, whether or not they are information-related workers, to cope with information overload. [41]

The informal, unwritten social contract the author describes is a perfect example of homeostatic processes theorized by cybernetics. Utility originates from the acknowledgment that every piece of information forwarded from a sender to potentially interested receivers will be counter-balanced by other pieces of targeted information that the original sender will receive from former recipients. Given the marginal cost of forwarding which tends to null, the value for the original sender will outweigh the resources spent in producing value that benefits receivers. Like in a social homeostat, altruism, and self-interest go hand in hand.[42]

This cybernetic explanation, however, should not seem fully convincing to Rheingold, if he feels the need to add references to the gift economy:

> reciprocity is a key element of any market-based culture, but the arrangement I'm describing feels to me more like a kind of gift economy in which people do things for one another out of a spirit of building something between them, rather than a spreadsheet-calculated quid pro quo. When that spirit exists, everybody gets a little extra something, a little sparkle, from their more practical transactions; different kinds of things become possible when this mind-set pervades.[43]

---

39   C. Formenti, *Cybersoviet. Utopie postdemocratiche e nuovi media*, Milano: Raffaello Cortina Editore, 2008.

40   Saxenian, *Regional Advantage*.

41   Rheingold, *The Virtual Community*, p. 46.

42   This is indeed the way peer-to-peer (P2P) networks work. As it is well known, P2P clients operate on the basis of a contract embedded into code, according to which the higher your upload bandwidth, the faster your download.

43   Rheingold, *The Virtual Community*, p. 49.

Here, Rheingold implicitly borrows from anthropological studies on exchange in pre-modern societies where the gift is seen as a means for the establishment of social order. According to a well-known anthropological tradition, gifts originate cycles of exchange that result in the establishment of structural relations between givers and recipients.[44] This is possible because the gift embeds multiple meanings that ultimately work to turn material resources into social capital.[45]

In the case of virtual communities, resources are mainly knowledge-based and immaterial. As such, they are indefinitely reproducible at null or negligible cost. This peculiar feature of informational resources is of crucial importance for the emergence of the communitarian paradigm. If valuable resources – conceived of as gifts whose ultimate role is the establishment of structural relations – can be reproduced at very low cost, then the entrance barriers for setting up online relations turn out to be considerably reduced. This argument would explain the proliferation of online communities that Rheingold saw as a biological necessity.

What is noticeable here is that this explanation refers to elements which fall outside of the cybernetic paradigm. To explain how virtual communities proliferate, Rheingold must resort to analytical patterns borrowed from structuralism, which conceive of informational resources as currency in a gift economy. Here is where virtual communities à la Rheingold and its underpinning libertarian paradigm show their limits. In order to not only describe how virtual communities work, but also to explain how they are constantly upkept, essentialist references to a sense of belonging are not sufficient. The material characteristics of the resources being co-produced become key to clarify how a sense of belonging emerges as a result. As FLOSS[46] development communities are upkept by exchange forms which set code as the main currency (see next sections), so virtual communities are reproduced through gift economies which set information as currency.

In summary, Rheingold's virtual communitarian framework is not only rooted in, but also contributes to perform a U.S. cybercultural libertarian paradigm characterized by sharp separation between cyberspace and physical world, localism and/or cultural proximity, grassroots commitment, distrust in hierarchically organized institutions and professional powers, trust in technocentric forms of decentralized organization based on reputation, and homeostatic social relations. On close analysis, Rheingold's book can be conceived of as a rhetorical, performative effort to merge multiple cultural traits and experiences in a coherent account of online sociability, along the lines of the dominant U.S. libertarian paradigm. The virtual communitarian framework was crafted as pliable enough to allow this converging effort. Given this monopolizing attempt, it is not surprising that in those same years techno-social feminism

---

44   M. Mauss and W. D. Halls, *The Gift: The Form and Reason for Exchange in Archaic Societies*, New York: Norton, 1990.

45   P. Bourdieu, *Méditations pascaliennes: Éléments pour une philosophie négative,* Paris: Seuil, 1997.

46   FLOSS is the acronym of *Free/Libre Open Source Software.* It is considered to be the politically correct expression that merges the 1998's controversy between Richard Stallman, initiator of the Free Software Foundation, and Eric Raymond, promoter of the 'open source' philosophy as a business model. For details on the controversy, see C. DiBona, S. Ockam, and M. Stone, *Open Sources: Voices from the Open Source Revolution*, Sebastopol: O'Reilly Publishing, 1999.

issued warnings against totalizing technological narratives. Donna Haraway's *Cyborg Manifesto*, for example, was an ironic act against binary distinctions between the physical and the semiotic, and against holistic communitarianism: 'The cyborg does not dream of community on the model of the organic family, this time without the oedipal project. The cyborg would not recognize the Garden of Eden.'[47]

On the other hand, when it comes to explaining how virtual communities are upkept and reproduced, the communitarian paradigm falls short of convincing theories. Rheingold thus needs to resort to structuralist paradigms that originated outside the U.S. communitarian tradition. The need to resort to explanations that transcend the libertarian approach provides a hint to start delineating the main argument of this book. As we have seen, Rheingold's understanding of virtual communities qualifies communitarian ties in essentialist terms. In this chapter, we shall see how some of the libertarian assumptions and communitarian traits had to face empirical counter-evidence in the early 2000s. Instead of claiming the ontological death of digital communitarian ties, however, this book suggests that empirical counter-evidence requires as much of an empirical, anti-essentialist epistemological approach to digital communites.

Yet before that, we are going to see how other paradigms have contributed to the understanding of online communities through different classificatory attempts.

1.2 1980s' Internet Imaginaires as Attempts to Classify Early Virtual Communities

Being concerned with advocating the community cyberspace to outsiders, by mid 1990s Rheingold's effort had turned outdated. With the internet overdrive, GUIs and hypertext, CMC systems had become directly accessible to a much wider population, as the author himself acknowledges in the new edition of *The Virtual Community* (2000).[48] Nevertheless, many of the features that characterized the communitarian culture sketched in that early book were translated into new internet logics between mid 1990s and early 2000s.

Rheingold might be considered an exponent of that 'third layer' of the internet culture that Manuel Castells lists the 'virtual communitarians': users of the net who – while not being techies – nonetheless mould its uses. Castells adopts a linear evolutionary perspective according to which innovative behaviours percolates from élites to wider portions of society through concentric waves.[49] He also highlights the correlation between designers' culture and technological developments. In so doing, he has identified four hierarchical 'layers' contributing to internet cultures: techno-meritocratic, hacker, virtual communitarian, and entrepreneurial

---

47   D. Haraway, 'A Cyborg Manifesto. Science, Technology, and Socialist-Feminism in the 1980s', *Socialist Review* 80 (1985): 65-108. Reprinted in D. Haraway (ed.) *Simians, Cyborgs and Women: The Reinvention of Nature,* New York: Routledge, 1991, pp.149-181; p.151.

48   Rheingold, *The Virtual Community*, pp. 323-391.

49   Castells, *Internet Galaxy*.

culture.[50] The key concept underpinning all these layers – Castells argues – is the openness of the source code, as FLOSS has been the crucial technological element in the development of the internet.[51]

What Castells names 'techno-meritocratic culture' corresponds to the cold-war academic technological research mentioned in the previous section. It is characterized by the trust in scientific and technological development as a key component of the progressive improvement of the human condition.[52] The crucial features of techno-meritocracy are the pursuit of technological advancements in computer networking, seen as commons benefitting the whole community of researchers/peers. The object-driven nature of valuable knowledge; peer-review system for reputation building; attribution of managing functions to figures recognized as authoritative among the community of peers; refusal to use common resources for individual purposes and; open communication to the whole community of the results achieved through networked collaboration, are some of the features specific to techno-meritocracy.

According to Castells, these values have been well adopted by hacker ethics, the second layer of internet culture. Hacker cultures share with the techno-meritocratic paradigm the goal of technological excellence – which requires a peer review system for open source code; the intellectual freedom to create, manipulate, and redistribute technical knowledge; and the denial of money and formal property rights as source of authority and reputation; the values of cooperation, reciprocity, and a specific kind of gift economy, in which reputation is linked to the practical relevance of the gift (i.e., the innovative code) for the community of developers..

Castells highlights some distinctive features of the 1980s hacker ethics vis-a-vis the academic system of value: the independence of projects, the use of computer networking as the technological and organizational foundation for this autonomy, informality and virtuality as key elements in the process of identity building. He thus provides a more specific definition of 'hacker' than those proposed by Himanen and Raymond.[53] Hackers are

> actors in the transition from an academically and institutionally constructed milieu of innovation to the emergence of self-organizing networks transcending organizational control. In this restricted sense, the hacker culture, in my view, refers to the set of

---

50   Castells, *Internet Galaxy*, pp. 36-37.
51   As examples of key open technologies, Castells quotes Apache server programs, TCP/IP protocols, Unix and GNU/Linux operating systems, Mosaic and Netscape Navigator browsers and partially Java language.
52   On this topic, Mattelart, *Histoire de la société de l'information* wrote about the origins of the technocratic culture and of the same notion of 'Information Society', referring them back to Francis Bacon's *scientia utilis*.
53   P. Himanen, *The Hacker Ethic and the Spirit of the Information Age*, New York: Random House, 2001; E. Raymond, *The Cathedral and the Bazaar: Musings on Linux and Open Source by an Accidental Revolutionary*, Sebastopol, CA.: O'Reilly, 1999.

values and beliefs that emerged from the networks of computer programmers interacting on-line around their collaboration in self-defined projects of creative programming.[54]

Further elements characterizing hacker ethics are the sheer joy of creation that draws the
hacker culture up to the art sphere, and the political involvement in favour of rights such
as freedom of expression and privacy. We shall address the closeness between art, politics,
and hacking in sections 1.3 and 1.4. For the time being, I'd like to focus on the role of the
communitarian dimension, acknowledged by Castells as a key component of this second
layer of internet culture.

Castells suggests that in the hacker community the sense of belonging is indeed rooted into
an organizational form – although extremely informal. The co-existence of informality and
organizational mechanisms is made possible by technological mediation. Conflict and harmo-
nization are negotiated online through collectively-reinforced rules and, eventually, sanctions
in the form of 'flaming', public blame, and exclusion from the community of collaborative
software creation. Computer-mediated sociability and labour organization thus are deeply
intertwined in the interpretation that Castells gives of hacking communities.

The third layer of internet cultures according to Castells are virtual communities. They have
adopted from academic techno-meritocratic culture and hacker ethics values such as mer-
itocracy, freedom to use and manipulate technological artefacts, many-to-many patterns of
communication, *unus inter pares* forms of leadership based on internal reputation, and an
open-sharing approach to the commons produced by the community itself. Crucially, they
have also borrowed decentralized organizational patterns embedded in distributed networks.

In turn, this layer has contributed to previous cultures an orientation towards society-at-large,
thus watering down the focus on technology for technology's sake. BBSs, Usenet, Fidonet,
The Digital City Amsterdam, the Institute for Global Communitcation (igc), and the WELL,
shaped innovative uses and social practices on the net, although their promoters had limited
technological skills. According to Castells, while software-oriented cultures provided the technological basis for the internet, communitarian culture moulded its social processes and uses.

Similarly to Turner,[55] Castells recalls the cultural affinity between early virtual communities
and the counterculture of the 1960s: 'many of the early on-line conferences and BBSs seem
to have grown out of the need to build some kind of communal feeling after the failure of
countercultural experiments in the physical world'.[56] However, over the years – he argues –
the link was deadened, to the point that nowadays it is impossible to identify countercultural
heritage with digital communitarian culture. Despite this, Castells singles out two features
shared even by highly diverse online communities: the value of horizontal, many-to-many
grassroots communication in a world dominated by media concentrations, and a kind of

---

54 Castells, *Internet Galaxy*, pp.41-42.
55 Turner, *From Counterculture to Cyberculture*.
56 Castells, *Internet Galaxy*, p. 54.

entrepreneurial attitude to network, self-publish, self-organize, and induce new networks.[57]

In summary, while for Rheingold communitarian ties are specific types of social relationships characterized by a sense of belonging, Castells reconnects the origins of a sense of belonging to the decentralized form of network organization, which fosters individualism and entrepreneurship as characterizing features of digital communities.

The fourth and last layer identified by Castells corresponds to those entrepreneurs that in the 1990s fostered the new economy and led the diffusion of the internet to wider parts of society. New economy firms were a driving force for the expansion of the internet from closer circles of techies and communitarians to society writ large. At the same time, entrepreneurs, innovators, and venture capitalists developed – and were moved by – autonomous values, rather different from those of the previous actors.

First, the economic realization of the power of the mind was a cornerstone of the emerging Silicon Valley entrepreneurial culture. Second, large financial assets represented not only success, but also independence from the traditional corporate world. The stock option mechanism was functional in this regard, allowing the convergence between individual freedom and entrepreneurship. Third, money was a means to earn the respect of peers. This is were the distance with the other internet cultures described by Castells becomes more evident. While for scientists, hackers and communitarians the respect of peers depended upon the degree of excellence of the innovation proposed to the community, for internet entrepreneurs the financial market was the ultimate judge of the company's innovating performance. Fourth, while traditional Wall Street corporations used to create value by betting on future market behaviour, internet entrepreneurs used to sell the future which they believed they were able to determine. As a consequence, more than a full-blown business man, the internet entrepreneur acted as a self-fulfilling-prophecies vendors. Fifth, for the internet business culture the reward-system did not follow a deferred gratification model but rather an immediate hedonistic pattern of superfluous consumption accompanied by an informal working behaviour. Even here, the difference with the humble life style of hackers like Richard Stallman is manifest.

To conclude, one might suggest that Castells marks a clear distinction in the systems of value of excellence-oriented scientific, hacking and communitarian cultures, on the one hand, and of internet entrepreneurs, on the other hand. It should also be noticed that this point contrasts with Turner's argument, conversely stressing the seamless translation of the New Communalists' culture into the early experiences of online communities of the 1980s and, through them, into the internet business logic of the 1990s. As we have seen in the previous section, according to Turner the counterculture movement of the 1960s provided the emergent internet business world not only with a cultural framework oriented to informality and self-entrepreneurship, but also with new organizing logics derived from cybernetics.[58]

---

57   Castells, *Internet Galaxy*.
58   Turner, *From Counterculture to Cyberculture*.

1.2.1 Flichy's Classification of Online Communities

Another author who has stressed the debt of the virtual communitarian culture to the counterculture of the 1960s – although avoids extending the analogy further – is Patrice Flichy.
Flichy parts with establishing a diachronic classification of the different cultures whereby the
internet was constituted, and prefers to focus on the origins of virtual communities between
the late 1970s and early 1980s.[59]

Flichy distinguishes an understanding of information technologies seen exclusively as intellectual tools, on one hand, and their conception as instruments to be made widely accessible
to everybody, on the other hand. If the first understanding is typical of the closed academic
world, the second attitude towards networking technologies was fostered by computer programmers working at the margins of the university. Following Levy and very closely Castells'
definition, Flichy adopts the term *hackers* to indicate independent computer amateurs moved
by values like open access to information technology, decentralized organization, freedom of
information, reputation capital based solely on the excellence of the products, and trust in
the capability of computers to enhance the quality of human life.[60]

However, differently from Castells, Flichy does not limit this definition to developers, but
extends it to online communitarians. According to him, hackers can be sorted into three
principal currents: those involved in the wider project of counterculture and the hippie movement, those stressing technical performance (*hackers* in the strict sense), and those involved
in community projects oriented towards civil society at large. Among the countercultural
experiences, Flichy remembers *Community Memory* – an 'utopia embodied onto the first
technological steps', that started in 1973, whose goal was to provide personal computers
for all and a network of communication among peers; *CommuniTree* – a conference system
started in 1978 in the San Francisco area, aiming to build a community whose freedom of
communication should be inscribed into software; and the WELL itself.

The second current gets closer to hackers *stricto sensu*. Hobbyists networks were mainly
focused on technical objectives, like enhancing the capability to communicate at a distance
by means of computing systems. Here, Flichy includes the *Computer Hobbyist Bulletin Board
System* (1978) and *Fidonet* (1983). The *Computer Hobbyist BBS* was an electronic board
for goods exchange. Being a system for experimenters, the developers freely released the
code in order to enable other people to create their own BBSs as nodes of a wider network.[61]

Nevertheless, it was *Fidonet* that in 1983 realized the intuition of early BBS designers. Developer Tom Jennings released a software enabling the networking of two BBSs running on
micro-computers. Fidonet's architecture was based on the principle of maximum decentralization: every node was self-standing and could automatically communicate with all the other

---

59   Flichy, *L'imaginaire d'Internet.*
60   S. Levy, Hackers: *Heroes of the Computer Revolution*, New York: Dell Book, 1985.
61   Christensen and Suess, 'Hobbyist Computerized Bulletin Boards', quoted in Flichy, *L'imaginaire
     d'Internet.*

nodes, in a much more anarchist way than Usenet and Arpanet. Freedom of Fidonautes was limited by a minimalistic ethical principle: don't be annoying in order not to be annoyed.

As for radio amateurs, Jennings' goal was primarily technical: to create a 'non-commercial network of hackers willing to play and find new uses for data transmission networks'.[62] Yet Flichy argues that Fidonet – a project defined by technical objectives – turned out to be a social project, as well. Indeed, 'techies' and social currents soon diverged as far as the control of the network and the focus on content transmission vs. technical performances were concerned.

Differently, the third type of communitarian *imaginaire* acknowledged by Flichy explicitly looked at ICT as tools for community development. He recalls that the idea of neighbourhood communities using grassroots media to grant free expression to citizens appeared in early 1970s in the U.S., with the diffusion of public access cable TV and video. The *People's Video Theatre* and *Alternative Media Center*, for instance, were projects aimed at giving communities, especially the most disadvantaged, the opportunity to independently produce information about themselves. Video-making was conceived of as a tool for community development.[63] Similar projects aggregated around principles like universal access to media, refusal of mainstream media distortions, lack of top-down control.

Among these initiatives, Flichy includes the *Free-Net* (1984), *Big Sky Telegraph* (1987), and *PEN* (1989). The Cleveland Free-Net was founded by Tom Grundler, a professor in education, as a BBS focused on health-related issues. By 1989, it had turned into a multi-topic community network (the National Public Telecomputing Network) directly managed by the 250 community volunteers. Differently from the WELL and commercial services, the NPTN was not based on an information-pull model: free information was published according to the desires of the senders and not to the needs of the receivers. Additionally, the logic underpinning Cleveland Free-Net was that of the digital public library based on universal free access to knowledge. Like physical libraries, the virtual one was conceived of as a founding element of local identity and as a tool for the re-humanization of urban life.

Big Sky Telegraph's rationale was fairly different. BST was a network that digitally interconnected dispersed schools and businesses in rural communities in the West. It was aimed to facilitate community integration in rural middle-classes traditionally suspicious of big governments and big businesses.[64] Here, the distrust towards big powers echoes Rheingold's opposition between top-down and bottom-up digital networks.

Lastly, Flichy quotes Santa Monica's Public Electronic Network as an experiment in local electronic democracy. The PEN was a local municipality-led digital assembly where citizens, disadvantaged individuals, and local authorities could engage in open discussions. However, while acknowledging the communitarian scope of this early experiment for a digital city, Flichy argues that this network did not succeed in constituting a place for political confrontation.

---

62 Jennings, 'Fidonet History and Operation', quoted in Flichy, *L'imaginaire d'Internet.*
63 For a similar perspective shown in this research's sample, see the dotSUB case study in section 6.4.
64 Dave Hughes, quoted in Rheingold, *The Virtual Community*, p. 242.

To conclude, Flichy has suggested that it was at the early prototypical stage that the internet *imaginaires* were being constructed. Bypassing both Rheingold's converging account and Castells' materialist perspective, Flichy has proposed not a univocal understanding of online sociability, but a taxonomy in which early virtual communities can be classified accord-ing to three features: geographical proximity, institutional belonging, degree of face-to-face knowledge. As to geographical proximity, BBS, Free-Nets, and the WELL (mainly based in the San Francisco Bay Area) replaced the claims for universal, de-localized communication introduced by hackers and technology amateurs with a local perspective. As to institutional belonging, while CommuniTree was fully open, BBS and community networks required some formal subscription and a shared vocabulary as strong identity markers. Finally, reciprocal face-to-face knowledge was a very variable element, depending upon the dimension and regularity of participation.

Nevertheless, an understanding of networking technologies as tools to be made accessible to wider segments of population was a unifying element of much diverse experiences. And this is one of the traits that can also be recovered in the communitarian experiences of the 1990s.

1.3 The Network is the Message: Networking as a Form of Art and the Mailing List Culture of the 1990s

In addition to the early experiences discussed up to now, which are widely recognized as key instances of online forms of socialization, other kinds of computer-mediated social practices were developed during the 1990s. While contributing elements to the more recent under-standing of digital communities, new media art practices running on mailing list systems and political movements commonly subsumed under the umbrella term 'No/New Global' cannot be traced directly back to New Communalism and the North-American libertarian tradition. This is why some authors have preferred to expunge them from online communitarianism's genealogical tree. Differently, given this book's anti-essentialist approach, I suggest that includ-ing these experiences can contribute to a richer framing of online sociability.

With the internet overdrive, the graphic interface and hypertext, in mid 1990s the World Wide Web emerged for non experts as a powerful broadcast (i.e., one-to-many) medium for information retrieval. However, online groups assembled through decentralized, peer-to-peer technologies continued to constitute an important amount of the activities carried out on the internet. Avoiding the World Wide Web, these activities used to take place in self-organized digital environments, like BBSs, mailing lists, streaming channels, and internet chats. Only in late 1990s open publishing web platforms started being implemented.

Despite the diffuse efforts to devise business plans whereby to extract monetary value from the internet, many artists and activists kept looking at the net as a place for designing collective projects in a non-profit way. As Antonio Caronia has pointed out, the 1990s were years of coexistence where the expansion of freedoms went hand-in-hand with economic chances: 'the Net was seen as a means to multiply experiences, to extend freedom, to share. A space where not only broadening the opportunities for interpersonal relations was possible, but also subduing the logic of profit to these relations was feasible, without denying the possibility to create income from online activities, but looking at this possibility as the result of the logic of sharing'.[65]

Such a sense of potentiality was sustained by a peculiar type of coalition. It is widely accepted that the 1990s witnessed the alliance – however never overtly declared – between immaterial capitals and knowledge workers, libertarian capitalism and the rebels on the net. Formenti, for instance, named this heterogeneous coalition 'Fifth State'.[66] More than economic powers, government attempts to shrink the spaces of autonomous action online were seen as the main obstacle to the development of the net. The 1990s thus were a decade where TAZ – Temporary Autonomous Zones[67] – mingled with start-ups.

It is well-known that this phase of expansion woke up in the ruins of the Dotcom burst. As we discuss in chapter 2, the net economy burst not only killed the illusion of medium and small companies to compete with big traditional sectors, but also marked the end of the alliance between venture capitalists and creatives of the net. However, given their non-profit nature, this sudden awakening seemed to exert less influence on those practices of independent networking that were situated at the confluence of digital technology, art, and politics.

Actually, networked forms of artistic collaboration did not appear with the internet. In the 1960s' neo avant-gardes' experimental networked practices took place across distances, using traditional mail, television, radio. As Norie Neumark recalls, 'in the second half of the 20th century, artists turned communication media into their art media. At that moment art, activism, and media fundamentally reconfigured each other – at a distance. The projects they engaged with ranged from mail art to radio art to satellite art and beyond and between'.[68] Artistic and activist practices joined forces in the critique of communication institutions: 'many artists were concerned more with challenging the institutions not (just) of art, but of communication, from the mail system, to publishing, to radio and television. This challenge to the institutions of communication was a nodal point of connection between artists and activists'.[69]

From *Fluxus* to mail art, from *Neoism* to *Mini-FM*, the minimal common denominator was the possibility to experiment with art as collective inter-action where every actor was at the same time user and producer of information. This principle brought with it a radical critique of the artist/spectator distinction, the notion of originality in the art work, the same idea of individual author, and the distinction between amateur and professional. As Tatiana Bazzichelli has pointed out, these insights were subsequently inherited and further developed by the antagonist art practices of the 1970s and 1980s. By claiming the autarchy of media and the

65   A. Caronia, 'AHACamping: Le Trappole del Social Networking', *Digimag* 38 (October, 2008) http://isole. ecn.org/aha/camper/doku.php?id=antonio_caronia_-_ahacamping._le_trappole_del_social_networking (*Author's translation from Italian*).

66   C. Formenti, *Mercanti di Futuro*, Torino: Einaudi, 2002.

67   H. Bey, *Temporary Autonomous Zones*, Brooklyn: Autonomedia, 1992.

68   N. Neumark, 'Art/Activism', in A. Chandler and N. Neumark (eds) *At a Distance: Precursors to Art and Activism on the Internet*, Cambridge, Mass: MIT Press, 2005, p.3.

69   Neumark, 'Art/Activism', p. 12.

possibility to self-produce art outside commercial circuits, cyberpunk, graffitism, hacking, and squatting aimed to create infrastructures of communication that could be alternatives to those dominated by market logics and commercial content.[70]

In the 1990s this system of values and practices found full deployment in the practices of so called 'digital networking'. Artists, hackers, and activists seamlessly integrated nomadic media projects, decentralized forms of organization and critical issues as elements constituting coherent meanings and modes of action. International public discussion lists like *Nettime, Rhizome, Xchange, Recode, Syndicate* provided decentralized communication networks, open access policies, low-profile moderation, and media criticism.[71]

By freeing the artistic process from the one-to-many technological restraint of broadcast media, the internet came to embody the ideal of inter-active artwork creation and replaced the artist/spectator distinction with that of host/guest.[72] Net, ascii, and software art marked the transition from an aesthetics of representation to an aesthetics of interaction, from image and intention to interconnection and interaction. In these forms of art, the creative act was not oriented to the creation of objects, but rather to the development of networks, share procedures and protocols, and shared knowledge *corpora*. Art theorist Andreas Broeckmann has labelled 'machinic aesthetics' this new media art subfield located at the convergence of the social, the political, the cultural and the economic.[73]

One of the pioneers in this field was *The Thing* (http://bbs.thing.net), a BBS-based discussion platform that soon became a reference point for new media art and net.art. Founded in 1991 in New York by Austrian artists Wolfgang Staehle and Gisela Ehrenfried, in 1992 The Thing Köln and The Thing Vienna joined the network, followed by The Thing Berlin, Amsterdam, Frankfurt, Basel and Rome. As Marco Deseriis and Giuseppe Marano (founders of The Thing Rome) recall,

> in 1995, The Thing New York <bbs.thing.net> and Vienna <www.thing.at> migrated on the Web, thanks to an interface created by young Viennese developer Max Kos-satz. *This interface kept the communitarian features of the BBS*, providing members with additional chatting, comments posting and discussion list reading facilities. By gathering a rich archive of artistic projects, sound documents, radio transmissions, reviews, articles and interviews, over the years The Thing became a fundamental

---

70   Bazzichelli, *Networking*.
71   G. Lovink, *My First Recession: Critical Internet Culture in Transition*, Rotterdam: V2_/NAi Publishers, 2003.
72   E. Hobijn and A. Broeckmann, 'Techno-parasites: bringing the machinic unconscious to life', *Lecture at the 5th Cyberconference*, Madrid 1996, http://v2.nl/archive/articles/techno-parasites. I am referring here in particular to their understanding of net.art as 'techno-parasite'. Like a parasite, net.art endlessly migrates from host to host and net.artists homepages are constituted, in turn, by links to other artists.
73   A. Broeckmann, 'Towards an Aesthetics of Heterogenesis', *Convergence*, 3.2 (1997): 48-58. DOI: 10.1177/135485659700300207; A. Broeckmann, 'Public Spheres and Network Interfaces', in S. Graham (ed.) *The Cybercities Reader*, London: Routledge, 2004, pp. 378-383.

reference point for both the underground scene and the Avant-garde art.[74]

Between 1994 and 1996 other initiatives joined The Thing in offering discussion platforms on critical net culture.[75] Moreover, from 1995 onwards, this discussion could also rely on international mailing lists. The culture of the lists was originally born among university researchers as a way to reach agreement on standards and software development. Then, in mid 1990s mailing list software turned out to be adaptable to the needs of media artists, theorists and technology designers. *Nettime* (www.nettime.org) was the first mailing list devoted to the development of an environment for Net critique. It was founded in 1995 at the Venice Biennale by artists, media theorists and activists Nils Roeller, Pit Schultz, Tommaso Tozzi, Vuk Cosic, Kathy Rae Huffman, Geert Lovink, David Garcia, Diana McCarty, Siegfried Zielinski, Roberto Paci Dalò, and Alessandro Ludovico. In a few months the list became the reference point for the European digital avant-garde, with hundreds of subscribers. Net.art, public space, digital democracy, media activism were issues of interest. Among the goals of Nettime, was the effort to renew a 'leftist' European political agenda of the 1990s by fostering an approach towards ICT that overcame the 'Californian Ideology' as well as the cynicism of 'old media' intellectuals.[76] Further mailing lists focused on net culture were *Rhizome, Syndicate, Cybermind, Xchange, 7-11, Faces.*[77]

Media theorist Geert Lovink has introduced the label 'critical[78] internet culture' to indicate this 'emergent *milieu* made of no-profit initiatives, cultural organizations and individuals mainly

---

74 Deseriis and Marano, Net.Art, p.196. Author's emphasis. Author's translation from Italian.

75 *De Digital Stad Amsterdam* was founded in 1994, *Public Netbase* was born in Vienna in 1995, *Ljubljana Digital Media Lab* started in 1995, *Backspace* was founded in London in 1996. A detailed description of the rise and fall of *De Digital Stad* can be found in G. Lovink, *Dark Fiber*, Cambridge, Mass: MIT Press, 2002.

76 D. McCarty, 'Nettime: the legend and the myth', *EduEDA. The Educational Encyclopedia*, 1997, http://www.edueda.net/index.php?title=Nettime:_the_legend_and_the_myth (in Italian).

77 *Rhizome* (www.rhizome.org) was founded by American artist Marc Tribe in Berlin in 1996. It is now based in New York. On top of the newsletter, Rhizome has developed a Web 2.0-like archive for net.art works. The *Syndicate* (http://v2.nl/archive/organizations/syndicate/) mailing list was founded by media art critics Inke Arns and Andreas Broeckmann in 1996 as a branch of the V2_East initiative aiming at involving new media art professionals active in East and West Europe in a common discussion space. This list witnessed the controversies arisen during the war for Kosovo and was closed in 2001 under attacks by trolls and net.artists. *Cybermind* was founded in 1994 with a focus on online identity construction: arguments spanned from French theory to Mud and Moo, from cybersex to the theory of films. It closed down during US invasion of Iraq in spring 2003 because of overwhelming tensions arisen from national identity-related controversies. *Xchange* was initiated in 1997 as a no-profit, independent network experimenting grassroots solutions for internet streaming. For an extended account on international networking platforms and mailing lists, see Deseriis and Marano, *Net.Art.*

78 Lovink, *My First Recession*, p. 11 of Italian edition. *Author's translation from Italian*. With 'critical' Lovink did not refer to continental critical theory developed by the Frankfurt School, but rather to an intellectual practice that pushed internet cultures to root in more solid ground than the 1990s' hype. '"Critique", in this contest, refers to the urgent need to reflect and think, combined with action. In the 1990s many felt that taking action was essential in order to contrast an emphatic information obsessed by slogans. What was needed was an informed discourse that could transcend daily slogans and combine a diffuse orientation towards the public, free software, and open standards with a self-critical understanding of economy and of the role of culture in the building of the "net society"'.

based in Europe, United States, Canada and Australia and in an increasing number of other countries [...] that lies at the crossroads between visual art, social movements, pop culture, journalism and academic research.'[79] It is this inter-sectoriality that characterizes critical internet culture. Its goals pertain to artistic practice as much as to a critique of media institutions, to political activism as much as to technological design. On one hand, critical media culture aimed to establish long-term media infrastructures independent from mainstream media corporations and governments. On the other hand, it aimed to directly intervene in the early phases of technological innovation. It reversed engineer network architectures and their code, software-designed social relations and their technical standards.

While its attention to decentralized, self-organized platforms – coupled with a challenge to communication institutions – overlaps with earlier experiences described in the previous sections, Lovink is reluctant to describe critical internet culture as digital communitarianism. This is mainly due to his suspicion towards the idea of harmony, consensus and order entailed by the term 'community'. This rejection of an essentialist vision of community is shared by this author. Nevertheless, I suggest that contemporary understanding of digital communities is deeply in debt to media art platforms, which blurred artist and spectator, amateurs and professionals. Those experiences constituted the link translating the avant-garde critique of authorship into the emerging digital realm. Many present-day community initiatives analysed in the second part of this book could not be understood without the move from an aesthetic of representation to an aesthetic of interaction brought about by 1990s media art experimentations.

1.4 Mediactivism and the Early Web Platforms for Open Publishing

In early 2000s, mailing lists' techno-political agenda integrating political, media and artistic critique witnessed the emergence of a new collective actor. As American film professor and activist Dee Dee Halleck pointed out, from the so called 'battle of Seattle' onwards, a growing number of world-spanning appointments ratified the welding of two currents that up to that moment had rarely met. During the protests in Seattle, Davos, Geneva, Nice, Genoa and Prague, the anti-neoliberist movement for social justice and the alternative media scene integrated their agendas, thus setting the bases for the birth of a globally widespread network of Independent Media Centres (IMC or *Indymedia*).[80]

The hybrid movement that emerged to worldwide visibility in 1999's rallies showed the common will to resist neo-liberalist policies imposed by Western countries on developing ones. One further unifying trait was the capability to gain global visibility starting from grassroots conditions by 'tactically' using media and the internet.[81] 'Don't hate the media, become the

79   Lovink , *My First Recession*, p. 32.
80   D. D. Halleck, 'Una tempesta coinvolgente: Il cyber-forum aperto Indymedia', in M. Pasquinelli (ed.) *Media Activism. Strategie e pratiche della comunicazione indipendente*, Roma: DeriveApprodi, 2002.
81   M. Pasquinelli (ed.) *Media Activism: Strategie e pratiche della comunicazione indipendente,* Roma: DeriveApprodi, 2002.

media' soon became the motto of Independent Media Centres.

Multiple cultural strands contributed to the *Indymedia* experience, and to early-2000s media activism in general: *World Social Forum* activists and pirate radios, hackers and journalists, fanzine editors, and artists from the punk scene. As Pasquinelli has observed, early century's media activism was constituted along 'two geopolitical faults – the Latin and the Anglo-Saxon – that collide in the global scene of independent communication [...] Media activism explodes at the junction of Internet and Seattle, at the convergence of self-organized networked information with the global movement network'.[82]

For many commentators, media activism constituted the encounter between two different attitudes towards bottom-up media, namely the second and third type of online community identified by Flichy as 'techno-narcissism'[83] of the *techies* – programmers, hackers, media designers, and the technological naivety of local community networks, mainly from the so called 'Global South'.

Concerning the use of technologies, media activism reproposed Fluxus's 'intermedia' practices that used to combine different media and languages.[84] Often under precarious conditions, mediactivists produced grassroots information by combining low- and high-resolution media: web radio and podcasts, video streaming and FM microradios, open channels and communitarian televisions, satellite transponders and weblogs.[85] For example, the anti-WTO protests in Seattle were both TV-broadcast by *Deep Dish TV*, an independent satellite video network founded in mid 1980s by U.S. artists, activists and academics and web-cast by the Indymedia website using FLOSS software *Active* developed by the *Catalyst* community in Sidney.[86] [87]

The Indymedia web platform developed by Catalyst was particularly flexible and scalable: contents were automatically ordered by the software, the news section was constantly updated and the publishing system was open to everyone's contribution. While new users could consult a web guide to get started with video editing and news publishing, members of the nodes used to coordinate through public mailing lists and Internet-Relay-Chat (IRC) channels. As a matter of fact, Indymedia's adoption of an open publishing web platform, sustained by mailing lists and IRC channels, anticipated the massive advent of weblogs in mid 2000s.

---

82 Pasquinelli, *Media Activism*, p. 10.
83 Flichy, *L'imaginaire d'Internet*.
84 Bazzichelli. *Networking*.
85 A. Pelizza, 'Dall'Auditel al General Intellect. Un modello evolutivo del pubblico televisivo', in P. Adamoli, and M. Marinelli (eds) *Comunicazione, media e società. Premio Baskerville 'Mauro Wolf' 2004*, Bologna: Baskerville, 2005; 'Comunicare l'immediatezza: Una televisione dal basso a Rotterdam' [Communicating Immediacy: A grassroots TV broadcaster in Rotterdam], *Inchiesta. Rivista di Studi Politici* 152 April/June (2006): 12-18.
86 For a reconstruction of the history of Indymedia's Weblog and the *Active* software, see G. Meikle, *Future Active*, Sydney: Pluto Press Australia, 2002.
87 J. Drew, 'From the Gulf War to the Battle of Seattle: Building an International Alternative Media Network', in A. Chandler and N. Neumark (eds) *At a Distance*.

Thanks to their capacity to organize collective activity through web platforms, between 1999 and 2003 Independent Media Centres established themselves as models for multi-media production, as well as actual examples of decentralized organization and online consensus building. The global network of local IMCs was run according to some principles typical of hacker ethics: decentralization, self-management of autonomous local collectives, do-it-your-self (DIY) attitude towards media and technology at large, free access to information and free, and collaborative knowledge sharing.

Many organizations started using Indymedia software to coordinate protests. During the 2001 G8 rallies in Genoa, for instance, the constellation of self-organized, grassroots media gathered through Indymedia Italy acted as the principal source for information also for mainstream broadcast media. As a consequence, the visibility of the digitally-mediated global movement triggered the interest of political studies, as well.[88]

Their ability to provide actual models of grassroots collective organization and online consensus building by using open web publishing platforms suggests including Indymedia and the media activist movement into the composite landscape of communities aggregating through the internet. As Andreas Hirsch, the designer of the *Prix Ars Electronica* Digital Communities competition, has suggested:

> the basic ideas of the internet about 'giving' and 'taking' are not only present on the meme level, but are also coded into the basic protocol architecture of the internet. It would probably be bold to argue that the 'basis' of such protocols shapes the thoughts of users, but to a certain degree it might, if certain other factors come to help. Among those 'other' factors I see the drastic increase in usership of the net between the 1990s and today, a backswing away from the neoliberal ideology together with a certain renaissance of leftist positions, the anti-globalization movement and an entirely new generation of users, who grew up with computers. [89]

Despite these developments, over the last years the 'second super-power' (as the *New York Times* called the anti-war media-activist movement in March 2003, after the global rallies against the war in Iraq) proved to be unable to exert significant influence on international political choices made by the US-UK coalition. On the contrary, the new measures associated with the 'War on Terror' marked the strengthening of control over internet by governments. As a matter of fact, in mid 2000s the neo-anarchic grassroots credo (or better, credos) looking at the internet as a major channel for the liberation of individuals, the enforcement of democracy and social justice, the proliferation of critical communities or simply the creation of supportive ties on the net was at a crossroads, as we are going to discuss in the next chapter.

---

88   Della Porta, D. et al. (2006), 'Searching the Net: An Analysis of the Democratic Use of Internet by 266 Social Movement Organizations. WP 2', *Democracy in Europe and the Mobilization of Society Research Project*, http://demos.iue.it/PDFfiles/PressReleaseMay06.pdf.

89   Personal e-mail exchange with the author, 28 September 2007.

2. FROM THE PRAIRIE TO THE BATTLEFIELD

If there is a decision to be made,
and an enemy to be singled out,
it's the techno-libertarian religion of the "free".[1]

Despite a general agreement among scholars about the historical experiences that marked the birth and development of the digital communitarian paradigm, in the last sections of the previous chapter, I suggested broadening the scope of experiences that contributed to digital communitarianism. As a matter of fact, in late 2000s the understanding of digital community has spread to so many domains that one might wonder whether it retains some semantic value, whether it is still possible to distinguish a particular essence behind the label 'online community'.

In chapter 3 we shall engage with a few authors who tried to answer this question. Before that, however, in order to understand some aspects of this dilution, we need first to recognize how the internet anarchic prairie has turned into a battlefield, a conflictual field not very different from the brick-and-mortar world. My argument is that over the recent years libertarian cyberculture that nurtured the virtual communitarian utopia came to a crossroads. Since early 2000s, many of the beliefs that the digital communitarians inherited from cyberculture have either revealed their inconsistency or had to face empirical counter-evidence. This chapter confutes, in particular, three myths: the coalition between creative and economic actors, the uncontrollability of the internet, and its freedom from commercial dynamics.

2.1 The Dotcom Burst and the Crisis of the Creatives-Internet Entrepreneurs Coalition

The first communitarian myth that had to face the new climax of early 2000s was the one associated with the emergence of an autonomous creative class. It was believed that their lifestyle and economic weight could influence global markets towards informal and more equal organization of labour and production. Politically too, they would perhaps push towards post-democratic forms of direct participation.

Let's follow the genesis of this myth. As we have seen in the previous chapter, in mid 1990s' net culture, leftists' positions tended to coexist and share resources with neo-liberalist agendas. This coexistence is reflected by the literature on 'immaterial work'.[2] Over the years, actors who led the digital revolution have been called alternatively 'creative class', 'hacker class',

---

1   Lovink and Rossiter, 'Dawn of the Organized Networks'.
2   E. Rullani, 'Lavoro immateriale e società della conoscenza', in Gosetti G. (ed.), *Il lavoro: condizioni, problemi, sfide*, Angeli, Milan 2011, pp.13-34. Rullani defines 'immaterial work' as 'cognitive and explorative work that produces knowledge. Modern work is both self-organizer (it moulds a subjectivity which is self-generated through experience) and reflexive (it is done by human beings who are, above all, in search for a meaning). [...] [Cognitive work's] role consists in explaining the growing complexity of life and production'.

'creative workers', 'cognitarians'.[3] While these labels share some common traits as to the new relevance of knowledge-related assets, they quite differ as far as their rationales are concerned.

According to Richard Florida, the creative class is an emerging subject whose power lies in its capacity to produce knowledge.[4] His argument is based on two assumptions: that techno-economic innovation is more and more fed by artistic creativity, and that knowledge-based capitalism is pushed to extend its scope in order to grasp the creative potential of those social actors who were at the margins of the old system of production. According to this argument, the new class does not own nor control material means of production, but rather bases its economic power on the immaterial capital of the mind. Furthermore, in Florida's argument internet companies' executives are themselves part of the creative class. As a consequence, the conflict between capital and labour is reduced to the tensions between creativity and organization, informality and old hierarchies.

Differently, Wark's hacker class includes creative workers that have been expropriated of their own immaterial means of production.[5] According to this perspective, internet companies, the cultural industry, and telcos executives belong to a distinct 'vector class' which founds its economic power on a system that struggles to extend intellectual property rights to all forms of immaterial production. By extending the intellectual property regime with help from the juridical apparatus, the vector class reduces immaterial commons into goods, thus producing that principle of scarcity which is necessary to the proliferation of the capitalistic market. By conceiving of the hacker class as a by-product of this process, Wark's argument proposed an (at that time) original elaboration of the Marxist opposition between capital and labour.

Florida's and Wark's divergent perspectives as to the ownership of immaterial means of production and intellectual property reflect the coexistence of different souls in the internet cultures of mid and late 1990s.[6] This coexistence was made feasible first of all by a cultural compatibility. In mid 1990s, the internet perfectly fitted the libertarian anti-state and market-oriented agenda which was popular at that time. Embodied by Newt Gingrich's 'Contract with America', that agenda was meant to give massive power to financial institutions.[7] Furthermore, sections 1.1. and 1.2 above have suggested ever more profound cultural similarities. As we have seen, libertarianism had fostered forms of organization of labour that were perfectly suited to neoliberalism. Creative workers and internet entrepreneurs shared a decentralized

---

3   Lovink, *My First Recession*; R. Florida, *The Rise of the Creative Class: And How It's Transforming Work, Leisure, Community and Everyday Life*, New York: Basic Books, 2002; M. Wark, *A Hacker Manifesto*, Cambridge, Mass.: Harvard University Press, 2004; F. Berardi, *Il sapiente, il mercante, il guerriero*, Roma: DeriveApprodi, 2004.
4   Florida, *The Rise of the Creative Class*.
5   Wark, *A Hacker Manifesto*.
6   The attentive reader could call this assertion into question by noticing that the two books mentioned were published at the beginning of 2000s. However, we are not saying that the authors were directly involved in the Dotcom culture, but rather that their works 'reflect' a coexistence that was first experienced in the 1990s. After all, as Lovink, *My First Recession*, recalled, the Dotcom hype used to travel at such a speed that there are few books that were published *during* the phase of expansion. The first studies started being published only in 2000, in concomitance with the NASDAQ slump.
7   Lovink, *My First Recession*, pp. 63-64.

organizational paradigm and self-entrepreneurship ethics that they both had inherited from cybernetics and excellence-oriented peer communities. They also shared Wiener's suspicion towards big powers as opposed to grassroots organizations: as Castells has recalled, in the New Economy system of values, money became a symbol of independence from that traditional corporate world from which both digital wizards and entrepreneurs felt the greatest distance.[8]

Economic interests sustained the coexistence between creatives and internet capitals, as well. The non-profit internet communitarian culture has rarely developed economic models for its sustainability. Or better, its economic models have been mainly based on the concept of 'heterarchy'. Introduced by David Stark in order to explain the behaviour of firms in post-Soviet Eastern Europe, the concept of 'heterarchy' is recovered by Turner and associated with the methods of evaluating value on the WELL:

> within a heterarchy one encounters multiple, and at times competing, value systems, principles of organization, and mechanisms for performance appraisal. "Heterarchies create wealth by inviting more than one way of evaluating worth". [...] On the WELL, users' abilities to characterize their postings as having value in both the social and the economic registers depended on both the computer technology of the WELL and the cultural legacy of the New Communalist movement.[9] [10]

In substance, while voluntarily contributing to the creation of common knowledge, WELLites invested in their reputation capital that ultimately led to a number of working opportunities.

Turner limits the application of the heterarchy concept to the WELL. However, it is not difficult to recognise a similar mechanism at work among developers and creatives participating in 1990s' digital communities. It is well-known that reputation capital and knowledge that had been acquired through communitarian activities started being made productive elsewhere in the new euphoric high-tech industry by digital creatives.

To indicate an emergent social class whose roots lay at the convergence of cultural values and economic interests between internet entrepreneurs, on one side, and the social actors that led the digital revolution, on the other, Formenti introduced the concept of 'Fifth State'.[11] In his work following the Dotcom burst and 9/11, Formenti put forward a hypothesis overtly in counter-tendency with those developments. He suggested that – although knowledge workers were undergoing a severe loss of contractual power because of the burst – there still existed some chances to reconstitute the coalition between creatives and entrepreneurial power. If that hypothesis had turned out right – Formenti argued – there would have been

8   Castells, *Internet Galaxy*.
9   The inner quotation is taken from D. Stark, 'Ambiguous Assets for Uncertain Environments: Heterarchy in Postsocialist Firms', in P. J. DiMaggio, *The Twenty-first Century Firm: Changing Economic Organization in International Perspective*, Princeton, NJ: Princeton University Press, 2001: 69-103.
10 Turner, *From Counterculture to Cyberculture*, p.156.
11 Formenti, *Mercanti di Futuro*.

a good chance for western democracies to evolve towards post-democratic political systems in which forms of representational democracy could mingle with forms of direct participation.

Nevertheless, by 2008 Formenti had to admit that his hypothesis would have never come true.[12] With the collapse of 500 dotcoms, half million jobs lost in the high-tech industry, and three trillions dollars ending up in smoke at NASDAQ, the Dotcom burst not only had venture capitals take to their heels, but had also marked the end of dreams for bottom-up alliances. The Dotcom burst ratified the failure of the coalition between the rebels of the net and emerging internet entrepreneurs. If later on the net economy did recover from the burst, the coalition between knowledge workers and internet companies had sunk.

While the ideological alliance between techno-anarchism and neoliberism broke into fragments in 2000, another alliance, based on completely different presuppositions, was appearing on the horizon and became solid with 9/11: the alliance between governments and those internet companies that had survived the burst and had become giant corporations.

2.2 The Territorialization of the Net

We saw in section 1.1 that one of the pillars that the digital communitarian culture inherited from cybernetics is the possibility to keep the virtual and the brick-and-mortar domains separated. The idea of a virtual network unassailable by old 'hard' powers emerged together with efforts to build a network architecture that could survive nuclear attacks.[13] It is a leading principle not only of J.P. Barlow's Declaration of Independence, of Electronic Frontier Foundation's campaign against the Communications Decency Act and of Rheingold's reports from the WELL, it also characterizes Indymedia's efforts to create self-organized digital infrastructures. That is, the separation of virtual and real domains is a foundational principle not only of digital communities directly informed by the U.S. libertarian paradigm, but also of those inspired by more heterogeneous sources.

This separation is based on the notion of a completely de-territorialized internet, an intrinsically borderless network that can escape efforts to reduce it to nation-state boundaries, sovereignty and laws. However, pressures for political control and surveillance introduced after 9/11 and the so called 'War on Terror' have put this assumption under considerable strain.[14]

---

12   Formenti, *Cybersoviet*.
13   At least, this is the mythology that accompanies the birth of Arpanet. For a confutation of it – that nonetheless does not affect our discussion, see Hafner and Lyon, *Where Wizards Stay Up Late*.
14   I cannot account here for the numerous studies that since 2001 have been investigating the threats to privacy constituted by technologies of social sorting and control backed by TIA (Total Information Awareness, the global surveillance project designed by Pentagon in 2002 to substitute Echelon) and similar governmental initiatives worldwide. On the value of privacy confronted to national security see, among others, H. Nissenbaum, 'Privacy in Context', in G. Stocker, and C. Schöpf (eds) *Goodbye Privacy. Ars Electronica 2007*, Ostfildern: Hatje Cantz Verlag, 2007; B. Rössler, *The Value of Privacy*, London: Polity Press, 2005.On dataveillance technologies and the patterns of human coexistence that they enable, especially in the urban domain, see S. Graham, 'Introduction: Cities, Warfare, and States of Emergency', 'Software-sorted geographies', *Progress in Human Geography* 29.5 (2005): 1-19; D. Lyon, *Surveillance as Social Sorting: Privacy, Risk and Automated Discrimination*, London: Routledge, 2002. I

Already in 1999 Lawrence Lessig warned against the architectures of regulation exercised by technologies of 'smooth' commerce, backed by the rule of law.[15] More recently, Stanford's researchers Goldsmith and Wu have depicted a more and more controlled and territorialized internet. They argue that since mid-1990s the internet has been transformed 'from a technology that resists territorial law to one that facilitates its enforcement'.[16] Instead of imposing its cosmopolitan culture on local milieus, the global net seems to be adapting to local conditions and norms. According to the authors, the 'Balkanization of the Net' is made possible by close teamwork between governments and global internet companies, which formally foster the cult of networking freedom. Three factors are pushing this course.

First, users themselves ask for culture-targeted internet browsing: 'geographical borders first emerged on the internet not as a result of fiats by national governments, but rather organically, from below, because internet users around the globe demanded different internet experiences that corresponded to geography'.[17] The primary demand concerns language. While in late 1990s 80% of internet contents were in English,[18] by 2002 English web pages were only 50% of the total amount.[19] On 30th June 2008, the percentage of non-English native internet users worldwide was 70,6%.[20] While the amount of English-speaking internet users grew 203.5% from 2000 to 2008, in the same period the amount of Chinese-speaking internet users grew 755.1%, Spanish-speaking internet users grew 405.3%, Portuguese-speaking internet users grew 668% and Arabic-speaking internet users grew 2.063,7%. With these demand rates for non-English information, content providers are more and more pushed to offer services that meet local linguistic and cultural needs.

The second factor follows as a consequence. The need to meet local needs can now rely upon geo-identification technologies that automatically localize the user and provide targeted information or block 'forbidden' contents. While geo-ID technologies have at first been developed in order to filter information for commercial purposes, the alliance between internet companies and governments that followed the War on Terror has in fact shown new surveillance-oriented applications.

---

wrote about urban planning challenges and technologies of social sorting in 'Stretching the Line into a Borderland of Potentiality. Communication technologies between security tactics and cultural practices', in A. Aurigi and F. De Cindio (eds) *Augmented Urban Spaces. Articulating the Physical and Electronic City*, Aldershot: Ashgate, 2008. For some lucid reflections about the interrelation of privacy and copyright issues, see V. Grassmuck, 'Copyright Instead of Data Protection', in G. Stocker and C. Schopf (eds) *Goodbye Privacy*.

15 L. Lessig, *Code and Other Laws of Cyberspace*, New York: Basic Books, 1999.
16 Goldsmith and Wu, *Who Controls the Internet?*, p.10.
17 Goldsmith and Wu, Who Controls the Internet?, p. 49.
18 B. Wallraff, 'What Global Language?', *Atlantic Monthly*, November 2000, Quoted in Goldsmith and Wu, *Who Controls the Internet?*.
19 D. Crystal, *The Language Revolution*, Cambridge, Mass.: Polity, 2004. Quoted in Goldsmith and Wu, *Who Controls the Internet?*.
20 Source of these and of the following statistics: Internet World Stat, 'Internet World Users by Language', http://www.internetworldstats.com/stats7.htm, accessed 30 October 2008.

Goldsmith and Wu dedicate a whole chapter to the Chinese case. Here, the 'Great Electronic Wall' could not have been built without Cisco's gateways and Google's filtering systems. These same internet corporations that elsewhere are champions of the 'free flows of information' ideology, in China subscribed a binding self-discipline pact according to which they cannot 'produce or disseminate harmful texts or news likely to jeopardize national security and social stability, violate laws and regulations, or spread false news, superstitions and obscenities'.[21]

Chinese internet writers' arrests demonstrate how virtual life can have dire consequences on physical life once geo-ID technologies allow to associate a physical address to an IP address. Furthermore, they reveal that there is no internet architecture which is 'naturally' uncontrollable:

> [the Chinese Government] is trying to create an Internet that is free enough to support and maintain the fastest growing economy, and yet closed enough to tamp down political threats to its monopoly on power. [...] Only time will tell whether the China strategy will work, or whether the sheer volume of information will erode the government's influence and render the Internet in China open and free. But so far, China is showing the opposite: that the Internet enjoyed in the West is a choice – not fate, not destiny, and not natural law.[22]

The third factor for the Balkanization of the Net concerns western control policies backed by ID technologies. Democratically elected governments worldwide have found ways to impose their laws on internet as a transnational territory as well. Even if a nation-state can exert coercive power only within its borders, Goldsmith and Wu note that global internet companies usually 'hit the ground' in local branches that can be subjected to government pressures. Dow Jones, Yahoo, eBay, Pay Pal, Google, and MasterCard are examples of large firms present in many nations that had to comply with national laws of countries where they do business.

As their book title suggests,[23] once the internet is subjected to nation-state sovereignty, the core issue shifts from techno-pundits' concerns about internet controllability to legitimizing the sources of law. As Italian former head of the Privacy Authority, Rodotà pointed out, lack of rules would hand the internet over to the same big powers against which it was originally born.[24] According to Rodotà, freeing the internet from juridical control established by democratically elected parliaments means turning it into a space where the only rules in force are those made by the most powerful actors, according to their specific needs.[25] As a consequence of a similar privatization of regulatory functions, law would lose its *super-partes* nature.[26]

---

21 AA.VV, '"Living Dangerously on the Net": Censorship and Surveillance of Internet Forums', *Reporters without Borders*, May 12 2003. Quoted in Goldsmith and Wu, *Who Controls the Internet?*,
22 Goldsmith and Wu, *Who Controls the Internet?*, pp. 89-90.
23 Goldsmith and Wu, *Who Controls the Internet?*.
24 Turner's reconstruction of how *Wired*'s editorial board turned out to sustain conservative politicians from 'the Big Old Party' is exemplary in this respect.
25 S. Rodotà, *Tecnopolitica*, Roma-Bari: Laterza, 1997.
26 Even if we cannot account here for the juridical literature on the sources of Law when acting on a

In summary, at the end of 2000s, techno-political developments have shrunk the gap between virtual and physical domains. As a matter of fact, cyberculture's libertarian credo of an intrinsically ungovernable internet has turned out to be an illusion. In spite of declarations of independence, today geography matters more than ever.

2.3 Web 2.0, the Renaissance of Community on the Net and the Quest for Value Creation

The third libertarian belief that has faced scepticism over the last years postulates that information sharing empowers individuals and communities vis-a-vis governmental and commercial powers. As we saw in chapter 1, the ethics of sharing is a cornerstone of internet architecture. While this is true of internet protocols and standards, however, it is less ascertained for data produced by net surfers, the so called 'user-generated contents' (UGC). The assumption that online interactions produce diffuse wealth, stronger political participation, reduction of inequalities, empowerment of disadvantaged sectors of population needs to be demonstrated.

This assumption gained momentum soon after the Dotcom burst, when internet pundits and cyberculturalists denied the economic models they had followed over the previous years, and recalled the inherently open and sharing-oriented nature of the internet. In the words of Kevin Kelly,

> so much money flew around dot-coms, that it hid the main event on the Web, which is the exchange of gifts. While the most popular 50 websites are crassly commercial, most of the 3 billion web pages in the world are not. Only thirty percent of the pages of the Web are built by companies and corporations like pets.com. The rest is built on love, such as care4pets.com or responsiblepetcare.org. The answer to the mystery of why people would make 3 billion web pages in 2,000 days is simple: sharing.[27]

These words might constitute the first implicit reference to so called 'Web 2.0', that is, web platforms where information is supplied by users themselves.[28]

---

transnational level, it should be mentioned that Rodotà talks about the privatization of governance functions on the internet (*Lex Informatica*) in a way that very much resembles Saskia Sassen's concerns about the privatization of the regulatory functions in transnational politics and trade (*Lex Mercatoria*). See S. Sassen, *Territory, Authority, Rights: from medieval to global assemblages*, Princeton: Princeton University Press, 2006, pp.184-271. This similarity could be seen as a further element suggesting the artificiality of any distinction between virtual and physical realms, as they both have to face similar challenges.

27   K. Kelly, 'The Web Runs on Love, not Greed', *The Wall Street Journal*, 4 January 2002.

28   For the original definition of 'Web 2.0' see T. O'Reilly, 'What Is Web 2.0. Design Patterns and Business Models for the Next Generation of Software', *O'Reilly*, 30 September 2005, https://www.oreilly.com/pub/a/web2/archive/what-is-web-20.html. For a further, condensed definition see P. Graham, 'Web 2.0', 2005, http://www.paulgraham.com/web20.html. Paul Graham describes the origins of the term from the title of a series of $2800-fee conferences oriented to 'throngs of VCs and biz dev guys' organized by O'Reilly Media and Medialive International in 2004-5. Graham also provides a definition of Web 2.0 as user-oriented 'Ajax' web-based applications that can rely upon high-quality free contents thanks to systems of selection based on the vote of crowds ('voters do a significantly better job than human

Between 2004 and 2005, 'online community' had turned into a much inflated concept, and the opportunity was appropriate to replace it with terms like 'social networks', 'mobs', 'swarms'.[29] Simultaneously, the recovered ethics of sharing contributed to the success of UGC-driven web, a new business model expected to better fit the inherent openness of the medium. According to Tim O'Reilly – who introduced the successful expression – 'Web 2.0' constituted an effort to devise a business model that respected the sharing-oriented nature of internet, after the dotcom's failure demonstrated the inadequacy of old pay-per-view business models. Indeed, Web 2.0 introduced new business models that rely on online sociability as a fundamental source of value:

> Web 2.0 is the business revolution in the computer industry caused by the move to the internet as platform, and an attempt to understand the rules for success on that new platform. Chief among those rules is this: Build applications that harness network effects to get better the more people use them. (This is what I've elsewhere called "harnessing collective intelligence.") Eric Schmidt has an even briefer formulation of this rule: "Don't fight the internet." That's actually a wonderful way to think about it. Think deeply about the way the internet works, and build systems and applications that use it more richly, freed from the constraints of PC-era thinking, and you're well on your way. Ironically, Tim Berners-Lee's original Web 1.0 is one of the most "Web 2.0" systems out there – it completely harnesses the power of user contribution, collective intelligence, and network effects. It was Web 1.5, the dotcom bubble, in which people tried to make the Web into something else, that fought the internet, and lost.[30]

This long quotation is useful to recall a key aspect often forgotten by the UGC hype. Social network services were first and foremost a response to the need to produce value on internet in new ways. This historical evidence is usually underestimated in accounts dealing with Web 2.0 platforms. The December 2006 *Time* cover, for example, is a compendium of much Web 2.0 rhetoric on renewed democracy, solidarity, and grassroots cooperation. *Time*'s December 2006 cover story nominated the crowds contributing UGC as 'Person of the Year':

> we're looking at an explosion of productivity and innovation, and it's just getting started, as millions of minds that would otherwise have drowned in obscurity get backhauled into the global intellectual economy. Who are these people? Seriously, who actually sits down after a long day at work and says, I'm not going to watch *Lost* tonight. I'm going to turn on my computer and make a movie starring my pet iguana? [...] The answer is, you do. And for seizing the reins of the global media, for founding and framing the new digital democracy, for working for nothing and beating the pros at their own game, TIME's Person of the Year for 2006 is you. [31]

editors').

29   D. M. boyd, and N. B. Ellison, 'Social network sites: Definition, history, and scholarship', *Journal of Computer-Mediated Communication*, 13 (1) 2007, 210-230; H. Rheingold *Smart Mobs: the Next Social Revolution*, New York: Basic Books, 2002.
30   T.O'Reilly, 'Web 2.0 Compact Definition: Trying Again', 2006, http://radar.oreilly.com/2006/12/web-20-compact-definition-tryi.html.
31   L. Grossman, 'Time's Person of the Year: You', *Time*, 13 December 2006.

One might wonder about the rationale according to which shooting an iguana-starring movie is related to founding the new digital democracy. Similarly the assumption, that including millions of minds into the global intellectual economy would cause an explosion of innovation and seize the reins of global media, is all but tested. As some authors have argued, the blogosphere can actually be very conservative, and prefer to promote rather than compete against mainstream media.[32]

Time's article recovers cyberculture's duality between institutions and individuals, top-down power and bottom-up communities:[33]

> look at 2006 through a different lens and you'll see another story, one that isn't about conflict or great men. It's a story about community and collaboration on a scale never seen before. It's about the cosmic compendium of knowledge Wikipedia and the million-channel people's network YouTube and the online metropolis MySpace. It's about the many wresting power from the few and helping one another for nothing and how that will not only change the world, but also change the way the world changes.[34]

Despite the high-sounding rhetoric, the article's theory of action is explicit: Web 2.0 deals with small contributions that – when assembled together on a web platform – gain a higher influence than professional contents, and thus 'wrest power from the few' and give it back to the many.

It is noticeable that this theory of action does not mention *which* power to do *what*, nor what is supposed to keep the community together. It does not show *in which direction* the world is changing its way of changing, nor *who* will benefit from these changes. In other words, the article replaces technological determinism with sociological determinism, but refrains from questioning the cause-and-effect explanatory model underpinning the alleged correlation between collaboration and empowerment. Questions about *why* strangers collaborate and how collaboration is supposed to lead to empowerment remain unanswered.

Counter-evidence to this ideological theory of action comes from political studies and political economy. First and unexpectedly, Web 2.0 platforms (said to empower individuals by providing tools for self-expression and collaboration) are scarcely used by political movements (supposed to be the champions of free speech and grassroots organization). Indeed, empirical research has shown that political movements are very reluctant to adopt multi-interactive services on their websites.[35]

For example, 'Searching the Net: An Analysis of the Democratic Use of internet by 266 Social Movement Organizations' analysed the main website features of 266 Global Justice Movement organizations in Italy, France, Germany, Great Britain, Spain, and Switzerland, as well as at the

---

32   Lovink, *Zero Comments*.
33   See section 1.1.
34   Grossman, 'Time's Person of the Year'.
35   Della Porta, et al., 'Searching the Net'.

transnational level. Results revealed that internet is used to satisfy five functions: diffusion of alternative information, identity-building, debate and discussion, improving the transparency and accountability of the organization, online, and offline mobilization. Despite efforts to foster participation and empowerment constitute a large amount of movements' online activities, the research showed that multi-interactive tools other than forums and mailing lists are rarely implemented. Only 10% of social movement's websites use UGC technologies.[36]

As the *Networked Politics* think tank has highlighted, social movements make limited use of Web 2.0 technology. For example, while Wikipedia started using wiki software in 2001, it was only in 2004 that the first wiki platform was used in social forums. Furthermore, Indymedia – which introduced open-publishing platforms in political action[37] – is now losing popularity, and recent initiatives aimed to build interactive websites to organize social forums have had very limited diffusion.[38] As a matter of fact, these pieces of evidences call into question the capability of Web 2.0 tools to foster bottom-up political participation and empowerment.

Second, as Formenti has pointed out, the notion of empowerment underpinning the Web 2.0 hype makes it difficult to distinguish between democratic engagement, cyber-ideology, 'cyber-soviet'[39], and 'cyber-pop'. Formenti provocatively wonders whether empowerment coincides with the possibility to publish a post among million others, or whether it even coincides with an alleged wisdom of the crowds. While libertarian techno-enthusiasts claim their absolute confidence in the capacity of Web 2.0 platforms to select the best contributions out of millions, according to Formenti the definition of 'best' is never 'natural' nor objective, but is embodied in code. Google's Page Rank, for instance, does not measure the quality and reliability of the information contained in the pages indexed, but rather reflect a sort of 'popularity index'.[40] [41]

Furthermore, Formenti points out that empowerment does not relate to the use of ICT for entertainment purposes, like for most Web 2.0 applications, but rather to the possibility of exploiting internet's potential for life-long learning, work, cognitive enrichment, and democratic participation.[42] The author proposes the notion of 'cultural divide' to indicate the distinction between enthusiast consumers of information technology that show low overall cultural consumption rates (*technofans*), and those who combine technological interest with other forms of cultural consumption (*eclectics*). While the latter users retain the cultural skills that allow them to bend ICT to their needs, technofans are more likely to enthusiastically adopt ICT

---

36   Della Porta et al., 'Searching the Net'.

37   See section 1.4.

38   Fuster i Morell, 'The new web communites and political culture'.

39   With 'cybersoviet' Formenti (2008) names self-organized initiatives run by hackers and digital
      communitarians debating internal direct democracy and governance issues.

40   Since when this research was first written in 2007-2009, much literature has developed around this
      issue, starting with E. Pariser, *The Filter Bubble: What the Internet Is Hiding from You*, New York:
      Penguin Press, 2011. (Note to the 2018 Edition).

41   Ippolita collective, *Luci e ombre di Google*, Milano: Feltrinelli, 2007, quoted in Formenti, *Cybersoviet*.

42   Formenti, *Cybersoviet*, 244.

without developing the ability to harness its potential for personal enrichment. According to Formenti, this cultural divide can easily be transformed into a new class divide.[43]

Third, the most elaborate counter-argument to Web 2.0's claims to empower individuals and communities come from the labour economy. While the openness of the digital architecture – of code, protocols, practices, and standards – is a *condicio sine qua non* for the same existence of the internet, the question of how a digital commons-driven economy should distribute resources and wealth is still matter of dispute. As a matter of fact, not only do online relationships constitute a highly-targeted audience for profits based on adverts and data mining, they also act as content producers in a newly New Economy founded on the 'cult of the amateur'. Still, only very rarely do forms of value distribution correspond to the voluntary supply of UGC.

Formenti numbers seven cases of Web 2.0 business models which have succeeded in 'harnessing the collective intelligence' of users by deploying participatory technologies: from readers' book reviews to commercial intermediaries like e-Bay which create value by providing the technological infrastructure for trust; from free footage shot with prosumer technologies to UGC as ways to monitor cultural trends; from traditional advertising finding new stimuli in fans' posts to talent-scout activities online, to the spontaneous activity of collaborative categorization performed by millions of individuals online. However, probably the most inter- esting example of a business model based on UGC comes from $ 15bn *Facebook*.[44] [45] This popular social networking site in November 2007 had *Coca-Cola, Blockbuster, Verizon, Sony Pictures, Condé Nast*, and seven other global brands make large advertising investments on its platform. Furthermore, it is fresh news that *Facebook* is launching a new generation of commercials called 'engagement ads'.[46] With engagement ads, users will be asked to respond to ads popping up when they log in, by evaluating a product. Their reply will then be shared with their *Facebook* friends.

As Guardian's journalist Tom Hodgkinson has pointed out, the interest of companies towards 59 millions potential advocates of their brand is usually framed as 'sharing':

[the creators of the site] simply sit back and watch as millions of Facebook addicts voluntarily upload their ID details, photographs and lists of their favourite consumer objects. Once in receipt of this vast database of human beings, Facebook then simply has to sell the information back to advertisers, or, as Zuckerberg puts it in a recent blog post, 'to try to help people share information with their friends about things they do on

---

43   In his argument Formenti quotes the results of the 'Liquidi & Mutanti. Industrie dei contenuti & consumatori digitali' survey conducted by AC Nielsen for the Italian Permanent Observatory on Digital Contents. A summary of the results of the survey are available at http://aie2007.advansys.it/Portals/22/ File%20allegati/OCD_sintesiindagine.pdf.
44   As of 2008, Facebook board is composed of its young creator Mark Zuckerberg, venture capitalist Jim Breyer and neocon futurist and hedge fund manager Peter Thiel.
45   Formenti, *Cybersoviet*.
46   J. Boorstin, 'Facebook's New Ad Play In a Down Economy', *CNBC.com*, http://www.cnbc.com/ id/27682302. [Not anymore available on 02 September 2018].

the Web'. [...] 'Share' is Facebook speak for 'advertise'. Sign up to Facebook and you become a free walking, talking advert for Blockbuster or Coke, extolling the virtues of these brands to your friends. We are seeing the commodification of human relationships, the extraction of capitalistic value from friendships.[47] [48]

Similar arguments focusing on the production of value from non-economic activities touch upon an unresolved issue of the new New Economy. Although UGC are sources of value in Web 2.0 business models, none of the most popular Web 2.0 platforms provides for the remuneration of amateur authors.[49] According to Lovink, the 'ideology of the free' is systematically avoiding the crucial issue of a distributed economy in the so-called 'knowledge society'.[50] While 'liberal communists'[51] evade questions about their own business models, they mention users, developers, citizens that would need to be 'liberated', rather than enabled to earn a living from their creativity:

in order to open new social spaces for action, it is necessary to get rid of the religion of the free: 'social media' need to develop their own economy. Giving one's own contents for free should be a voluntary, generous act and not the only option available. Instead of celebrating the amateur, we should develop a culture of the Internet that help young amateurs to become professionals. And this cannot happen if we preach to them that the only choice they have is to make ends meet through a McJob during daytime, so

---

47   That Hodgkinson's tone is all but exaggerated is demonstrated by the same firms' representatives commenting the agreement: 'with Facebook Ads, our brands can become a part of the way users communicate and interact on Facebook' (Carol Kruse, vice president, global interactive marketing, the Coca-Cola Company); 'we view this as an innovative way to cultivate relationships with millions of Facebook users by enabling them to interact with Blockbuster in convenient, relevant and entertaining ways. This is beyond creating advertising impressions. This is about Blockbuster participating in the community of the consumer so that, in return, consumers feel motivated to share the benefits of our brand with their friends' (Jim Keyes, Blockbuster chairman and CEO). Comments quoted in T. Hodgkinson, 'With friends like these...', *The Guardian*, 14 January 2008.

48   Hodgkinson, 'With friends like these...'.

49   T. Weber, 'YouTubers to get ad money share', *BBC News*, 27 January 2007, http://news.bbc.co.uk/2/hi/business/6305957.stm. One of the few exceptions is the video sharing platform *Revver*. Another case is the *AdSense* service by Google allowing targeted adverts banners to be published on personal websites and blogs. Already on 27 January 2007, during the World Economic Forum in Davos, Switzerland, *YouTube*'s founder Chad Hurley announced that a revenue-sharing system was being developed in order to 'reward creativity'. Even if at that time the system was said to be expected in few months, almost two years later there is no trace of it.

50   Lovink, *Zero Comments*.

51   This expression, quoted by Lovink, *Zero Comments*, 11, of Italian edition, was originally coined by Olivier Malnuit in his 'Ten Liberal Communist Commandments' published by French magazine *Technikart*. The term indicates an economic paradigm that sees copyright as an impediment to knowledge-based economic flows and fosters the creation of immaterial commons while recovering Adam Smith's theory of the invisible hand. See S. Zizek, (2006), 'Nobody has to be vile', *London Review of Books*, available at http://www.lrb.co.uk/v28/n07/zize01_.html.; Y. Benkler, *The Wealth of Networks: How Social Production Transforms Market and Freedom*, New Haven, CT: Yale University Press, 2006 has probably elaborated the most complete version of this post-modern eschatology: he foresees a new form of capitalism freed from private property. For an accurate analysis of the theoretical bases of this school of thought, see Formenti, *Cybersoviet*.

that they can celebrate their "freedom" during the long night hours spent online. A redistribution of money, resources and power is necessary.[52]

If amateurs encounter difficulties in becoming professionals, the other way round is not easier. A further limit of the emerging sharing economy is the loss of influence by cultural industry professionals, as they are replaced by amateurs. While networked organizations outsource more and more risks and responsibilities to freelance contributors, they shrink R&D resources for professionals. The concern that the cult of the amateur constitutes a threat to creative workers is shared by ICT analyst Nicholas Carr, as well. Carr has questioned the effective quality of Wikipedia's articles, while admitting that the search for quality tends to be overwhelmed by the search for free contents:

the Internet is changing the economics of creative work – or, to put it more broadly, the economics of culture – and it's doing it in a way that may well restrict rather than expand our choices. Wikipedia might be a pale shadow of the Britannica, but because it's created by amateurs rather than professionals, it's free. And free trumps quality all the time. So what happens to those poor saps who write encyclopedias for a living? They wither and die. The same thing happens when blogs and other free on-line content go up against old-fashioned newspapers and magazines. [...] Implicit in the ecstatic visions of Web 2.0 is the hegemony of the amateur. I for one can't imagine anything more frightening.[53]

Yet authors' loss of contractual power is not only due to their replacement by amateurs. Organizational changes in the creative industry also have a role. In a different article about the theory of disintermediation, Carr argues that in the UGC production and distribution chain, the most profitable position is that of the intermediary. Contrary to cyberlibertarian claims celebrating the end-to-end pattern of communication enabled by the web, 'internet continues to be a rich platform for intermediation strategies, and it's the intermediaries who stand to skim up most of the profits to be made from Web 2.0'.[54]

Venture capitalist David Hornik has linked the renewed relevance of intermediaries to the Long Tail paradigm.[55] He argues that there are essentially two types of technology (and actors, I would add) that benefit economically from the Long Tail: aggregators and filterers. While aggregators and filterers rely upon the increasing volume and diversity of content to boost

52 Lovink, *Zero Comments*, p. 37.
53 N. Carr, 'The Amorality of Web 2.0', *Rough Type*, 3 October 2005, http://www.roughtype.com/archives/2005/10/the_amorality_o.php.
54 N. Carr, 'Hypermediation 2.0', *Rough Type*, 28 November 2005, http://www.roughtype.com/archives/2005/11/hypermediation.php.
55 C. Anderson, *The Long Tail: Why The Future of Business in Selling Less of More*, New York: Hyperion, 2006. The well-known 'Long Tail' economic paradigm illustrated by *Wired* editor Chris Anderson (Anderson 2006) asserts that products that are in low demand or have low sales volume can collectively make up a market share that rivals or exceeds the relatively few current bestsellers and blockbusters, if the store or distribution channel is large enough. Examples of such mega-stores include Amazon.com and Netflix.

their value, 'that growth of content will not have a material impact upon the value of any one piece of content floating somewhere in the Tail'.[56] That is, the value produced by filtering and aggregating activities will all go to the benefit of intermediaries, not of content producers.

If these anticipations are confirmed, they will not only shape the crisis of 21st century sepa-ration between labour and non-economic activities, but will also call into question the same foundations of the internet libertarian culture. Readers probably remember that in 2001 Lawrence Lessig numbered the features upon which the openness of the internet relies. Among these, Lessig saw the peer-to-peer architecture as the crucial element in the design of commons. Peer-to-peer architectures led Lessig to assert that the wisdom of the network lies on individual clients, and not on the network itself. Now that Web 2.0 platforms aggregating and filtering contents have centralized the wisdom of the network, one could wonder which new principles the openness of the internet is expected to rely upon.

In summary, many see the appropriation of the communitarian, techno-libertarian vernacular by internet corporate companies at the origin of the paradox of an informal gift economy turned into a hundred-million-dollars machine. While the 'ideology of the free' has pushed millions of people to upload their contents on Web 2.0 platforms, there is a endemic lack of business models that foster an impartial, distributed, and decentralized internet economy. The point is not so much to question Web 2.0 models that seek to make profits out of users' contents. Late 1990s' bubble has brought with it a much more disenchanted gaze than that shown by the prophets of digital harmony and gift economy. Rather, the point is about understanding what remains of the 'digital community' once communal ties based on soli-darity and the gift economy are invoked as the cornerstone of commercial activities whose revenues are kept in the hands of few corporations. While the benefits for aggregating and filtering internet companies are quantified by analysts in terms of millions of dollars,[57] the theory of action according to which participating in Web 2.0 open-publishing should foster community empowerment, produce diffuse wealth, and boost stronger participation to political processes is not as self-evident.

According to emergent scholarship on social network sites (SNSs), participation in services like *Friendster, Orkut* or *Facebook* provides resources for identity-building and reputation management. Donath and boyd have shown that SNSs allow users to negotiate presentations of self, and have suggested that the 'public display of connection' serves as an important identity signal that helps people navigate the networked social world.[58] Furthermore, Choi has

---

56   D. Hornik, 'Where's the Money in the Long Tail?', *Venture Blog*, 13 December 2005, http://www.
      ventureblog.com/2005/12/wheres-the-money-in-the-long-tail.html.
57   For instance, in 2008 *YouTube* is expected to produce $ 100 millions of revenue in US and between
      $ 200 and 250 millions worldwide, while *Google* paid 1,65 billions to take it over in 2006. Source:
      Bradshaw and Garrahan (2008). In 2007 *Facebook*'s revenue amounted to $150m millions, while they
      are expected to reach $ 265 millions in 2008. K. Swisher, 'Chatty Zuckerberg Tells All About Facebook
      Finances', *All Things Digital*, 31 January 2008, http://kara.allthingsd.com/20080131/chatty-zuckerberg-
      tells-all-about-facebook-finances/.
58   J. Donath and D. M. boyd, 'Public displays of connection', *BT Technology Journal* 22.4 (2004): 71-82.

found that 85% of respondents to a Korean study 'listed the maintenance and reinforcement of pre-existing social networks as their main motive for Cyworld use'.[59]

If we consider these studies, the question then becomes whether sociability in itself can be considered as an empowering factor, or whether it acts as a means to reach further resources at different sites. On one hand, sociability per se might be a meagre outcome, if paid for in that precious currency of privacy.[60] On the other hand, studies that identify the nature of further resources are still few, and mainly based at production sites.[61]

To conclude, the skeptical perspectives we have reviewed in this section have the merit to focus the discussion on the means of production in a domain that has for long celebrated dematerialization. They also introduce a conflictual perspective into digital utopianism. Similar approaches help to raise the question as to whether the supposed empowerment of individuals and communities through Web 2.0 tools belongs only to the immaterial domain, or does it also apply to living resources and wealth. At the same time, I suggest that the recovery of a materialist perspective should avoid reproducing the virtual vs. real dichotomy inherited from libertarian cyberculture. Claiming that the knowledge dimension works as 'parasite' of the material dimension of living in extracting value from creative workers only shows the other side of the cyberculturalist coin.[62] Rather, I argue that we cannot understand what digital communities have become if we do not jointly take into account their semiotic and technical character. After all, knowledge communities do not thrive in a *vacuum*, but rely on infrastructural layers that shape possible forms of interaction.

Finally, in the light of the breakdown of some of the internet libertarian culture's funding myths, this chapter has shown that the advantages of online interaction for individuals and communities cannot be simply postulated, but needs to be investigated by asking actors themselves about their own theory of empowerment. This is what this book will do in the second part. Before embarking on this task, though, we need to first review two theories that try to answer the question about what remains of online communities once the techno-libertarian belief in an immaterial economy of the free has come to a crossroads.

Box 1: The manifesto of the 'No Screw Tube' campaign numbering seven good reasons not to upload videos on YouTube-like Web 2.0 platforms. The campaign was promoted by Transmission.cc, a global network of citizen journalists, video makers, artists, researchers, hackers, and web producers who developed online video distribution tools for social justice and media democracy

59 J. H. Choi, 'Living in Cyworld: Contextualising Cy-Ties in South Korea', in A. Bruns and J. Jacobs (eds) *Use of Blogs (Digital Formations)*, New York: Peter Lang, 2006, p.181; boyd, and Ellison 'Social network sites'.
60 S. Barnes, 'A privacy paradox: Social networking in the United States', *First Monday* 11 (9), 4 September 2006, http://www.firstmonday.org/ojs/index.php/fm/article/view/1394/1312.
61 See for example, Saxenian, *Regional Advantage*.
62 M. Pasquinelli, *Animal Spirit. A Bestiary of the Commons*, Rotterdam: NAi Publishers, 2008.

Why NOT Just Use YouTube?

The 'No Screw Tube' campaign is beginning...

1. Exploitation: ScrewTube exploits your free videomaking to gain ad revenue.

2. Surveillance: Posting on YT risks surveillance and IP tracking, both by corporations and the state. For example in 2004 Yahoo collaborated with Chinese authorities to identify dissident blogger Shi Tao. He is now serving 10 years in jail. Many sites record your IP address, not just corporate projects.

3. Censorship: Posting on YT opens the door to censorship since they will do take-downs at State request or for copyright violations.

4. When sharing isn't really sharing: Sites like YT only allow sharing with other members, or by embedding YT videos in your site or blog. There is no re-distribution via p2p networks, or availability of high-resolution downloads for screenings.

5. When free isn't really free: Though free to use, the platform is closed – using YT technology entails using YT. With free software platforms, anyone can create their own video-sharing site.

6. When a community isn't really a community: YouTube was sold to Google for $1.65 billion in Google stock. If it can be bought and sold, is it really a community? Editorial and software control should be in the hands of the user community. Control of Screw-Tube sites is organised by the profit motive.

7. Intellectual Property: Sites like ScrewTube place exploitative terms and conditions on your contributions, allowing them to re-sell and remix your work.

Using existing ethical and pirate technologies, we can do much, much better... Projects like VisiononTv, Ifiwatch.tv, Engagemedia.org (Australia) and numerous Indymedia video spin-offs, coordinated through Transmission, are linking up their databases to create decentralised search tools. This will greatly increase the profile and possibilities for social justice video online.

Using open source tools these projects hope that once you start watching in this way you won't go back! Miro allows subscription to different channels of video content; some themed and some the pick of channel editors. You can even subscribe to You-Tube channels and it sneakily downloads those videos for you.

Independent Media is not stagnant, it's mutating. We'll start to see the fruits of this mutation soon... so stay tuned.

3. IN SEARCH OF COMMUNITY

By arguing that the anarchic internet prairie has turned into a battlefield, the previous chapter has shown how over the last decade the utopias that digital communitarians inherited from libertarian cyberculture revealed their empirical inconsistency. The opposition between lay citizens and big powers that Rheingold and the WELL community inherited from cybernetic culture faced the hype of crowds voluntarily contributing their contents and personal data to internet corporations. Instead of aggregating and exchanging information on peer-to-peer networks, more and more people rely upon few corporations in order to socialize online. New Communalists' decentralized organizational paradigm as well as the ethics of self-entrepreneurship and informal labour outsources content-production to amateurs, while shrinking resources for professionals. In this light, the gift economy fostered by academic networks and FLOSS communities has sustained the business model of new internet powers who gain revenues by promoting old brands through user-generated-contents. On a different level, early academic and hacker confidence about the uncontrollability of the Net faced geo-ID technologies for law enforcement, and sorting technologies that challenged privacy rights.

In summary, three early myths have been confuted by these developments: an imagined coalition between the rebels and entrepreneurs of the net, and related dreams of grassroots cultural alliances; the vision of the net as an uncontrollable space detached from the brick-and-mortar world, not subject to governments' sovereignty; and the belief that the sharing of information would empower individuals and communities against governmental and commercial powers.

Such dystopic evidence has led many internet scholars to acknowledge that the utopia of an internet rooted in communitarian harmony has left room for conflicts and competitions not too different from the ones affecting the brick-and-mortar world. Many wonder whether we can still talk about internet communitarianism, and, if so, under what conditions.

This chapter attempts to engage with social sciences scholars and media theorists who have formulated different responses to this question. On one hand, there are those who highlight the structural variations in the wider notion of 'community' in late modernity. On the other hand, other authors argue for new forms of communal ties on the net, on condition that the communitarian effort gets rid of the libertarian paradigm.

3.1 From Groups to Networks

The conviction that communitarian ties have been facing structural changes is shared by two of the most influential social scientists shaping the field of internet studies: Castells and Wellman. Yet their position is not only focused on online communities, nor is it limited in time to the evolution of the internet, rather, it tackles deeper societal transformations.

By using the expression 'networked individualism', Castells and Wellman call into question the possibility of identifying communitarian ties online. More precisely, they both argue that the traditional notion of online community as bounded groups have been replaced by networks of individuals interacting online in one-to-one patterns of communication. In Castells' 'space of flows', the individual is the hub of different kinds of streams that move from the place to the subject and vice versa.

According to Castells, social relationships are over determined by the technical organization of the means of production brought about by informational capitalism. That is, sociability is moulded in the shape that the dominant mode of production takes in the Information Age. Since the dominant form of organization of informational capitalism is the network, social relations reflect a similar structure.[1] 'Networked individualism' is thus a specific model of sociability rooted in the relationship between labour and the networked enterprise typical of the Information Age:

> Now the dominant trend in the evolution of social relationships in our societies is the rise of individualism, in all its manifestations. [...] Social scientists, such as Giddens, Putnam, Wellman, Beck, Carnoy, and myself, have emphasized the emergence of a new system of social relationships centered on the individual. After the transition from the predominance of primary relationships (embodied in families and communities) to secondary relationships (embodied in associations), the new, dominant pattern seems to be built on what could be called 'tertiary relationships', or what Wellman calls 'personalized communities,' embodied in me-centered networks. It represents the privatization of sociability. This individualized relationship to society is a specific pattern of sociability, not a psychological attribute. It is rooted, first of all, in the individualization of the relationship between capital and labor, between workers and the work process in the network enterprise.[2]

Me-centred networks can establish themselves offline and/or online: it is not the dichotomy of material vs. virtual that concerns Castells the most, rather the opposition between traditional (and somewhat mythological) territorial communities structured around dwelling proximity and social ties based on cultural affinity. According to Castells and other influential scholars he quotes, territoriality plays a less and less relevant role in shaping social relationships in advanced societies, being replaced instead by similarities of interests.[3] [4]In particular, Castells tends to associate the territorial type of relationship with the label 'community' and the cultural one with the term 'network'. As a consequence, Castells argues, we are witnessing the substitution of communities with networks as the primary form of social interaction:

> communities, at least in the tradition of sociological research, were based on the sharing of values and social organization. Networks are built by the choices and strategies of social actors, be it individuals, families, or social groups. Thus, the major transforma-

---

1   Castells, *The Rise of The Network Society*.
2   Castells, *Internet Galaxy*, p.128.
3   See among others, B. Wellman and M. Gulia, 'Netsurfers don't ride alone: virtual communities as communities, in B. Wellman (ed.) *Networks in the Global Village*, Boulder, Col.: Westview Press, 1999.
4   See among others, Wellman and Gulia, 'Netsurfers don't ride alone'.

tion of sociability in complex societies took place with the substitution of networks for spatial communities as major forms of sociability. [5] [6]

The principal model of sociability is thus constituted by a centre – built around the household nucleus – that spreads in many non-territorial directions according to individuals' interests. Castells tends to associate this kind of affinity-based ties with Wellman's 'weak ties'.[7]

If networked individualism is the model for both online and offline sociability in the Information Age, according to Castells internet only provides a material support for the spread of networked individualism as the dominant form of sociability. While social networks based on weak ties are not new, ICT have allowed them to become dominant. In so doing, Castells distances himself from technologically deterministic explanations and introduces a multi-causality model. Only once online networks get stabilized into social practices, can they build virtual communities.[8] However, stable virtual communities like the WELL or Nettime – Castells adds – are exceptions and it would be easier to understand them if we used the term 'networks of sociability'.[9]

Wellman shares with Castells some insights on networked individualism that he further develops by focusing on the interplay between urban space and social practices enabled by mobile media.[10] He suggests that research on online sociability should be carried on with attention to a wider context investigating the transformation of sociability patterns at large. According to Wellman, the proliferation of personal networks happened well before the advent of ICT: computer-mediated-communication (CMC) has only supported the emergence of individualized networks as the dominant form of social organization.

This approach allows Wellman to distance himself from cybercultural utopias, and to empirically examine the transformations triggered by computerized communication networks. Like Castells, Wellman carefully avoids mono-causality and technological determinism and outlines a retro-active mechanism to explain the relationship between technology and society:

> the technological development of computer networks and the societal flourishing of social networks are now in a positive feedback loop. Just as the flexibility of less-bounded, spatially dispersed social networks creates demand for the world wide web and collaborative communication, the breathless development of computer networks nourishes societal transitions from little boxes to social networks. [11]

---

5   Actually, this argument's logical consequentiality is not fully deployed, as it can be noticed from this quotation: it is not clear why community's 'values and social organization' should be seen as opposed to network's 'choices and strategies', as if networks were not built on common values. After four pages, in fact, Castells himself asserts that 'individuals build their networks, on-line and off-line, on the basis of their interests, values, affinities, and projects', Castells, *Internet Galaxy*, p. 131.
6   Castells, *Internet Galaxy*, p. 127.
7   Castells, *Internet Galaxy*, pp. 127-128.
8   This latter point is evidently in opposition with Rheingold's biological (and deterministic) understanding of virtual communities.
9   Castells, *Internet Galaxy*.
10   Wellman, 'Physical place and cyberplace'.
11   Wellman, 'Physical place and cyberplace',p. 2.

In Wellman's approach, technology does not 'cause' social transformations, but 'supports', 'enables', 'allows' them. Crucial in this regard is the introduction of the concept of 'social affordances' as 'the possibilities that technological changes afford for social relations and social structure'.[12] Notably, Wellman argues that portability, ubiquitous computing, globalized connectivity, and personalization are supporting the movement from place-to-place communities to person-to-person communities.

Place-to-place interactions[13] are centred on the household, where visits and telephone calls are received. This pattern of sociability links households and family nucleuses that are not in the same neighbourhood: home is the base for relationships that are more selective than the neighbourhood communities of the past. Furthermore, being based on inter-household networks, place-to-place connectivity creates a fluid system for accessing material and cognitive resources: by switching among networks, people can use ties in one network to bring resources to another one.[14]

The place-to-place model of sociability has enabled communities of affinity less constrained by territoriality yet it preserved some sense of social context. Conversely, person-to-person connectivity drastically reduces the sense of place. With 'person-to-person connectivity', Wellman indicates an emerging pattern of sociability enabled by innovations in communication technologies, notably by the development of mobile ICT centred on the individual:

> when someone calls a telephone wired into the telephone network, the phone rings
> at the place, no matter which person is being called. Indeed, many place-to-place
> ties have connected households as much as individuals. By contrast, mobile phones
> afford a fundamental liberation from place, and they soon will be joined by wireless
> computers and personalized software. Their use shifts community ties from linking
> people-in-places to linking people wherever they are. Because the connection is to the
> person and not to the place, it shifts the dynamics of connectivity from places--typically
> households or worksites--to individuals.[15]

The evolution from place-to-place to person-to-person connectivity introduces the second aspect which Wellman's paradigm shares with Castells'. Like Castells, Wellman conceives of the dichotomy between territorial and de-territorialized social ties as the most pertinent category for analysis, that cuts across the material/immaterial dichotomy.[16] He distinguishes,

---

12   Wellman, 'Physical place and cyberplace', p. 2.
13   Household-based place-to-place connectivity evolved from neighbourhood-based door-to-door interaction. 'Community interactions have moved inside the private home--where most entertaining, phone-calling and emailing take place--and away from chatting with patrons in public spaces such as bars, street corners and coffee shops', Wellman, 'Physical place and cyberplace, p.6.
14   We have already seen in section 2.1 that Turner, *From Culture to Counterculture*, calls the structure arising from this behaviour 'heterarchy'. Yet Turner refers only to online communities like the WELL.
15   Wellman, 'Physical place and cyberplace', pp. 8-9.
16   'The cyberspace-physical space comparison is a false dichotomy. Many ties operate in both cyberspace and physical space, used whatever means of communication is convenient and appropriate at the moment. [...] Myopically fixating on the rapidly-developing internet, hypesters, pundits, and wired

in fact, two main types of community: spatially defined community vs. a socially defined one. They roughly correspond to Castells' 'territorial community' and 'interest-based network' respectively. Actually, Wellman identifies four main uses of the term 'community', but he concentrates on only one: 'I define "community" networks of interpersonal ties that provide sociability, support, information, a sense of belonging, and social identity'.[17]

According to Wellman,[18] with the shift to mobile connectivity it is the individual, and not the household nor the group, that becomes the principal unit of interaction. It is around the individual that communities providing support, sociability, information, and a sense of belonging aggregate. This is why they are named 'personalized communities'.

A third aspect in common with Castells, relates to the dichotomies territorialized/affinity-based community and household/individual-centred community. On this, Wellman superimposes the structural distinction between group and network following his own early distinction between strong and weak ties.[19] Networks are sparsely-knit (i.e., few people are directly connected), far-flung, loosely-bounded (i.e., few ties stay within the densely-knit cluster), and fragmentary. In networked societies 'boundaries are permeable, interactions are with diverse others, connections switch between multiple networks, and hierarchies can be flatter and recursive'.[20] Conversely, groups are densely-knit, tightly-bounded and multithreaded (i.e., most ties contain many role relationships).

Group and networks are not necessarily opposed: 'formally, a group is a special type of network'.[21] However, Wellman prefers to simplify and fix an opposition: 'in practice, it is linguistically convenient to contrast groups and networks'.[22] Wellman also tends to identify the group/network dichotomy with the territorial/affinity-based community dichotomy: he basically uses the term 'group' to indicate neighbourhood-bounded door-to-door connectivity while the place-to-place and person-to-person models of interaction are structured as 'network'.

On one point Wellman's and Castells' positions differ. According to Wellman, community can resemble groups or networks or both, while for Castells it is opposed to networks and corre-

---

scholars have all wrongly proclaimed it to be a place apart. Yet systematic research shows that physical space and cyber space interpenetrate as people actively surf their networks online and offline', Wellman, 'Physical place and cyberplace', p. 19.

17   Wellman, 'Physical place and cyberplace', p. 2.

18   Apart from Castells, this argument is shared also by other scholars like, for instance, T. Kopomaa, *City in Your Pocket: Birth of the Mobile Information Society*, Helsinki: Gaudeamus, 2000.

19   B. Wellman, 'The Community Question: the Intimate Networks of East Yorkers', *American Journal of Sociology* 84: 1(1979): pp. 201-31; 'Structural analysis: from method and metaphor to theory and substance', in B. Wellman, and S. D. Berkowitz (eds) *Social Structures: A Network Approach*, Cambridge: Cambridge University Press, 1988; B. Wellman, P. J. Carrington and A. Hall, 'Networks as personal communities', in Wellman and Berkowitz (eds) *Social structures*; B. Wellman and B. Leighton, 'Networks, Neighborhoods and Communities: Approaches to the Study of the Community Question', *Urban Affairs Quarterly* 14 (1979): 363-90.

20   Wellman, 'Physical place and cyberplace', p.1.

21   Wellman, 'Physical place and cyberplace', p. 26.

22   Wellman, 'Physical place and cyberplace', p.26.

sponds rather to Wellman's definition of 'group'. Actually, for Wellman 'community' does not refer to a specific social structure, but it seems to be related to a particular type of substance that characterizes social ties through a sense of belonging.[23] As a consequence, given the current trend towards networks, Wellman concludes that nowadays we do not find community in bounded groups anymore, but rather in loose networks: 'arguments and evidence converge in thinking about the transformation of community from solidarity groups to individualized networks', today there is a 'predominance of networks (rather than groups) in communities'[24]

Castells' and Wellman's arguments are of merit in developing the crucial intuition that society and technology are intertwined in ways that are much more complex than simple causality models would imply. In Wellman, the multi-causality explanation model allows him to take distance from cyberculture's utopias underpinned by a simple cause-and-effect theory of action, and to introduce more variegated forms of interaction between technology and society. Yet in these authors' approaches these two dimensions are conceived of as distinct domains.

From another perspective, their approach set binary types of aggregation ('territorial community' vs. 'affinity-based community', 'collective' vs. 'individual', 'group' vs. 'network') that are to be used as starting points for sociological inquiries. However, it is not clear whether these categories only partially overlap, or whether one overlays/excludes the others. In Wellman's argument, for instance, bounded groups made of strong ties characterize door-to-door neighbourhood communities ('group' overlays the 'territorial community' category), while loose networks made of weak ties characterize communities based on common interests ('network' overlays the 'affinity-based community' category). Furthermore, networks as a structure characterize also person-to-person networks of individuals as well as place-to-place household-based communities. That is, 'network' overlays the 'individual' category and it also overlaps with 'collective' as far as household communities are concerned, but not as far as neighbourhood communities are concerned. In other words, while the 'territorial vs. interest community' dichotomy corresponds to the 'group vs. network' one, the 'collective vs. individual' dichotomy seems to be transversal to the previous ones.

On a different level, it is not evident why territorial, neighbourhood communities should be completely identified with bounded groups, while studies have usually shown that street corners and coffee shops are the 'third places' where mainly weak ties proliferate.[25] Similarly, it is not obvious why the intersection between 'group' and 'affinity-based community' is not taken into consideration. After all, it is at least as much likely that strong ties emerge from cultural affinity and similarity of interests as that they emerge from mere physical dwelling proximity.

---

23   See Wellman's definition of 'community' above. Actually, the way Wellman uses the term 'community' is fluctuating and sometimes contradictory. While most times it seems to refer to a substance that characterizes social ties based on solidarity and not to a structure, in some occasions it is used as synonymous of neighbourhood-based bounded group. For instance, 'where high speed place-to-place communication supports the dispersal and fragmentation of *community*, high speed person-to-person communication goes one step further and supports the dispersal and role-fragmentation of *households*', Wellman, 'Physical place and cyberplace', p. 9, *Author's emphasis*.

24   Wellman, 'Physical place and cyberplace', p. 7.

25   Oldenburg, *The Great Good Place*.

Such a terminological ambiguity is probably partly due to the two, divergent meanings that are associated with 'social': 'social' as related to human beings and thus opposed to 'technology', and 'social' as 'collection of human beings', thus opposed to 'individual'.[26] As to this point and to the notion of 'community' as a peculiar type of substance, we shall see in the next chapter how a shrunken meaning of 'social' could lead the researcher astray.

On the relationship between technology and society, Wellman's argument seems to lack logical consequentiality in its conclusions. Wellman acknowledges that internet facilitates the maintenance of weak ties and that mobile technologies' affordances enable the individual to be the hub of different flows of communication. However, this does not logically imply that 'networks of individuals' are the dominant type of aggregate making up the social world, nor that they can be seen as the best type of grouping with which to start a sociological inquiry. Logically speaking this is an inference that does not follow the premises. Apart from the fact that it minimizes the constraints related to the digital divide,[27] this inference follows a linear evolutionary model according to which dominant forms of sociability progressively replace non-dominant ones. Yet, as we shall see in section 4.3, different models of sociability do not need to be mutually exclusive, but can co-exist and fulfil different functions.

The point here is understanding whether 'group', 'network of individuals', 'territorial community', 'personalized community' are conceived of as ideal types that intertwine in the actual world, or whether Wellman looks at them as macro-structural trends that sharply cut society in terms of 'groups' or 'networks', place-to-place or person-to-person connectivity according to an evolutionist model that sees bounded groups withering in favour of me-centred loose networks.

3.2 Towards Organized Networks

Not all scholars who have addressed the question on whether digital communities are still relevant actors of the virtual world have turned to focus on the individual as the hub of contemporary computer-mediated models of sociability. Different solutions (and questions) come from the domain of media studies and software development.

Internet commentator Clay Shirky, for instance, has pointed out that the de-coupling of groups in space and time[28] allowed by the internet has ushered in a host of new social patterns which are embodied in social software. According to Shirky, what makes social software different from other communication tools is that through social software *groups* are brought into existence as entities in their own right.

---

26   Wellman, 'Physical place and cyberplace'.
27   'The "digital divide"--the income/locational/cultural gap between those comfortable with computerization and those not--is shrinking within the western (sic) world; the gender gap has already disappeared', Wellman 'Physical place and cyberplace, p. 3.
28   While Shirky does not mention him, it should be recalled that one of the first scholars that focused on space-time decoupling as a feature of 'late modernism' was Giddens, *Modernity and Self-Identity.*

A group of people interacting with one another will exhibit behaviours that cannot be predicted by examining the individuals in isolation, peculiarly social effects like flaming and trolling or concerns about trust and reputation. This means that designing software for group-as-user is a problem that can't be attacked in the same way as designing a word processor or a graphics tool.[29]

Since the software interface rearranges the regimes of access and visibility, 'social software is political science in executable form'.[30] This argument is a key one, as it draws an interpretation of 'the political sphere' which is immanent to digital media: handling the procedures and protocols whereby people aggregate, social software always embodies political decisions.

From a similar perspective, Geert Lovink and Ned Rossiter's 'organized networks' combine the efforts to assemble collective agents with that of addressing organizational impasses typical of digital communities, such as accountability, sustainability, and scalability. We have already seen how Lovink re-examines the notion of virtual communities as social networks and focuses on how they reflect society as well as anticipate new forms of social interaction.[31] Making a step forward, Lovink and Rossiter argue that online forms of cooperation are still possible, on condition that communitarian efforts distance themselves from the libertarian ideology.[32] [33]

First, Lovink and Rossiter specify that 'organized networks' are not a new type of social actor resulting from statistical analysis, but should be read as a proposal or guidelines aimed at replacing the inflated term 'virtual community'. Albeit on a theoretical level, the authors try to address many of the impasses we reviewed in the previous pages. The notion of 'organized networks' recognizes the limits that virtual communities and tactical media have been unable to deal with, and tries to figure out new strategic directions for techno-social assemblages that aim at experimenting forms of social interaction.

To do this, organized networks first need to acknowledge that instability, conflict, heterogeneity, passivity are the norm, and collaboration, unity and cooperation are exceptions. Freedom of refusal and 'notworking' are put at the very heart of any collaboration:

> organised networks are "clouds" of social relationships in which disengagement is pushed to the limit. Community is an idealistic construct and suggests bonding and harmony, which often is simply not there. [...] Networks thrive on diversity and conflict (the notworking), not on unity, and this is what community theorists are unable to reflect upon.[34]

---

29   C. Shirky, 'Social Software and the Politics of Groups', posting to Networks, Economics, and Culture mailing list, 2003, http://shirky.com/writings/group_politics.html.
30   Shirky, 'Social Software and the Politics of Groups'.
31   Lovink, *My First Recession*.
32   Lovink and Rossiter, 'Dawn of the Organized Networks'.
33   Lovink and Rossiter, 'Dawn of the Organized Networks'.
34   Lovink and Rossiter, 'Dawn of the Organized Networks, p. 2.

Despite claims for participation and interactivity, in the digital society passivity rules: activities like browsing, watching, waiting, surfing and long periods of 'interpassivity' characterize online life. Total involvement would mean billions of replies from all to all and the implosion of any network. Therefore – the authors argue – networks are kept together by a 'shared sense of potentiality' and at the same time are kept by the fact that this potentiality is realised only in part.

Furthermore, disagreement and distrust do not imply the disruption of the flow of dialogue. Rather, they act as productive principles, as 'disputes condition [...] internal to the creation of new institutional forms'.[35] To explain this point the authors introduce the notion of a 'constitutive outside' as a 'process of post-negativity in which rupture and antagonism affirm the future life of the network.[36] The tension between internal dynamics and external forces comprises a new ground of "the political"'.[37] [38] In other words, in organised networks the 'outside' always plays a constitutive role in determining the direction, actions and shape of the network, which is always situated. The 'other' is visible, present and active.

Similar to the approaches reviewed in the previous section, organized networks are made of loose ties, forms of collaboration are always temporary, voluntary and subjected to disengagement: 'networks foster and reproduce loose relationships. They are hedonistic machines of promiscuous contacts. Networked multitudes create temporary and voluntary forms of collaboration that transcend but do not necessary disrupt the Age of Disengagement'.[39]

Here is where Lovink and Rossiter meet Wellman. Yet there is a relevant difference between them. On one hand, while he disregards conflict, Wellman conceives of networks as structures and considers community as a sort of psychological substance – characterized by 'sense of belonging' – that nowadays is embodied in networked structures rather than in bounded groups. On the other hand, Lovink and Rossiter abandon the structuralist distinction between form and substance and, with it, the idealist construct of a community kept together by solidarity, harmony and support: conflict is as constitutive for networks as inner harmony is. In addition, the two authors specify that organised networks 'are specific in that they are situated within digital media'.[40]

By blurring the distinction between 'horizontal' and 'vertical' models of organization, organized networks aim at constituting themselves as new hybrid formations where tactical media encounter institutions: 'all forms of techno-sociality combine both horizontal and vertical forms of organization. Our argument is not so much that a hard distinction separates these modes of

---

35   Lovink and Rossiter 'Dawn of the Organized Networks, p. 3.
36   N. Rossiter, 'Creative Industries, Comparative Media Theory, and the Limits of Critique from Within', *Topia: A Canadian Journal of Cultural Studies* 11 (2004).
37   As well as for other scholars like Sassen, *Territory, Authority, Rights,* for instance, 'the political' is a very wide concept that transcends the formal political system made of parties and political institutions. An example provided by the authors is the activity of linking in blogs (see below).
38   Lovink and Rossiter, 'Dawn of the Organized Networks', p. 6.
39   Lovink and Rossiter, 'Dawn of the Organized Networks, p. 2.
40   Lovink and Rossiter, 'Dawn of the Organized Networks, p. 1.

organization, as a degree in scale.'[41] As in Turner's concept of heterarchy, their hybrid nature would allow organized networks to obtain benefits from both the tactical and the institutional domains. In particular, in order to develop their own form of organisation, emergent organised networks must address three crucial aspects: accountability, sustainability, and scalability.

As to accountability, Lovink and Rossiter do not leave room for much ambiguity: 'networks disintegrate traditional forms of representation [...] it is time to abandon the illusion that the myths of representational democracy might somehow be transferred and realised within network setting. That is not going to happen'.[42] Nor do process-oriented forms of governance like those experimented by hackers seem to be sustainable in the long haul. According to the authors, the issue of accountability and transparency are crucial and need to be addressed starting from a set of questions: 'Where does it [i.e., the organised network] go? How long does it last? Why do [sic] it in the first place? But also: who is speaking? And: why bother? A focus on the vital forces that constitute socio-technical life is thus required'.[43]

Another major issue is sustainability. Here is where organised networks distance themselves the most from their precursors of the 1990s – lists, collaborative blogs, alternative media[44] – that rarely put business models on the agenda. Lovink and Rossiter on the contrary break some taboos associated with early independent digital communities. The first is planning. According to the authors, current independent digital networks must overcome their self-destructive tendency and accept the challenge of cautious planning. Defining a collaborative value system that is able to address issues like funding, internal power management, accountability, and transparency constitutes the first step.

The second taboo to be faced is legal status. The constitution of an organization with legal status should not be excluded. Third, as work has to be paid, it is necessary to face economic reality and to outline how networks can be funded over time. The economy of the free can work for free software geeks that develop their own coding projects, but not necessarily for cultural, artistic, activist projects, content editors, and web-designers. Fourth, as attracting funding from private philanthropy, governments and business tends to be a hard task, complementary currencies need to be devised.[45] Devising alternative currencies would also allow organised networks to refuse the cybercultural logic of free labour and free contents.

Lastly, another issue that organized networks have to face is scalability. It tackles a well-known aspect of online communities: the tendency to split up in myriad micro-conversations when they reach a few thousand participants. According to Lovink and Rossiter, this issue lies at the convergence between software architecture and internal power structures. In this regard, the notion of the 'constitutive outside' is crucial: it is exactly because organised networks

---

41   Lovink and Rossiter, 'Dawn of the Organized Networks, p. 10.
42   Lovink and Rossiter, 'Dawn of the Organized Networks', pp. 3-4.
43   Lovink and Rossiter, 'Dawn of the Organized Networks', p. 4.
44   See sections 1.3 and 1.4.
45   *Note added during the 2018 revision.* It is striking to note how Lovink and Rossiter's intuition was to become one of the most disruptive innovations, even well outside internet cultures, almost ten years later with cryptocurrency experimentation and successive hype.

need to open up new horizons within which 'the political' find a space of expression that the requirement of scalability has to be addressed. If in the digital organised network the 'outside' has to play a constitutive role in determining the actions of the network, then software needs to embody this principle by allowing the 'other' to be always visible and present.[46] However, addressing this demand for scalability means to overtly recognize internal informal power structures and to go beyond the dominant assumption of decentralization that prevents the discussion about new forms of organization – the authors argue.

Once the taboo of decentralisation has been called into question, for Lovink and Rossiter it is easy getting rid of the last legacies of the techno-libertarian cyberculture. First, they point out how blogs and social networks are based on software that refuses antagonisms. Similar software does not leave any other choice than accepting an inflation of friends: 'this is New Age revivalism at work, desperately insecure, and in search of a "friend".'[47]

Second, the authors observe that while wiki software allows the collaborative creation of 'collective intelligence', this specific social-technical model will probably not work in all cultures and countries, as, for instance, those where public work and full visibility are not appreciated. Despite free culture's claims, sharing knowledge is not a universal value.

Third, Lovink and Rossiter point out the naivety of those initiatives, like the Creative Commons, that seek to conquer institutions and cultural industries to their cause by recalling their 'non-political' character, while, on the contrary, 'there is no escape from politics'. According to the authors, the rhetoric of openness hides the political motivations and economic interests at work in these projects: 'the provocation of organised networks is to unveil these mechanisms of control and contradiction, to discuss the power of money flows, and to redirect funds [...] the organised network has to break with the "information must be free" logic'.[48]

3.3 The Proliferation of 'Community'

At the end of this long *excursus*, the reader might feel puzzled, wondering whether in the first decade of the 21st century talking of communitarian ties being developed online makes sense at all. She would have good reasons to be justified in her puzzlement.

Despite the radical ongoing transformations discussed in chapter 2, nowadays references to 'community' are more numerous than ever. According to the *2007 Digital Future Report*

---

46   Contrarily to what happens with blogs – the authors argue, where the 'enemy' is invisible and only
     friends are present. This is possible because the logic of blogs is that of the link. It is links that enhance
     visibility through a ranking system, and links correspond to 'friends', to the blog's cultural enclave.
     All what is outside the zone of affinity simply does not exist. With blogs 'the political' corresponds to
     the moment of linking. 'The fact that I do NOT link to you remains invisible. [...] Blogs can thus be
     understood as incestuous networks of auto-reproduction', Lovink and Rossiter, 'Dawn of the Organized
     Networks', 7. Blogs are not organised networks because they are not open, they close themselves to the
     potential for change. See also Lovink, *Zero Comments*.
47   Lovink and Rossiter, 'Dawn of the Organized Networks', p. 8.
48   Lovink and Rossiter, 'Dawn of the Organized Networks', p. 8.

elaborated by USC Annenberg School Center for the Digital Future, 67.2 percent of members of online communities[49] answer their community is very or extremely important to them, while 46.1 percent of members say they benefit a lot from their community and only 3.8 percent find no benefit from their online community.[50] Under different forms, online communities are recognized as key social aggregates in diverse fields of activity. While 'cyber-communities' are disappearing from the top of the digital culture's hot concepts list, articles about 'social networking sites' colonize high-tech magazines' columns, 'communities of practice' constitute the backbone of corporate knowledge management policies, while almost every venture capitalist and internet marketer invokes participation through 'Web 2.0 community tools' as a strategic component adding value to internet companies' investments.[51]

While the cyberculture paradigm underpinning the notion of online community is showing its limits, other domains are taking over this concept. As a consequence, its boundaries have become fuzzy. In late 2000s, online communities are becoming more and more difficult to identify, and the relationship between access to digital media and empowerment hard to disentangle. It is not clear anymore whether there exist ties that are specific enough to be called 'communitarian' and that can be assembled together in constituting a special assemblage. 'Community' seems to be watered down: it is diffused everywhere and yet nowhere in particular.

To a phenomenological observation, one can see three currents that are rippling the apparently flat ocean's surface of digital communities. First, to the new popularity of digital communities an ever-widening meaning of community corresponds. There is a clear etymological trend in the successive variations of this expression. It goes from the most specific and context-related meaning of the 1980s' underground scene to the most generic one. As a matter of fact, the definition of digital communities has been ranging up to include almost every form of aggregation through ICT: RSS feeding, tagging, blogging, bookmarking associate multimedia objects as well as digital *personae*.

What is thus at stake is not only the possibility to identify communities, but the meaning of the same notions of collaboration and the nature (human/machinic) of those actors supposed to collaborate. Can individuals using the same tags in order to organize and share their own pictures through a web platform be considered a community or, at least, a network? Which kind of collaboration is conveyed by a video posted in order to critically respond to a previously published one? Are the bonds arising from blog cross-linking similar to those originated through USENET? Ultimately, these questions lead to ask whether it is possible to extend agency to technological artefacts.

---

49   The Digital Future project defines 'online community' as 'a group that shares thoughts or ideas, or works on common projects, through electronic communication only'.

50   Jeffrey I. Cole et al., 'The 2007 Digital Future Report: Surveying the Digital Future. Year Six.' USC Annenberg School Center for the Digital Future. 2007. https://www.digitalcenter.org/wp-content/uploads/2013/02/2007_digital_future_report-year6.pdf

51   Bazzichelli, 'Stalder'.

Second, it might be affirmed that the term 'online community' has been growing in popularity as the range of potential shared interests has widened. The Berkshire Encyclopaedia of Human Computer Interaction indicates that digital divide reduction, open access to ICT, local communities' empowerment, and revitalized democracy were the issues that were mostly addressed by 'cybercommunities' during late 1990s and early 2000s. With social networking sites and Web 2.0 the identification of an explicit interest focus – beyond sociability itself – has become increasingly hard. If early digital communities were glued together exactly by a common mission, this doesn't seem the case anymore. In her effort to classify text-based virtual communities, for instance, Mascio recognizes that 'since it is usually very generic, the interest focus cannot be considered a prolific category for research'.[52]

Likewise, echoing Wellman's vocabulary, boyd and Ellison argue that social network sites mark a shift from interest-centred networks to me-centred networks and that this shift 'mirrors' a new organizational structure of online communities:

> the rise of SNSs indicates a shift in the organization of online communities. While websites dedicated to communities of interest still exist and prosper, SNSs are primarily organized around people, not interests. Early public online communities such as Usenet and public discussion forums were structured by topics or according to topical hierarchies, but social network sites are structured as personal (or "egocentric") networks, with the individual at the center of their own community. This more accurately mirrors unmediated social structures, where "the world is composed of networks, not groups".[53] The introduction of SNS features has introduced a new organizational framework for online communities, and with it, a vibrant new research context.[54]

Third, we are witnessing the explosion of the *gemeinschaft* well beyond the domain of sociology and computer science – towards economics and management, as well as beyond academic institutions – towards market and corporate media. It has crashed the boundaries of social sciences and urban planning to shore on the crowded coast of business, internet companies and media discourse. Amin and Thrift argue that while the concept of 'community' is called into question inside its native urban studies domain, paradoxically it seems to gain new relevance as a key element of success for economic systems.[55] In order to explain why some cities have turned out to be more competitive than others, for example, scholars like Storper and Scott have stressed the role of community-based non-economic ties in economic processes of adaptation and knowledge sharing.[56] Similarly, a number of works have argued that the key to success with online businesses is the development of virtual communities.[57]

---

52   L. Mascio, 'Le comunità virtuali *text-based*', *Versus*, numero monografico sulla semiotica dei nuovi media, 2003, p.157.
53   Wellman, 'Structural analysis', p.37.
54   boyd and Ellison, 'Social network sites', p.10.
55   A. Amin, and N. Thrift, *Cities. Reimagining the urban*, Cambridge: Polity Press, 2001.
56   M. Storper, *The Regional World*, New York: Guilford Press, 1997; A.J. Scott, *Metropolis*, Los Angeles: University of California Press, 1988.
57   L. Downes and C. Mui, *Unleashing the Killer App: Digital Strategies for Market Dominance,* Boston, Mass.: Harvard Business School Press, 1998; J. Hagel, and A. G. Armstrong, *Net Gain: Expanding*

As a consequence of these movements, it is by no means certain that nowadays what is meant by the term 'online community' in all these domains relates to the same thing. As we have seen in chapter 1, Rheingold's foundational book can be conceived of as a rhetorical performative endeavour to merge multiple streams in a coherent account of online sociability. Such an endeavour converged along the lines of the dominant U.S. cyberlibertarian paradigm, and conceived communal ties as a sort of 'substance'. This explains why early researchers in the 1990s could quite straightforwardly not only postulate specific definitions of digital communities, but also classify them on the basis of their kind of interface (text-based/graphics) or of time modalities (synchronous/asynchronous).[58]

However, when it came to explaining how digital communities are upkept and reproduced, the digital communitarian paradigm fell short of convincing theories. Scholars and practitioners have thus attempted to explain sense of belonging not as a substance, but in terms of the structural form of the network,[59] as a shift from an aesthetics of representation to an aesthetics of interaction,[60] as a form of consensus building embedded in software platforms,[61] or even by negating any predetermined sense of belonging.[62]

Some of these attempts were justified in the backdrop of recent developments in the economy of the internet and in the politics of information (see chapter 2), which have called into question the utopias that the digital community paradigm inherited from cyberculture. The shift from the prairie to the battlefield has been acknowledged by scholars and commentators who have renounced to acknowledge peculiar social aggregates kept together by communal ties. Influential sociologists discussed in this chapter, for example, have even replaced 'communities' with 'networks' of individuals.

Other scholars – like Lovink and Rossiter – are more optimistic towards the renaissance of communitarian ties online, provided that the collaborative perspective gets rid of the libertarian paradigm that postulates harmony, stability, homogeneity, and proactivity as the norm. Along this same line lies the main proposal of this book. Instead of claiming the ontological death of digital communitarian ties, it suggests that in the face of contemporary developments an anti-essentialist, materialist perspective has to be mobilized. Such an epistemological perspective entails the refusal of a priori definitions of 'community', and rather privileges asking actors themselves to provide accounts of what 'community' means for them.

Drawing on the developments accounted for in chapter 2, but avoiding swift conclusions, this book in other words suggests that such developments can constitute an opportunity to answer an open question by means of empirical analysis. Under what conditions is it possible to conceptualize online sociability in the first decade of the 21st century? Answering this

---

Markets Through Virtual Communities, Boston, Mass.: Harvard Business School Press, 1997.

58   Jones, *Cybersociety; Cybersociety 2.0;* Smith, *Voices from the WELL*

59   Castells, T*he Rise of The Network Society, Volume I: The Information Age.*

60   See section 1.3

61   See section 1.4, Shirky, 'Social Software and the Politics of Groups'.

62   Lovink and Rossiter, 'Dawn of the Organized Networks'.

question would liberate the communitarian perspective from many of the misunderstandings that dragged it into such a blind alley.

The chapters that follow answer this question by avoiding a macro account and by investigating the theories of actions that have underpinned the development of techno-social assemblages for online collaboration after the fade of the 'golden age' of digital communities. In so doing, it returns a multi-faceted picture of contemporary sociability online. The next chapter starts with an analysis of the notion of 'digital communities' in the words of their spokespersons.

4. WHAT REMAINS OF COMMUNITY

4.1 A Relational Definition of 'Digital Community'

When it comes to a definition of 'online' or 'digital community', actors currently involved in similar initiatives retain some aspects inherited from early experiences. This chapter explores the elements associated with 'digital community' in the applications submitted to Ars Electronica Digital Communities competition from 2004 to 2007. In other words, it 'asks' social actors themselves what they meant by this expression when they participated in a competition for 'digital communities'.

To do so, I have initially relied on textual analysis applications, and then conducted more fine-grained, qualitative analyses.[1] *Leximancer* is a data-mining software originally developed at the University of Queensland in Brisbane. It can conduct both thematic analysis, by identifying main concepts based on their frequency, and relational analysis, by measuring how often concepts occur close together within the same text.

A combination of thematic and relational analysis is ideal to address this book's main epistemological concerns, recalled in the introduction. The chosen software could perform concept extraction without forcing the researcher to define key concepts in advance,[2] nor did it borrow them from a predefined generic dictionary. It extracted its own dictionary for each document set from the co-variation among high-frequency words in the text collection. For each high-frequency word, the software extracted a thesaurus; through the thesaurus, concept classes were calculated so that co-occurrence patterns were maximized. While not being 'neutral', such a calculation had the advantage of defining a concept not by any substance, but by a list of associations.

Results can be displayed in three different ways. First, a conceptual map provides a bird's eye view, represents the most frequent concepts and how they co-occur. Furthermore, a ranked linked list summarizes the main concepts and gives access to their patterns of co-occurrence. Finally, a browsing function allows navigating through the textual excerpts of a concept or of a co-occurrence between two concepts. In summary, Leximancer provided a means of both quantifying and displaying the conceptual structure of a document set, as well as a means of using this information to qualitatively explore textual excerpts.

Differently from the analysis reported in the next chapter which did not profile any starting concept, the analysis in this chapter profiled the conceptual network associated with 'digital communities'.[3] The software was set in a way that words that often co-occur with this string

---

1   Furthermore, *InfoRapid Search and Replace* and a statistical application were used to conduct the last
     analysis reported in this chapter, namely the comparison between 'groups' and 'networks'.
2   This preliminary definition is nonetheless possible, depending on how the software is set.
3   In setting the software, I defined 'digital community' by merging the terms 'community', 'communities',
     'online', 'virtual', 'digital, so that online/virtual/digital community have been made methodologically
     indistinguishable.

made up a thesaurus. Words in the thesaurus displayed a high *relevancy value*: they tended to appear frequently in blocks of text where the string appeared, and to be absent elsewhere. The thesaurus for the concept 'digital community' included the following terms (in decreasing order of relevance): [4]

community, online, virtual, communities, [[takingitglobal]], combines, [[east_kilbride]], self-help, supportive, [[ubuntu]], telecentre, [[socrates]], librarians, aphasics, [[seniornet]], nonprofit, [[social_edge]], [[namma_dhwani]], nsw, orientation, community-builders, disenfranchised, [[icohere]], [[bawb]], -operation, [[tapped_in]], [[catcomm]], [[i-neighbors]], neighboring, qualitative, [[netco]], [[codetree]], gatherings, [[aboriginal]], aspirations, [[ngv]], place-base, [[war_zone]], [[budikote]], nurturing, customised, [[global_south]], [[modernist]], recognizes, complain, programmatic, delays, publicize, wisdom, astonishing, cares, king, promotions, instructional, [[new_town]], [[canonical]], [[minnesota]], war-affected, [[content_village]], [[fabasoft_egov-forms]], reservation, folksonomies, hometown, marginalised, [[commkit]], grrrl, zine, [[wbt]], first-hand, [[mongrel]], deepen, [[arrernte]], netznetz, investments, zines, affords, definitive, argue, descent, signifiers, legacies, courageous, [[nkca]], [[mol]], guesthouse, mediatheque, [[virtual]], [[official_proceedings_online]], [[econtent]], harnessed, impoverished, statewide, [[transmission]]

What strikes at first sight is the high percentage of proper names (39.3%). They mainly refer to digital initiatives and FLOSS development communities (e.g., *Transmission.cc, Ubuntu, Catcomm, Taking it Global, NGV*, etc.), while a limited number refers to geographical names (Minnesota, 'Global South'). At a deeper observation, some terms related to a potential 'grassroots empowerment' theme are visible: 'self-help', 'supportive', 'disenfranchised', 'nonprofit', 'marginalised', 'global_south', 'cares', 'communitybuilders', 'impoverished', 'nurturing'. There appear also some Web 2.0-related items ('folksonomies', 'customised', 'investments'), as well as some references to local, territorially bounded communities ('neighboring', 'i-neighbors', 'place-based').

However, words appearing in the thesaurus are only 'seeds' from which new concepts are 'learnt' through stochastic calculus. Indeed, the combination of thematic and relational analysis is aimed to cluster together concepts that co-occur often together and rarely with others. Four different types of metrics result: 1) the most frequent concepts (see Table 2 in Annex C); 2) the strength of links between concepts (i.e., how often they co-occur); 3) the centrality of each concept to the data set; 4) similarities in the context in which they occur. Figure 1 shows the conceptual map for 'digital community' as extracted from the Ars Electronica's data set. The strength of a concept's label relates to its relative frequency in the text, varying from black (highly frequent) to light grey (less frequent). The size of the concept point indicates its connectedness. Nearness in the map indicates that two concepts appear in similar conceptual contexts. The colour indicates thematic groups.

---

4   I am not reporting the whole thesaurus, but only the first, more often occuring terms with a relevancy value higher than 5.3. Items enclosed in double brackets are identified as proper names due to the amount of instances in which they are capitalized.

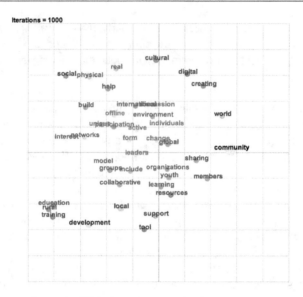

Figure 1: Conceptual map for 'digital community'. Bird's eye.

Taking a bird's eye view, some concepts tend to remain close to each other at every resetting and re-learning and to form clusters:[5]
- 'education', 'training', 'rural', 'development';
- 'community', 'members';
- 'social', 'physical', 'real', 'build', 'help';
- 'learning', 'resources';
- 'individuals', 'change';
- 'collaborative', 'include', 'model', 'groups';
- 'youth', 'organizations'.

Other concepts are more unstable: they travel across the map from time to time and do not establish permanent ties with any other concept. 'Tool', 'creating', 'support, 'cultural', 'world', 'network', and 'sharing' are instances of such loose concepts.

To understand the meaning of these behaviours it is necessary to take into consideration what nearness in the map represents for Leximancer. The map is initially built by placing the concepts randomly on the grid. Each concept pulls other concepts with a strength related to their co-occurrence value: the more frequently two concepts co-occur, the stronger will be the force of attraction (the shorter the spring that connects them), forcing frequently co-occurring concepts to be closer on the final map. However, because there are many forces of attraction acting on each concept, it is impossible to create a map in which every concept is at the expected distance away from every other concept. Rather, concepts with similar attractions to all other concepts become clustered together. That is, concepts like 'education', 'training', 'rural', 'development' that appear in similar regions in the map also appear in similar contexts

---

5   Being stochastic, the map needs to be reset and re-learnt several times before being stabilized.

in the data set, i.e. they co-occur with the other concepts to a similar degree. On the contrary, loose concepts like 'tool', 'network, 'support, 'cultural', 'sharing', although being quite relevant for the main concept profiled (their labels tend to black), exert different degrees of attraction on the other concepts. That is, they frequently co-occur with 'digital community', but do not so much appear in similar contexts with other concepts.

For this reason, the clusters above mentioned may be conceived of as recurring themes and might be renamed[6] as:
- rural/local development through education;
- community's organizational aspects;
- contribution of the digital realm to the physical one;
- knowledge resources;
- individuals as agents of change;
- models of inclusion through collaboration;
- youth organizations.

4.2 Recovered and Abandoned Paths

The attentive reader might recognize among those themes some of the topics that had accompanied the emergence and development of the digital communitarian culture, as recalled in chapter 1. First, Rheingold's early, foundational distinction between real world and virtual life is implicit in the 'contribution of the digital realm to the physical world' theme. This theme mainly focuses on empowerment possibilities entailed by the emerging virtual domain, expected to solve long-lasting issues plaguing the brick-and-mortar world, as illnesses, poverty, and lack of democracy.

Second, in the above list there is a clear mention of communitarian localism through the 'local development through education' theme. As Rheingold's computer networks find their communitarian dimension in the relatively small scale and in the sense of solidarity among peers, so improving local living conditions is a key goal for many submitters to the Ars Electronica's competition. Strictly related, suspicion towards institutions and hierarchical forms of reputation is to be found in references to bottom-up communitarian organization.

Finally, the focus on individuals as agents of change resonates with cyberculture's thrust towards decentralized, anarchic, and distributed forms of organization. However, early 2000s digital communities do not see decentralization as the outcome of technocratic delegation of control functions to machines.

Some remarkable evidence emerges when taking into account topics specific to early cyber-

---

6   Far from being arbitrary, the renaming proceeds from browsing into textual extracts in which the concepts clustered together co-occur. This is one of the cases in which the software's browsing function facilitates joint quantitative and qualitative analysis.

culture, which are conversely absent from the 2000s list/map of relevant concepts. Among the 60 concepts extracted from the data set there is no reference to biological metaphors, nor to other cybernetic themes like, for instance, 'decentralization'. Another semantic domain that looks absent is the one related to the Web 2.0: if some references appeared in the initial thesaurus, they have disappeared in the final concept list. Even more surprising is the absence of any explicit reference to technology: apart from a generic 'digital', that mostly features as an adjective of 'community', the only reference to technological artefacts, the web or software can be found under the label 'tool'.[7]

It should be recalled that an absence at this level of analysis does not mean that these topics are alien to the data set as a whole, but that they are not associated with 'online community'.[8] This is an outcome in itself. It is because these results number *only* the themes associated with 'online community' that we can trace the disappearance of some elements particular to 'online community' in early cyberculture from a nominally similar one (i.e., 'online community' in the Ars Electronica data set).

These shifts reveal to us which paths have been abandoned in our data set, with respect to original cyberculture: cybernetic discourse and its reliance on technology as a neutral organizational agency and the immaterial gift as a way to upkeep communities as a social homeostat. Conversely, if we investigate which new combinations are explored and which new elements are associated with 'online community' among the above themes, only one element is new, namely the reference to 'youth organizations'. A clear sign that new framings in 2000s have taken the place of the old 'online community'.

4.3 The Possible Coexistence of Groups and Networks

In the Ars Electronica data set, the concept that most frequently co-occurs with 'online community' is 'development', followed by 'local', 'world', 'members', 'digital', 'support', 'social', 'creating', 'tool', 'resources' (see Table 3 in Annex C). In figure 2, the co-occurrence pattern for 'online community' is also revealed by the brightness of the links, which represents to how often two connected concepts co-occur closely within the text.

---

7   Actually, 'tool' occurs quite frequently and, when browsing extracts, it works as an umbrella term for all kind of technological objects.

8   As we shall see in the next chapter, in fact, some of these absences will be filled up when we abandon the exclusive focus on 'online community'.

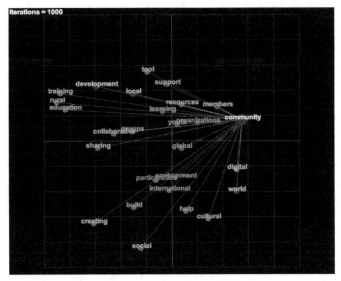

Figure 2: Co-occurrence pattern for the concept 'online community'.

The most interesting results concern the co-occurrence between 'online community' and 'networks'. This provides the opportunity to recall Wellman's argument about communities made up of networks rather than groups (see section 3.1). One can notice that in the Ars Electronica data set 'online community' co-occurs more frequently with the term 'groups' (2.4% of instances wherein 'online community' occurs) than with the term 'networks' (1.9%). Furthermore, in figure 2 'groups' corresponds not only to a single concept, but also to a thematic cluster including other concepts like 'collaborative', 'include', 'model', while 'networks' appears as a loose concept which does not co-occur with other concepts.

In order to verify a hypothetical counter-argument to Wellman's, I conducted a further co-occurrence analysis by means of Boolean textual software, *InfoRapid Search and Replace*. My aim was to test his distinction between communities as bounded groups vs. loose networks by translating his argument first into a set of hypotheses and then into logical strings.

Here are the hypotheses. If Wellman's argument was true, when one carries on a search into a data set made of accounts, the number of cases wherein the term 'online community' co-occurs with the term 'network' should be higher than the number of cases where the term 'online community' co-occurs with the term 'group'. Moreover, Wellman's sharp distinction between groups and networks would lead to expect that 'network' and 'group' be mutually exclusive and very rarely occur together. Even more, they should not jointly co-occur with 'online community'. Figure 3 visualizes these hypotheses and translates them into equations.

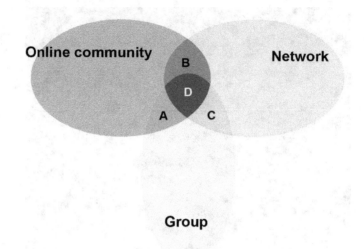

Figure 3: Logical intersections between 'online community', 'network', 'group'.

A represents the intersection of 'online community' with 'group', that is, the cases where both terms 'online community' and 'group' are present in the same submission. B represents the intersection of 'online community' with 'network', C the intersection of 'group' with 'network' and D the intersection of 'online community', 'group', and 'network'. Using this scheme, one can extract three hypothetical equations from Wellman's argument:

1 – A < B (intersection of 'OC' and 'group' is minor than the intersection of 'OC' and 'network')

2 – C = 0 (intersection of 'network' and 'group' equals 0)

3 – D = 0 (intersection of 'OC', 'network' and 'group' equals 0)

To verify these equations, I conducted text search with Boolean operators throughout the whole data set. I first replaced plurals and compound expressions, thus obtaining three strings – 'DIGCOM', 'network', 'group' – suitable to run the Boolean search. I then coded the equations into logical strings:

1.   As to the first hypothesis (A<B), I coded A as DIGCOM&group&!network (intersection of 'DIGCOM' and 'group' and not 'network') and B as DIGCOM&NETWORK&!group (intersection of 'DIGCOM' and 'network' and not 'group'). The resulting equation to be tested was DIGCOM&group&!network < DIGCOM&NETWORK&!group

2.   To test the second hypothesis (C = 0), I coded C as group&network. The resulting equation was group&network = 0

3.   To test the third hypothesis (D = 0), I coded D as group&network&DIGCOM. The resulting equation to be tested was group&network&DIGCOM = 0

As a matter of fact, all the three hypotheses derived from Wellman's argument were falsified. Running a Boolean search across the Ars Electronica data set, I found not only that 'group' and 'network' are not mutually exclusive, but also that 'digital community' occurs more often with 'group' than with 'network'. Let's see the results for the three hypotheses in detail.[9]

First hypothesis: A < B. Actually, it turned out that A > B. A (intersection of 'DIGCOM' and 'group' and not 'network') = 401 occurrences, while B (intersection of 'DIGCOM' and 'network' and not 'group') = 208 occurrences. In less formal terms, in the data set there were more cases in which 'group' and 'digital community' co-occured without 'network' than cases in which 'network' and 'digital community' co-occured without 'group'. Therefore, the first hypothesis was falsified.

Second hypothesis: C = 0. On the contrary, the Boolean search found that C (intersection of 'group' and 'network') = 3117 occurrences. In other words, in 3117 cases 'group' and 'network' co-occured together in the same submissions. Again, the hypothesis was falsified.

Third hypothesis: D = 0. The result of the second hypothesis found further confirmation when verifying the third one. The Boolean search found that D (intersection of 'group' and 'network' and 'DIGCOM') = 2144 occurrences. In less formal terms, I found 2144 cases in which 'group', 'network', and 'online community' co-occured together.

In summary, by running a Boolean search across Ars Electronica's Digital Communities archive, I found more cases in which 'group' and 'online community' co-occur than cases in which 'network' and 'online community' do. Furthermore, not only 'group' and 'network' are not mutually exclusive, but they occur very often together in accounts by social actors directly involved in online assemblages.

From these results three considerations may be drawn. First, loose networks are not the exclusive form of sociability when it comes to communal ties online. Rather, they co-exist with other models of sociability that actors label as 'groups', whatever it means. It is likely that different models of sociability fulfil different functions, even if this consideration remains at the level of hypothesis and does not follow from the results.

Second, as we know from technology studies, rarely is linear evolution the best model to explain techno-social change. Rather than a situation where newer forms of sociability progressively replace older ones, the results show their co-existence. The relationship between information technology and social forms is definitely much more variegated than one could expect, and social change cannot be linearly inferred from technological evolution. Just as internet and mobile technologies have not killed television yet, there are many probabilities that loose networks won't eradicate bounded groups in the coming years. For social scientists,

---

9   The complete results of all the searches are reported in Annex C, Tables 4-7.

avoiding sharp dichotomies that shrink the abundance of the social into predefined tracks might probably turn out to be more laborious, but it is well-known that approximation has always been an enemy of science.

Third, the results corroborate the appropriateness of the methodological choice to refrain from adopting any established type of aggregate as an incontrovertible starting point. Since 'network' and 'group' are not even seen as mutually exclusive by social actors themselves, it is difficult to figure out how one of the two should be a better starting point for inquiry. From the comparison of well acquainted sociological positions with rich and multi-faceted accounts the need to level up social actors' own accounts to academic arguments emerges. The results should thus not be read as a further demonstration of the inability of social actors to understand the macro-structural trends at work in the world they inhabit. Conversely, these results suggest the need to jointly investigate macro-structural trends and perception, *episteme* and *doxa*. 'Sociologists are on par with those they study, doing exactly the same job and participating in the same tasks of tracing social bonds, albeit with different instruments and for different professional callings'.[10]

---

10   Latour, *Reassembling the Social,* p. 34.

5. COMMUNITIES BEYOND 'COMMUNITY'

While the previous chapter has investigated the semantic profiling of 'online community', this chapter aims to analyse how communities are implicitly enacted through the data sets of submissions to Ars Electronica's Digital Communities competition. Drawing on an anti-essentialist, performative approach[1], it focuses on the way communities are said to exist by spokespersons to a major international competition.[2] Such an approach allows bypassing 1990s' discussions about what should be considered a 'proper' online community, and focusing instead on techno-social assemblages that are acknowledged as occurrences of digital communities by virtue of being presented to and admitted by one such competition.

To do so, the chapter retains a relational definition of digital communities, and identifies the relevant topics in the data set. As seen in chapter 4, the chosen software defines as 'relevant' those concepts which are not only more frequent, but also more often co-occurring in a cluster of other frequent words. In Leximancer a word is said to be 'part of' a concept if it often co-occurs with it and occurs not so often with other concepts (i.e., the relevancy standard deviation value is above a set threshold). This inclusion is achieved through 'learning', an iterative process in which the collection of terms defining a concept is updated, so that initially central terms can reach a peripheral position or even be lost when relevancy is normalised after a certain number of iterations. The aim of concept learning is to discover clusters of words which, when taken together as a concept, maximise the relevancy values of all the other words in the document.

Despite machine learning, the method followed in this research left the researcher much more room than using software automation would suggest. On one hand, the specific software techniques used were selected by attentively setting the software.[3] Very different results were obtained by changing only a few settings. For example, the analysis discussed in the previous chapter established 'online community' as seeding word, and results were considerably different from those discussed in this chapter, which were obtained by not setting any seeding word.

On the other hand, software-extracted concepts constituted only the starting point of the analysis. It was only by qualitatively comparing the relative strengths of concepts co-occurring with the most relevant ones that I came to identify full-blown topics and narratives. Actually, the effort to move from mined concepts to full-blown topics informs this whole chapter.

Figure 4 shows the conceptual map extracted from the data set without any word seeding

---

1   Given the steps ahead – and in parallel – in the performativity debate, during the revision for the 2018 edition the author has deemed appropriate to update the original manuscript with more recent, key references.

2   Note to the 2018 Edition. J. Butler, 'Performative Agency', *Journal of Cultural Economy* 3.2 (2010): 147-161; M. Callon, 'Performativity, Misfires and Politics', *Journal of Cultural Economy* 3.2 (2010): 163-169.

3   See Table 8 in Annex C. Key settings are emphasized in italics.

function.[4] The map's most remarkable characteristic is its stability: at every resetting, concepts aggregated in stable clusters. Differently from the conceptual map in the previous chapter, in which loose concepts were reshuffled at every resetting, here it was possible to identify recurrent and stabilized concept clusters.

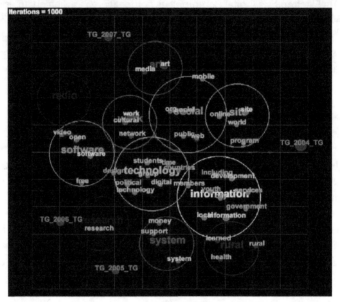

Figure 4: Conceptual map without word seeding. Bird's eye.

Concepts are clustered in thematic circles that form around the most connected ones: *information, (web)site, social, art, work, software, radio, research, technology, system* and *rural*. Here some technology-related concepts are crucial, that were absent when 'online community' was seeded as key concept (see previous chapter). For example, it is significant[5] that – when 'online community' was taken as a key concept – technological objects were conceived only as 'tools'[6]. Differently, in the unseeded analysis they are specified as 'technology', 'software', 'website'. In other words, while in discourses on online communities (i.e., the seeded analysis) the role of technology is black-boxed as mere tool, outside that discourse there seems to be more room for artefacts to be unpacked. It is only when the rhetoric about online communities is dropped, that artefacts can appear in their role as mediators keeping human relations going.

---

4   Resulting concepts are also listed in Table 9 – Annex C.
5   My aim is not to give an *explanation* of these results, but to *describe* the variations in the elements that constitute one or more aggregates. Indeed, this book's approach is not about providing a further theory about why social actors act in a certain way, but about tracing the minute shifts in meaning left behind by activities of group formation. As a consequence, the definition of 'significant' as 'having a particular meaning' (Oxford Dictionary) is the most precise: meaning is given exactly by the shifts in the elements that move from one association into another one.
6   Actually, in the previous analysis in chapter 4 'tool' was the only concept referring to technological artefacts.

Conversely, if we consider the concepts related to 'online community' in the seeded analysis, some of them are not present in the unseeded one. For example, in the concept list in Table 9 there is no reference to 'individuals' as agents of change, nor to the classical dichotomy between 'physical' and virtual realms. As we have seen in chapter 1, individualism and a sharp separation between the brick-and-mortar world and cyberspace were among the elements that digital communitarians inherited from early cyberculture. Indeed, these two concepts appear in the data set only when online community is taken as a seed, and not in the unseeded semantic profiling. It could thus be suggested that networked individualism and the physical/virtual separation are part of the discourse *on* digital communities, but they are not part of current practices *of* online assemblages.

5.1 From Concepts to Full-blown Topics

Figure 4 shows 'relevant' concepts, that is, frequent words that co-occur more often with some other words, and less often with other ones. In that map, broader themes form around a highly connected concept, from which they borrow the label, and aggregate less connected ones. For instance, the theme *Art* borrows the label from the highly connected concept 'art' and aggregates the concepts 'media' and 'music', as well. The relationship between the main concept/theme and the aggregated concepts is based on contextual similarity: they appear in similar contexts in the data set. However, to what extent do these themes develop into full-blown topics? How can narratives be identified from a list of co-occurring concepts? How can we account for the theories of actions involving artefacts that underpin techno-social online collaboration, that is, this book's main empirical question?

In order to address these requests, different methods than map visualization are needed. Co-occurrence patterns were thus systematically browsed, and corresponding textual excerpts thoroughly analysed in order to identify full-blown concepts and narratives. In so doing, I did not only consider the co-occurrences recurring inside thematic clusters, but opened up the analysis to the whole co-occurrence lists of highly relevant concepts. In this way, I tried to give reasons for those concepts being included in the more fragmented clusters, as well.

As an example of this method, the theme *Rural* aggregated the concepts 'rural', 'health', and 'learned'. These concepts were strongly related: 'rural' occurred very often with 'learned' and quite often with 'health', while 'health' and 'rural' were the concepts with which 'learned' most frequently co-occurred. The co-occurrence pattern between 'rural' and 'learned' singled out textual excerpts that could be browsed. Through browsing, a recurring narrative could be identified. that of information technologies conceived of as benefiting the quality of life of rural populations by allowing access to informal education. The rise of social networks was thus deemed the unmediated consequence of the possibility to access ICT. Conversely, lack of IT-mediated knowledge caused severe impairments:

> The farmers of the riverside remotest areas [of Bangladesh] do not have any access to the information society; consequently the conditions of 7,000 rivers and streams of the country are degrading day by day with negative impact on the overall health of the aquatic system, human health, biodiversity, rural economy, rural life etc. [...] Due to

the knowledge gap of the farmers on proper use of fertilizer and pesticide the usages went up a hundred times over the last thirty years, but with the education of the Mobile Units, thousands of farmers were trained on proper use of fertilizer and pesticides, agricultural productivity is increased and thousands of landless farmers did not have to leave their villages in search of work. [...] Technology contributes to the democratization of information and offers assistance to the underprivileged people of the remotest areas. This project has helped the people who had no right to be accessed to the information society. The rural people now can discuss their points of views and express their opinions. With the mobile unit activity their voices are disseminated in the distant areas and to other farming groups, and in this way they are able to think and decide the alternative ways for their local problems. Now they can look at the whole world, establish their relationships with it and, in this way they are building up a vision of development. [7]

This narrative corresponds to one of the topics identified in chapter 4: 'rural development through education'. Although this kind of narratives was quite recurrent, in our data set it followed a decreasing temporal trend. While several applications dealt with it in 2004, from that year onwards it became less and less popular, as figure 5 shows.

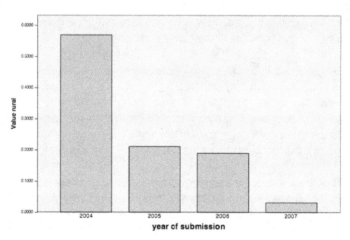

Figure 5: Temporal trend for 'rural'.

In summary, the qualitative analysis conducted for all themes (figure 4) shows that not all of them correspond to full-blown topics. Some of them (i.e., *Site, Social, Research, System*) turned out to be aggregates of concepts whose closeness in the map did not reveal any recognizable narrative. Conversely, some others showed meaningful associations and deserved further investigation. Notably, *Art, Information, Work, Software'* aggregated elements that co-occured with a certain regularity and suggested the following topics:

---

7   *Mobile Internet-Educational Unit on Boats* submission, 2004.

- free and open software
- local development and information
- cultural work
- media art

5.2 Social Software as Mediator or Intermediary

As with 'work' (see below), 'software' was a key concept over the four years of competition being analyzed, with only a light decrease in frequency in 2006 (figure 6). The theme *Software* aggregated the concepts 'software', 'video', 'open', 'free', 'collaboration'. Also 'collaboration' – not a frequent concept in itself – was part of this theme. Notably, a very strong co-occurrence pattern between 'software', 'free' and 'open' was recognizable.

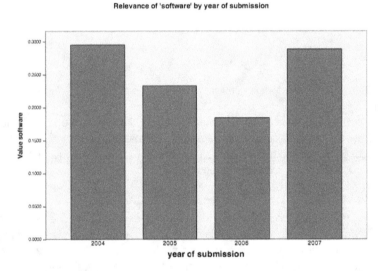

Figure 6: Temporal trend for 'software'.

'Software' was strongly related with 'free' (they co-occurred 11% of times in which 'software' appears) and 'open' (10,8%), while the strength of co-occurrence with 'social' was considerably lower (3,7%). Similarly, while 'open', 'free', and 'software' appeared in similar conceptual contexts in the map, 'social' and 'software' did not (see figure 7).

Iterations=1000

Figure 7: Co-occurrence between 'software' and 'free'/'open'/'social'.

This evidence leads to register a predominance in the data set of the FLOSS and hacker discourse over the Web 2.0 one, one of whose key expressions is precisely 'social software'. Further evidence is provided by Leximancer's entity vocabulary list: among the top thirty most frequent words appearing in sentences containing 'software', 'social' appeared 222 times, while 'open' 422 times and 'free' 420 times.

Textual excerpts browsing confirmed this insight and added further elements. On one hand, in all cases where 'software' occurred with 'free' and/or 'open', these terms were used to describe FLOSS initiatives participating in the competition: from *FSF-GNU* and *Linux* to *dyne. org* and epigones. On the other hand, less homogeneous narratives were identified by the co-occurrence of 'software' and 'social'. This lack of homogeneity is thus worth further analysis.

In the data set, three different meanings of 'social software' were distinguishable. First, software design was seen as constituting a moment for 'social inquiry'. As software design usually relies on knowledge of prior software, by definition software development is a collaborative process, and software is the artefact that crystallizes such social process.[8] See for an example the *Spring-alpha* project:

> Thematically, "spring-alpha" is an exploration of the relationship between software and social systems, focusing, in particular, on how issues in their design and implementation mirror one another. This is being realised practically, by taking the development of a game simulation world and exploring how the different issues involved in its design can form a process of social enquiry. [...] [The game] depicts a story in which the occupants of an industrial housing project attempt to establish their own autonomous society. The narrative acts as a kind of parable paralleling the themes and practice of the project. It will serve as a "conceptual kernel" which will be extended through collaborative public workshops. The content of the game is therefore also developed through a form of "Open Source" method. Many of the issues involved in designing such a game mirror those involved in constructing real-world social systems. In this way the development process will act as a form of critical social enquiry exposing the relationships of software and social systems. Objectives: To demonstrate the potential of software design as a process of social enquiry. To extend the collaborative, social principles of FOSS beyond programming into broader forms of participation and creative practice. To foreground the development of software as a fundamentally social process.[9]

A second, different understanding of social software was laid down by the *[meme.garden]* project. In this case, social software was conceived of as a peculiar kind of software that emphasizes the human dimension of networking. Here, 'social' was synonymous of 'human', as opposed to 'cold' computer systems:

> [meme.garden] functions as social software which explores an individual's interests (whether these interests be news topics, political phenomena, health, hobbies, etc) among a social group. The software emphasizes the human element inherent in networked tools. Artwork created with computerized systems often feels cold and impersonal to audiences. The [meme.garden] software blends social software, search tool, and aesthetic system to visualize participant's interests in prevalent streams of information, encouraging browsing and interaction between users in real time, through time. Our goal is to make a social software search engine tools that embody human themes.[10]

---

8   This is the crucial insight of net.art, software art and hacker practices (see section 1.3). I wish to thank Tatiana Bazzichelli for the stimulating discussions about this issue. ANT provides a further access to this approach by going back to the semantic root of the word 'thing' as 'assembly': 'long before designating an object thrown out of the political sphere and standing there objectively and independently, the *Ding* or Thing has for many centuries meant the issue that brings people together *because* it divides them. [...] The *Ding* designates both those who assemble because they are concerned as well as what causes their concerns and divisions.' Latour, 'From Realpolitik to Dingpolitik', p. 13, *italics in the text*). According to ANT, 'social' means 'collective' and things (also digital artefacts) are 'social' because they are 'assemblies', 'gatherings'.

9   *Spring-alpha* submission, 2004.

10   *[meme.garden]* submission, 2007.

A similar narrative was present in the *Barnraiser* submission. For this project, social software focuses more on the 'social conventions' than on 'software features'. It 'directly' benefits society by allowing people to interact and share knowledge. While providing hardware is not sufficient to assure development, having access to *social* software and knowing how to use it facilitates the development of society:

> We are a growing movement of people that want to contribute directly to a better soci-ety by pushing forward the boundaries of social software development and education. Social software is developed from social convention rather than software features. Social software facilitates interaction and collaboration and is changing how people communicate. Installing computers and supplying Internet connection is not enough when building capacity within society. We need software, software that allows that soci-ety to develop, allows the people within that society to share knowledge and contribute towards their information society. We facilitate this by creating free social software and ensuring that people can have access to it and the knowledge to use it.[11]

A third narrative associated with social software was provided for example by *World-Infor-mation.org*. Here, the Web 2.0 rhetoric was explicit. Indeed, social software's peculiarity was seen in allowing the convergence between sender and receiver, passive user, and content contributor:

> the [social software] content management system had to be specifically adaptable to support the different workflow models simultaneously because not only internal editors but also external parties such as institutions or single individuals must be enabled to join the editorial team. Also the very heterogeneous skill levels of the prospect users had to be kept in mind. Editors all over the world had to be given access to the system over the internet. The user interface had to give support during the research process as well during content entry.[12]

In summary, by following co-occurrence patterns for 'software', diverse narratives emerged, which can be compared to the communitarian rhetorics discussed in chapters 1 and 2. The most frequent narrative recalls hacker culture's focus on free and/or open software, as described in chapter 1. This discourse is dominant over less represented understandings of 'social software'. Social software can either refer to a type of 'human' substance opposed to machinic reasoning, or to a collaborative process of social inquiry. Additionally, the social networking narrative proper to the Web 2.0 rhetoric addressed in section 2.3 is a minor one.

The differences between these narratives allow introducing a key category of analysis, that will be crucial to the rest of the book. I suggest that we can read the difference among those narratives by recovering the distinction between *mediators* and *intermediaries*. While Human-Computer-Interaction (HCI) has usually focused on the 'immediacy' between input

---

11   *Barnraiser* submission, 2005.
12   *World-Information.org* submission, 2006

and output as a key concept for the evaluation of digital artefacts,[13] sociology of technology has suggested the notion of 'mediation' to overcome that dichotomy.[14] The two traditions entailed very different approaches towards agency. While for HCI agency pertains to a full-blown subject endowed with intentionality, sociology of technology questions the cognitive nature of intentionality, and sees agency emerging in interaction, distributed throughout an assemblage, a network of hybrid 'actants'[15]. For this scholarship, agency is not embodied in a single actor, nor in a single 'social cause', rather, it is dislocated.

On closer inspection, one could notice that this extended definition of 'action' as 'making someone do something' resembles HCI's notion of 'affordance' as an invitation to action that is embedded in the artefact.[16] Nonetheless, a crucial difference between the two approaches should not be overlooked: while for the theories based on situated action affordances emerge *during* action, for cognitive ergonomics the subject and the object are constituted *before* the interaction.

One of the ways to account for this difference is the distinction between 'mediation' – a relationship that constitutes actors while taking place, from 'intermediation' – a relationship in which a tool just transports agency from one pre-existing point to another pre-existing point. While in intermediation the inputs are enough to define the outputs, mediation exceeds its inputs and cannot be reduced to a relationship of cause-and-effect.[17] Putting it slightly differently, a mediator is an actant that translates, transforms, modifies the elements it is supposed to carry; a mediator is never a cause: it does not determine, but makes someone do something, it triggers further actions and activates new participants. Every time a mediator appears, it introduces a bifurcation in the course of action. Therefore, the chain of action

---

13 J. Nielsen, *Designing Web Usability*, Indianapolis: New Riders, 1999;
   D. A. Norman, *The Psychology of Everyday Things* New York: Basic Books, 1988; M. Visciola, *Usabilità dei siti web*, Milano: Apogeo, 2000.
14 M. Akrich, Des réseaux vidéocom aux réseaux électriques: machines, gestion, marchés, Paris: L'Harmattan, 1992; D. Haraway, Primate Visions: Gender, Race, and Nature in the World of Modern Science, New York: Routledge, 1989; L. A. Suchman, Plans and Situated Actions: The Problem of Human-Machine Communication, New York: Cambridge University Press, 1987.
15 Latour, *Reassembling the Social*. Latour uses the term 'actant' instead of 'actor' in order to gain higher pliability with respect to figuration. It might be said that an actant is an abstract agent endowed with a narrative function that on a discursive level gets embodied into an actor endowed with a figuration. Latour borrowed this distinction from semiotics, where it corresponds to the deployment of agency respectively on the narrative level (where we talk of 'actants') and on the discursive level (where 'actors' lie). Greimas and Courtés define an actant as 'the one that performs or undergoes the act, regardless of any other determination. Thus, quoting L. Tesnière whose work this term is borrowed from, "actants are the beings or the things that – under whichever qualification and in whatsoever manner, even as simple bit players and in the most passive manner – take part in the process". Under this perspective, the actant designates a type of syntactic unit, a peculiarly formal one, before any semantic and/or ideological investment'. See Greimas and Courtés, *Sémiotique,*, p. 40, *Author's translation into English*. It is interesting to notice that, under this distinction, 'loose networks', 'communities of practice' and 'groupware' differ on a discursive, figurative level, while they might fulfil the same logical function in a course of action.
16 J. J. Gibson, *The Ecological Approach to Visual Perception*, London: Hillsdale, 1986; Norman, The Psychology of Everyday Things.
17 Latour, *Reassembling the Social*.

becomes longer and the output is never predictable starting from the input. On the contrary, an intermediary only transports agency from an input to an output without transforming it; the output can therefore be easily predicted. With intermediaries, elements are usually linked through relationships of cause-and-effect and the chain transporting action is thus short, often made of only a couple of elements (i.e., the cause and the effect).

As to the social software cases above discussed, in the *[meme.garden]* and *Barnraiser* accounts, computer systems are supposed to be cold digital machines and social software acts as an intermediary that dilutes this coldness into the warmth of human interaction. Yet social software does not introduce elements that could interfere with the output, which is simply given by the encounter of the 'digital' with the 'social'. It is thus conceived as an intermediary. On the other hand, in the *Spring-alpha* project the software and the social system get constituted *through* their interplay. The gaming software is a mediator because it transforms the subjects involved: the output (the 'autonomous society') cannot be predicted by the input (the 'conceptual kernel').

This distinction is going to play a major role in examining the theories of action which underpin online collaboration, and the role of artefacts as mediators keeping human relations going, once the online communities rhetoric is definitely dropped.

5.3 Different Technologies for Different Territories

As far as the theme *Information* is concerned, it aggregated the concepts 'information', 'local', 'government', 'services', 'city', 'human', 'development', 'youth', 'including', 'map', 'life', 'members', 'created'. Among these concepts, 'information' co-occurred frequently with 'local', 'government', 'development'; 'government' co-occurred frequently with 'services' and 'development'; 'local' showed a strong co-occurrence with 'information' and 'development'; 'development' and 'members' co-occured frequently with 'local' and 'information'. As figure 8 shows, the concept 'information' was most relevant in the applications submitted in 2004, while it progressively decreased in importance in the following years.

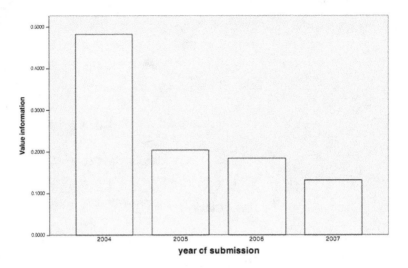

Figure 8: Temporal trend for 'information'.

In counter-tendency with the dominant internet discourse on de-territorialization (see sections 1.1, 3.1), and confirming more recent studies on the territorialization of the Net (see section 2.2), 'information' registers the emergence of a territorial topic. In the co-occurrence list for 'information', among the five concepts most frequently co-occurring three displayed a semantic reference to a territorial dimension ('local', 'government', 'rural'), while another one ('site') connoted both a physical and a virtual (website) portion of space (figure 9).

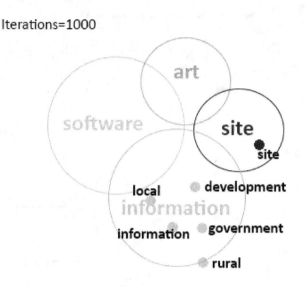

Iterations=1000

Figure 9: Co-occurrence map for 'information'.

The territorial topic was present also in the co-occurrence scheme for 'development', the fifth item in the list. The strongest item co-occurring with 'development' was 'local', followed by 'information', 'site', 'software', and 'technology'.

In most of these cases, a recurring narrative emerged, according to which information technologies are seen as empowering means for local, rural, disadvantaged communities:

> Namma Dhwani (Our VOICES in the Kannada language) is an initiative which has created a space for different rural social groups to utilize a combination of cable audio & digital technologies to put in place a local information and communication network owned and operated by members of the local community. [...] Namma Dhwani uses a unique model developed to suit local needs and circumstances. It not only combines cable audio with new digital media, but also combines these media tools with a network of local community groups, specifically poor women's self-help groups (SHGs), watershed groups made up of local farmers, and a local development resource centre. Namma Dhwani has enabled poor semi-literate, women, farmers, labourers, school drop-outs and other community members to use information & communication media & technologies to create: 1) Their own channels of information access, storage and dissemination 2) Their own platforms for communication and discussion [...] The network successfully addresses local information needs and has had a visible impact on local development and governance.[18]

---

18   *Namma Dhwani* submission, 2004.

Rural space was however not the only model of territoriality dealt with in the data set. A distinct relationship between territory and ICT involved urban spaces. Indeed, 'city' showed an absolutely peculiar semantic context aggregating around the urban territory, and a specific 'metropolitan' use of information technologies. While 'city' did never occur with any of the other territorial concepts (i.e., 'rural', 'site' or 'government', except 'local'), it showed a strong co-occurrence with 'mobile' and 'map'.

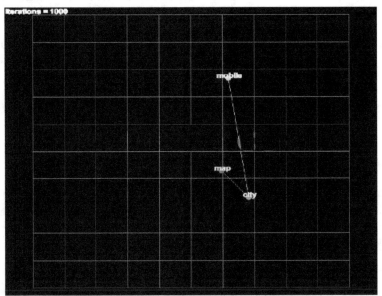

Figure 10: Co-occurrence map for 'city'.

Analysing the textual instances, they all dealt with geo-referenced mobile systems allowing the creation of unconventional maps of the urban space, and the bottom-up regeneration of a sense of place. Similar projects were usually subsumed under the umbrella term 'locative media'. Here is an example:

> Citypoems turns mobile phones in Leeds into widely distributed creative writing and publishing tools (70% of teenagers and adults in the UK own a mobile phone). Everyone in Leeds can read and write a Citypoem, experiencing and contributing to an enriched sense of their own place from wherever, and whenever, they are in the city. The Citypoems biography is made new by every reader, turning the pages in the order of their own daily lives as they move through the city, and transforming mobile phones into books with an infinite number of blank pages waiting to be filled.[19]

Summing up, different roles for information technologies were associated to different types of local territory. The qualitative analysis uncovered a first discourse in which ICT were depicted as empowering tools (i.e., intermediaries) fostering the development of disadvantaged, rural

---

19   *Citypoems* submission, 2004.

areas, in partnership with local governments, by sharing information accessible through websites. The second narrative conceives of information technologies as mobile and urban. They are seen as representational means that allow the creation of subjective maps of the urban space, of collectively generated psycho-geographies. With these different narratives, in our data set the mythological local community we discussed in chapter 1 hits the ground in two rather different forms, each of which attributes a different role to digital information technologies.

5.4 Knowledge Labour Between Sustainability and Gift Economy

'Work' is the third most frequent concept in the whole data set. It is also the second most central concept after 'art', meaning that – besides being frequent – it also often appears in contexts where other relevant concepts are present. Furthermore, despite a decrease in 2005, the concept 'work' remained frequent over the four years of the Digital Communities competition (Figure 11).

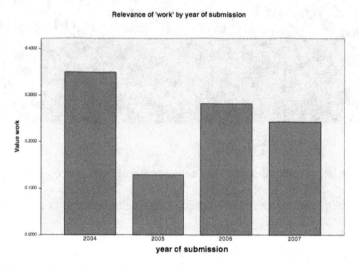

Figure 11: Temporal trend for 'work'.

The thematic circle *Work* includes the concepts 'work', 'cultural', 'international', 'network', 'text' (Figure 12). 'Work' more often occurs with 'art', 'media', 'software', 'open', 'online', 'video'. Notably, there is a strong co-occurrence between 'work' and 'cultural'. 'Cultural' and 'work' are also very close in the map, meaning that they appear in similar conceptual contexts. All in all, these co-occurrence paths show a dominant narrative about knowledge labour, testifying the reproduction of the creative class narrative well after the dotcom burst (see section 2.1).

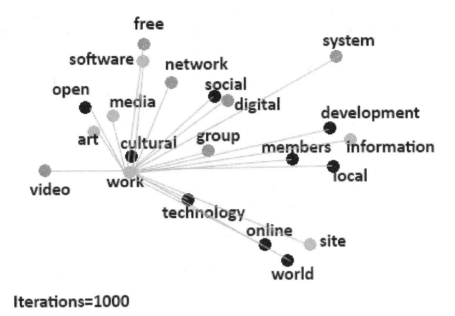

Iterations=1000

Figure 12: Co-occurrence map for 'work'.

However, that narrative survives in more articulated ways. When it comes to the models of remuneration of cognitive labour, two different meanings of 'work' emerge. The first deals with work as an economic activity, while the second one conceives of work as a voluntary act oriented to the production of common goods.

On one hand, 'work' appears quite frequently in the section dedicated to the planned use of the possible prize money (indicated by the recurring word 'money'). This testifies the intention to allocate some resources towards the sustainability of cognitive work and to go beyond the equation 'immaterial work' = 'amateur, unpaid labour' fostered by the Web 2.0 hype (see section 2.3). A proposal that addresses sustainability without abdicating to free knowledge is, for example, advanced by the *SerendiPd* project:

There are many people who dedicate substantial time and resources to making Pd better. We would like to enable such people to earn a living while working on Pd, while keeping it free. There are a number of methods of raising money for free software projects, including: project donations, selling support like RedHat does, and bounty systems like those used by GNOME. [...] the GNOME bounty system (http://www. gnome.org/bounties/) makes the most sense for the Pd community. One project that we would like to take on with the prize money would be to build a bounty board for Pd, where both user- and developed-initiated tasks could be posted. For user-initiated tasks, money collection via donations would continue until someone proved that the task had been completed; this individual would then receive the total collected sum for the work completed. For developer-initiated tasks, developers would include their minimum fee for execution. Pd users would give money to whichever tasks they deemed worthy; when a bounty is reached the developer would then work to complete the task, receiving payment upon completion.[20]

On the other hand, 'work' co-occurs very frequently with 'open' (see Figure 13). When browsing through the textual instances, it appears clear that 'open' is used in all the contexts wherein it co-occurs with 'work' as synonymous with 'free'. All these instances deal with the exaltation of volunteer cognitive work whose efforts allow the creation and distribution of immaterial commons. Volunteer workers are conceived of as community-engaged individuals contributing to the free/open knowledge:

> Ubuntu is a community developed, commercially supported Linux distribution with an emphasis on software freedom and making computers as easy and accessible for everyone. [...] Ubuntu has access to thousands of additional tools and applications, and a huge community who provide support and assistance to Ubuntu users. Ubuntu is commercially supported by Canonical Ltd, but a worldwide network of enthusiastic volunteers work together on all aspects of the system, providing a solid community orientated distribution.[21]

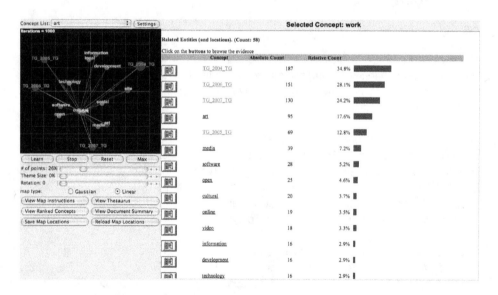

Figure 13: Co-occurrence list for 'work'.

All in all, in the data set the topic of labour is still wavering between the need for economic models that can assure an adequate remuneration to cognitive work and the push towards the creation and distribution of open and free commons. However, even when acknowledging

20   *SerendiPd* submission, 2004.
21   *Ubuntu* submission, 2007.

these contrasting narratives about 'work', a significant trend must be noticed. The entries where 'work' and 'open' co-occur were submitted mainly in 2004 (76% of cases), while the entries where 'work' and 'money' co-occur were submitted largely between 2006 and 2007 (60% of cases). This is sufficient evidence of a change in the runderstanding of work, from volunteer to paid activity, and a detachment from the rhetoric of user-based unpaid work that we have discussed in chapter 2.

5.5 'Public Media Art' as Politics

The last relevant topic emerging from the data set could be defined as 'public media art'. The theme *Art* aggregated the concepts 'art', 'media', 'music', that is, they co-occured in similar contexts. 'Media' and 'art' co-occured often together, especially in the expression 'media art'. 'Art' and 'music' showed a lower co-occurrence index. 'Media' and 'music' never occured together. Looking at the temporal trend for the concept 'art', we can see that in 2005 and 2006 the applications dealt less with 'art' than in 2004 and 2007, relatively to the total amount of submissions from each year (Figure 14).[22]

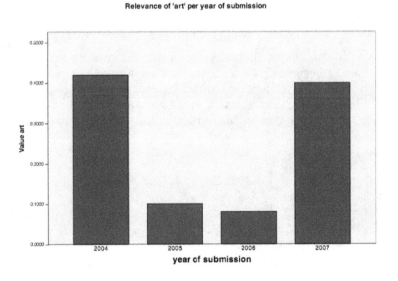

Figure 14: Temporal trend for 'art'.

A similar trend was shown by the concept 'media': after a strong frequency in 2004, it decreased until 2007, when it re-gained importance (Figure 15).

---

22   The result for 2007 might be explained by the new interest the *Prix Ars Electronica* put on artistic
     projects in that year's call.

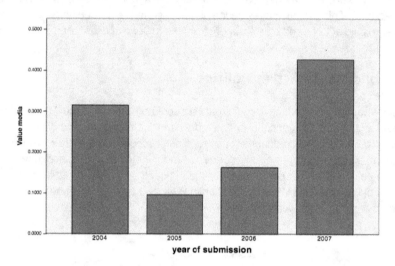

Figure 15: Temporal trend for 'media'.

Among the ten concepts most-frequently occurring with 'art', three were related to the type of medium ('media' in general, 'online', 'digital'), three were attributes of art itself ('international', 'open', 'public'), other three were part of frequent expressions ('cultural', art-'work', art-'world') (Figure 16). The last one, 'space', was alternatively included into expressions like 'public space', 'open space', and 'space of art'.

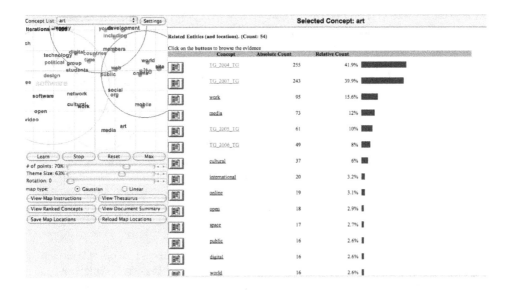

Figure 16: Co-occurrence map and concept list for 'art'.

Browsing through textual excerpts in more depth, three coherent narratives emerged when 'art' co-occured with 'public' and 'open'. The first conceived of art as public because it uses public space as a creative medium, as the space of exhibition. This was the case of projects like *Glowlab* – whose work on psycho-geography dealt specifically with urban spaces, and *52weeks52works* – whose artworks were deployed in public spaces worldwide.

The second narrative stressed the relationship between art and political engagement in social movements. In the *REPUBLICart* project, for instance, 'public art' was seen as retaining an organizational, theoretical and political role:

> the art of res publica is about experimental forms of organizing, which develop in precarious micro-situations for a limited period of time, testing new modes of selforganization and interplays with other experiments. The "organizing function" of art (Walter Benjamin) creates new spaces in the overlapping zones of art practices, political activism and theory production. [...] Joining the heterogeneous activities against economic globalization, the old forms of intervention art are being transformed and new ones are emerging. In the context of current political movements, art is becoming public again.[23]

The third narrative related to open/public art focused on a process-oriented aesthetic. Here, 'open art' is about collaborative creation eluding copyright regimes:

> The whole basis for the experience is 'intellectual generosity', the creation and supporting of an open environment for people to work on a project without being tied to

---

23   *REPUBLICart* submission, 2004.

any kind of restrictions of production created by the copyright. [...] Our goal is develop open art, produced in a collaborative way, within workgroups spread all over the world. [24]

Open art requires distributed learning and authorship. It is the response to the privatization of the Web and to the closure of the source code adopted by digital artists which followed the commodification of net-art:

a number of prominent artists have been experimenting with models for selling digital art, and dealers who smell money are scrambling to help artists package work into closed, exclusive forms. While there's nothing wrong in principle with making money off art, in practice this pressure has led some artists to move toward formats where code is hidden from view and where access is controlled by private collectors or gated communities. [25]

According to this narrative, while the blackboxing of code was to lead to the 'elitarization' of digital media and the exclusion of the many from such practices, the establishment of ethical procedures and the promotion of open standards initiated by the community of online artists was to empower individual artists:

the opportunity to create open yet enduring standards-and most important, a community ethic-offers creative individuals a chance to take control of their destiny and help shape the culture that nourishes them. The Open Art Network aims to empower artists working in digital formats by devising and promoting standards that encourage an open architecture for the Internet and digital media. [26]

In such accounts, empowerment proceeds from the opportunity for single artists not only to consume each other's works, but especially to mutually learn from each other's creative process. This possibility is designed in specific type of artefacts: access to mutual learning is assured by open standards and procedures. If we assume a definition of 'the political' as both the procedures that allow the assembly to gather as well as the matter of concern that has to be discussed in the assembly, in this third meaning 'open art' is eminently political, since it aims at setting the standards whereby an assembly may constitute. [27]

In summary, in the Digital Communities data set, art retains major relevance, albeit declining. Evidence confirms that the aesthetic interest that constituted one of the major thrusts for digital communitarianisms in the 1990s (see section 1.3) maintained its relevance for online sociability until 2007. Art has also kept an explicit political function as an opportunity for the empowerment of individuals through mutual learning. As such, it continues the tradition of

---

24   *Re:combo* submission, 2007.
25   *Open Art Network* submission, 2004.
26   *Open Art Network* submission, 2004.
27   Latour, 'From Realpolitik to Dingpolitik'.

individualistic empowerment á la Rheingold, while combining the decentralizing, self-organized efforts which characterized the 1990s' net art and mediactivism cultures.

At this point of the book, we have successfully attempted the tricky task of identifying relevant
topics and narratives in the data set without postulating actors and theories of action. This
shows the validity of our initial intuition about not rushing to conclusions about the disappearance of online communities but to conduct empirical investigation about the conditions
under which they can nowadays be re-conceptualized. Notably, when the early rhetoric about
'online communities' is dropped – i.e., when the concept is not 'sown' for analysis, narratives
enlighten theories of action that account for peculiar roles of artefacts as mediators of human
relations. In the next chapter we shall focus on some of these theories in more depth.

6. MEDIATORS UPKEEPING COMMUNITIES

Up to now we have struggled to extract meaning from a vast and variegated set of accounts. In order to deal with almost one thousand applications, we have been forced to reduce complexity to a manageable level by relying on co-occurrence patterns and relational analysis. In so doing, we've found a set of elements associated with 'online community' (chapter 4), demonstrated the appropriateness of not selecting a type of grouping in advance, and singled out some meaningful topics and narratives (chapter 5).

During these stages, we have always refrained from the temptation to add some explanation to what we were just describing. Every time this temptation came to our mind, we struck up loudly our *noli me tangere*[1] towards definitions, correlations, conceptual assumptions and methodological protocols. If such a lonely and renouncing Franciscan path was undertaken, it is because at the end of 2000s postulating a definition for a fuzzy object of study called 'online community' would have cast this research miles away from (second level) objectivity. Nothing would have been easier than starting from presuppositions. On the contrary, it was the incommensurable distance between much diverse initiatives – all defined as 'online communities' – that suggested the need to make a clean sweep and start on a much longer and laborious journey. Tracing back communities is still the goal of this journey, mapping the cartography of the different theories of action associated with them is the means.

The narratives discussed in the last chapter however suggest the need to investigate, in depth, the role of digital artefacts in upkeeping communities. The analysis conducted until now is half of the story, the half that had to reduce the complexity of the social when dealing with vast data sets. The other half lies in the opposite movement of addition, proliferation, and observation. At this point of the book, the time has come to increase the sensitivity of our analysis, and to privilege an articulated observation of a small number of applications, so that the role of artefacts may emerge in more detail than when addressing the whole data set.

This chapter attempts to deepen the investigation into different theories of action that underpin the development of digital communities through the role attributed to artefacts. It analyses the relationship between societal outcomes and digital artefacts, as it was laid down by communities' spokespersons.

To do so, following Haraway's suggestion to think about scientific and technological practice as story-telling, I conduct narrative analyses of a smaller number of case studies.[2] By focusing on the artefacts whereby groups are kept assembled, I describe the theories of action underpinning the rationale of the projects which from 2004 to 2007 were granted a *Golden Nica* (first prize) or an *Award of Distinction* (second prize) at Ars Electronica.

---

1   "Noli me tangere" ("do not touch me") was the Latin transation of the words spoken by Jesus to Mary Magdalene when she recognized him after resurrection. It is a topos in Western culture, as various paintings, novels and sculptures were so titled.
2   Haraway, *Primate Visions*.

Notably, in the following analyses I have borrowed Latour's list of traces left behind by activities of group formation[3] and the distinction between mediator and intermediary, already introduced in section 5.2.[4] From semiotics, the analysis has borrowed the notion of 'competence', the distinction between actants and actors and the notions of 'Addresser' and 'Addressee' (see Table 10 in Annex C)[5]. In particular, the patient work in search of mediators does not claim to be complete, even if, differently from chapters 4 and 5, here reduction is sacrificed to proliferation, comprehensiveness to articulation.[6]

6.1 Tonga.Online. Or of Rivers, Dams, Antelope Horns and Digital music

An amazingly rich case of proliferation of mediations is provided by the *Tonga.Online* application. This project won an Award of Distinction in 2004. It is an offspring of a cultural exchange

---

3   According to the French scholar, since the list of groupings composed of social aggregates is potentially infinite, it is easier for social enquirers to substitute it with the more abstract list of the elements which are always present in controversies about groups. These elements are: 1) a spokesperson who speaks for the group existence, defines it and argues for its uniqueness; 2) some anti-groups that can be compared with the group of interest, so that its consistency may be emphasized; 3) an element that originates the group boundaries, so that they are rendered durable and taken for granted. Usually *limes* are provided by appeals to tradition, law, nature, history, freedom, etc.; 4) professionals (social scientists, journalists, statisticians) who speak for the group existence. Any account by these professionals is part of what makes a group exist or disappear. On the generative role of journalists and pollsters in making social actors (for instance the 'public-opinion') exist, see also E. Landowski, *La société réfléchie*, Paris: Seuil, 1989.

4   Latour, *Reassembling the Social*, pp. 30-4.

5   Addresser and Addressee designate the two subjects of a process of communication. They correspond to the 'sender' and the 'receiver' of Information Theory, although this latter approach does not take into consideration the dynamic constitution of the subjects of communication. See the comparison between HCI, on one side, and sociology of technology and semiotics, on the other side, in chapter 5. While according to the first approach the subjects of communication pre-exist to the interactive process, according to the second school subjectivity gets installed *through* the communicational process. I cannot account here for the immense literature dealing with subjectivity and communication from 1950s onwards. As Mattelart, *Histoire de la société de l'information*, has pointed out, this literature traces indeed the history (and controversies) of what is meant by 'Information Society'. I thus only signal the origin of Informational Theory introducing the concepts of 'sender' and 'receiver' from a mechanical perspective in C. Shannon and W. Weaver, *A Mathematical Theory of Communication*, Urbana-Champaign, Ill.: University of Illinois Press, 1949.
    On the opposite side, post-structuralist and materialist authors have seen language as an action that transforms subjectivity *during* action. See for example, J. C. Coquet, *La quête du sens. Le langage en question*, Paris: PUF, 1997; L. A. Suchman, *Plans and Situated Actions: The Problem of Human-Machine Communication*, New York: Cambridge University Press, 1987; K. M. Barad, *Meeting the Universe Halfway. Quantum Physics and the Entanglement of Matter and Meaning*, Durham and London: Duke University Press, 2007.

6   'Articulation [...] does not expect accounts to converge into one single version that will close the discussion... Articulations, on the other hand, may easily proliferate without ceasing to register differences. On the contrary, the more contrasts you add, the more differences and mediations you become sensible to.' B. Latour, 'How to Talk About the Body?: The Normative Dimension of Science Studies, in *Body & Society* 10.2-3 (2004): 210-11.

program between Austrian and Zimbabwean artists and NGOs which has been running for
more than ten years. But let the spokesperson talk by herself:

In 2001/02 the Tonga.Online project has established the first community-based
Internet and Computer Centre in one of the remotest areas of Zimbabwe. Encouraged
by the response, the project is now striving to reach out to other villages and across
the waters of the Zambezi River into Zambia. The Tonga community – only fifty years
ago forcibly divided by the advent of modern technology and the building of Kariba
dam – has taken up the chance to use the most advanced communication technology
for rebuilding and improving links within the community and with the world abroad. A
truly local area network of telecentres is in the extension stage. One could perceive the
Tonga people as a digital community per se because of their music. Despite their harsh
living conditions the Tonga people have always adhered to their cultural heritage and
ways of communicating oral traditions that are generations old. Their unique Ngoma
Buntibe Music is a kind of binary or digital music in its own sense since one musician
is mastering one note only by contributing a short blow on an antelope horn to an
incredible storm of sound and stamping movements. Robert Bilek (a journalist with
ORF / Vienna) after an encounter in 2001: 'The music of the Tonga could be perceived
as a system of binary individual decisions, sound or silence, 1 or 0, within the matrix
of a creative group performance. Through this sound, through this seemingly wild and
chaotic order, the community reassures itself of its coherence... It appears that the
Tonga people's understanding of digital technology has its roots in their musical tradition. What could prevent them from covering new grounds using computers?' There is
a smart gadget which has proved to be very helpful in expanding the project beyond
the centres. It is a mobile device called Alpha Smart, a kind of expanded keyboard run
on batteries. Penny Yon and Theophorah Sianyuka are closely monitoring the establishment of two more telecentres in Sianzyundu and Siachilaba villages from May 2004
onwards. They will use the Alpha Smarts (and a digital camera) to provide and collect
messages and digital reflections on the effects of the project extension and send them
frequently onto the website www.mulonga.net. These contributions will create a kind of
social intervention sculpture by addressing stakeholders and the general public – from
Siachilaba pupils to the fishermen or smugglers on Lake Kariba, from basket weaving
women to the Chief's messenger on his bike or the Cuban doctor at Binga Hospital.
This exercise will be concluded with the festive opening of the Centres on 4th/5th
September 2004 (concurrent with Ars Electronica Festival) when Ngoma Buntibe musicians from Binga area and their counterparts from Zambia will complement the modern
means of communication and celebrate the smart X tension of the Tonga.Online project
in their own way.[7]

This account wonderfully testifies the flamboyant life of artefacts. From dams on the Zambezi
River to 'modern technology', from the Ngoma Buntibe Music to mobile devices, all these
entities take part in some way in the course of action whose goal is 'rebuilding and improving
links within the community and with the world abroad'. From this perspective, the extension

---

7   smart X tension/Tonga. Online submission, 2004. Author's italics

of the project across the waters of the Zambezi River provides the figuration into which the goal – the unity of the Tonga people – is embodied. Fifty years earlier, this unity was dismantled by 'the advent of modern technology and the building of Kariba dam': two actants in their own right which are endowed with figurations borrowed from the ranks of modernity.

In this account, three of the four kinds of traces left behind by the formation of groups are present. Apart from the spokesperson – obviously the one that submitted the project for evaluation and wrote the application – a professional enters the network in order to make possible the durable definition of the community. Austrian journalist Robert Bilek's account is itself part of what makes the group exist, since it provides the community with a theory of action (see below). As to the third trace left behind, boundaries are created and rendered durable by appealing to tradition and cultural heritage: 'despite the harsh living conditions the Tonga people have always adhered to their cultural heritage and ways of communicating oral traditions that are generations old'. It is the cultural heritage and the ways of communication that define the Tonga community as a stable entity, that make it hold against the centrifugal force exerted by the harsh living conditions and that ferry the community directly into the digital age.

Actually, the theory of action underpinning the project's vision of the digital community is overtly expressed through the journalist's voice: 'it appears that the Tonga people's understanding of digital technology has its roots in their musical tradition'. It is the traditional Ngoma Buntibe Music that act as a powerful mediator and translates agency from the 'short blow on an antelope horn' into a binary – and therefore digital – sound. The Ngoma Buntibe Music is not only what keeps the Tonga people united in spite of the diaspora started by modern technologies, but also the actant that carries this assemblage into the computer era.

Once the Tonga assemblage has shored on the quieter coasts of digital post-modernity, other adjutants get to march side by side with the Ngoma Buntibe Music to realize the goal of extending the project over geographical boundaries. Notably, the mobile device Alpha Smart 'proved to be very helpful in expanding the project beyond the centres'.[8] Here, information technology allows the project leaders to activate new mediators: 'messages and digital reflections' that, in turn, create new associations with geographically dispersed actants, stakeholders,[9] Siachilaba pupils, the fishermen or smugglers on Lake Kariba, basket weaving women, the Chief's messenger on his bike, the Cuban doctor.

The *Tonga.Online – smart X tension* project is an exemplary case where mediators proliferate and the chain that translates agency stretches out in many directions. Nonetheless, this is

---

8   *smart X tension/Tonga.* online submission, 2004.
9   What a better definition for the term 'stakeholder' than 'someone who participates in a course of action'? From the synonymy of stakeholder and mediator, the anti-democratic character of the use of this term follows. By using 'stakeholder', in fact, one may refer to an assemblage and still avoid making explicit who/what that assemblage in made of. Since 'politics' refers in half part to the procedures whereby groups are assembled and mediators legitimized to take part in that assembly, the use of the term 'stakeholder' relieves the one who uses it from publicly arguing who and what is to be included in that assembly. Conversely, in the Tonga.Online submission stakeholders are endowed with a list of figurations (pupils, fishermen, etc.).

a peculiar case: it may happen that the chain is arbitrarily short-cut before agency be fully unfolded, as we are going to see in the next section.

6.2 ICT and Developing Countries: Empowerment as a Cause-and-effect Relationship

The case studies discussed in this section do not represent the totality of the winning projects implemented in developing countries, but only those whose goals deal with empowerment of disadvantaged populations and/or consider belonging to the so called 'Global South' as a distinguishing element. We have already taken into consideration projects showing narratives of empowerment in chapters 4 and 5. Here, by analysing four cases in depth, I show how similar projects tend to be associated with short chains of action.

Differently from the *Tonga.Online* project, the *Akshaya* submission characterizes itself for the low number of mediators involved in the course of action. This project – that won the Golden Nica in 2005 – was developed in Kerala (India) to address the question of digital divide. It was implemented by the Government of Kerala through Kerala State IT Mission, the agency for implementing IT policies, and was run by local entrepreneurs.

In the submission,[10] four objectives and relative theories of action are mentioned. The first goal ('Universal IT Access') aims at setting and maintaining 4500 – 6000 Akshaya e-centres. Here, only one mediator is involved: entrepreneurs running the centres rely on e-literacy courses to assure self-sustainability to each centre. Other technological entities – broadband wireless, computers, scanners, printers, webcams, software, IP phones – appear as mere intermediaries, since their presence does not affect the outcome.

The second objective ('E-literacy') aims at familiarizing people with IT and improving their computer skills. There exist also a meta-goal: to 'create a 100% literate state'. Here, the theory of action is underpinned by an overtly causal relation: 'the process of providing the skill sets shall lead to the creation of a long lasting relation between the Akshaya centres and the families in the catchment, which on a macro level will generate a state wide data warehouse and repository' (*Akshaya* submission). In these words, it is not clear *through which means* the process of providing skills will cause a stable relationship whose ultimate outcome is a data repository. As we have seen, in the social domain stability is a costly exception. Face-to-face, unequipped interactions using only basic social skills pertain to a very limited sphere, namely to baboons.[11] Unequipped interactions alone cannot bear the weight of maintaining stable relationships that need to be ceaselessly negotiated. It is objects that allow long-standing relationships. However, in the *Akshaya* account there are no traces of the means whereby the long lasting relation between the centres and the families are supposed to be maintained.

---

10   It is reported as Document 2 in Annex A.
11   S. C. Strum, 'Un societé complexe sans culture materérielle: Le cas des babbouins', in B. Latour and P. Lemonnier (eds) *De la préhistoire aux missiles balistiques*, Paris: La Découverte, 1994.

A similar lack of mediators characterizes also the third ('Creation of Micro ICT Enterprises') and fourth ('Creation of ICT Service Delivery Points') objectives. As to the creation of micro IT enterprises, the theory of action is 'im-mediate': entrepreneurs emerged from the local community are seen as lending their 'entrepreneurial spirit' to the 'total development' of community. Here again, no mediators intervene either in the emergence of the entrepreneurs from the community, or in the opposite translation of this spirit from entrepreneurs to communities. Their 'skills and resources' just transport agency: they do not affect the outcome in one direction rather than another, nor trigger other mediators.

Summing up, in the *Akshaya* account there are some intermediaries and only one mediator. Agency gets stopped after few passages and may not rely on entities that translate the initial inputs. As a matter of fact, apart from their role as birth places of the entrepreneurs, there are few references to local communities and the relationship between technology and social ties is explained in terms of cause-and-effect, as one of 'empowerment' im-mediately proceeding from e-centres to families.

A less deterministic theory of action characterizes *Proyecto Cyberela – Radio Telecentros*, a Brazilian initiative that was granted an Award of Distinction in 2006. As it is explained in the submission,[12] this project was started in 1990 by the NGO *Cemina* as an initiative aimed at 'developing female communitarian leadership as an agent of social transformation'. Since this early commitment, the (analogue) radio has been conceived of as a strategic adjuvant, a media(tor) enabling women to promote human rights and gender empowerment: 'the radio as a medium was chosen for that purpose because it is the simplest and cheapest means of communication, and it reaches 98% of the population, being that women are the biggest listeners' (*Proyecto Cyberela – Radio Telecentros* submission, Author's translation). Over the years, female radio-makers attending Cemina's classes gathered in the *Red de Mujeres de Rádio (RMR)*: an assemblage born out of the desire to 'strengthen their activities'.

However, with the advent of digital information technologies new challenges arose and new mediators were needed. The new goal became to include women into the new digital realm:

> the scenario imposed by the new information and communication technologies (ICT) presented a great challenge for Cemina: either women are part of that process or they would be once again excluded from the equal participation to society. Including women in the world of information technology and the Internet, while continuing to use the radio, became a priority for the institution.[13]

On one hand, the change of the strategic goal from 'developing female leadership' to 'including women in the computer and internet domain' marks a major shift in the role of information technologies: from being instruments, ICT are transformed into 'skills' and become the main goal ('prioridad') of the course of action. On the other hand, gender-focused attention is transformed: from being the result of sensitization policies it becomes an intermediary (in the form

---

12   See Document 3 in Annex A.
13   *Proyecto Cyberela – Radio Telecentros* submission, 2006. Author's translation.

of 'contents') that can attract women. Notably, if the (now digital) radio continues to act as a mediator, it is because it renders gender-related contents available: 'www.radiofalamulher. com helped to intensify the strategy of attracting women to that universe with the availability of radio content with a focus on gender and human rights on the Internet' (*Proyecto Cyberela – Radio Telecentros* submission, Author's translation). If the internet radio 'helped' – and is thus a mediator -, there is no further specification about *how* contents attracted women to be included in the digital realm. This arbitrary restraint of the course of action shows that gender and human rights-focused contents act as mere intermediaries. Table 11 summarizes this analysis, stressing the changing role of communication artefacts.

	Before the advent of the digital domain	With advent of the digital domain
Radio	(Analogue)	(Internet radio)
	Mediator	Mediator
ICT	(Correspond to analogue radio)	(Seen as 'skills')
		Goal to be reached
Gender and human rights commitment	(Attention)	(Becomes 'Contents')
	Result of policies	Intermediary

Table 11: Proyecto Cyberela – Radio Telecentros. Variations in the role of radio, ICT and gender commitment following the advent of digital media.

Ferrying the radio-makers assemblage into the digital age requires more adjutants than before: the World Bank *Infodev* Program, the *Kellogg* Foundation and UNESCO thus sustained the newly born *Red Cyberela* with technical facilities (i.e., computers, audio editing software, high bandwidth) and support (i.e., training, technical assistance). It is interesting to note that in this submission a clear symmetry exists between humans (i.e., World Bank, *Kellogg* Foundation, UNESCO) seen as mediators and non-humans (i.e., technical facilities) seen as intermediaries.

To fully catch the theory of action underpinning this project, there is still a consideration to make. The project's great interest in the digital domain lies on the principle that ICT are causing major transformations in every field of human activity: 'the emergence of information and communication technologies (ICT) has transformed social relations, education, work, economy and even behavior'.[14] (As a consequence, access to ICT is seen as a pre-condition

---

14   *Proyecto Cyberela – Radio Telecentros* submission, 2006. Author's translation.

for development. The submission justifies this consideration through statistical data depicting women as deeply excluded from access to ICT, to the point that the United Nations and 'all the indicators of human development' have recognized women access to ICT as strategic. In other words, the gender perspective is legitimized by appealing to statistical data. It is statistics that provides the boundaries around which the group 'disempowered women' is made to exist.

Also the third project discussed in this section uses statistics as a source for setting up group boundaries.[15] *The World Starts With Me* focuses on young Ugandans between 12 and 19. This project – which won the Golden Nica in 2004 – provided a digital learning environment about sexual and reproductive health education and AIDS prevention. Its goal was double: to 'improve the sexual health of young people in East Africa while providing [computer] skills relevant to the job market' (*The World Starts With Me* submission). Here, too, entering the digital age by acquiring computer skills is one of the objectives. Nonetheless, differently from the previous project, in this case ICT skills are not only a 'necessity to enter the job market', but also something that 'stimulates curiosity to learn more'. That is, computer skills are not merely conceived of as the point of arrival, but as a competence that triggers other actions.

The *World Starts With Me* program is rather complex and gathers a lot of mediators, both human and non-human. There are five main groups involved in the project:

  - the WSWM development and program teams; Butterfly Works and WPF, Netherlands
  – The individual schools, teachers and students who use / run the program in Uganda co-ordinated by SchoolNet Uganda – The SRH partners for knowledge and counselling back up; WIDE and FPA, Uganda – The SRH partner for online counselling; Straight Talk, Uganda – The NairoBits project, who run the pilot in Nairobi, Kenya,[16]

The Dutch NGO *Butterfly Works* developed the project with local artists, health trainers and teachers supported by the *World Population Foundation* (WPF), a Dutch foundation supporting programs about sexual and reproductive health in developing countries. The *SchoolNet Uganda network* linked and supported 52 schools and telecentres throughout Uganda with computers. It included all types of schools: from male/female-only to mixed schools, from poor to rich, from urban to rural. Schools intervened not only as targets of the final product, but also at the pre-testing and pilot stages. WIDE was 'a small sexual health and training office of young Ugandan trainers'.[17] The *Family Planning Association* (FPA) used to have clinics throughout Uganda that supported people in SRH issues. *Straight Talk* provided online counselling on SRH. *NairoBits* was a digital design school for young people from slum areas in Nairobi founded by Butterfly Works In 2000. The trainers at NairoBits were themselves youth from the slums who became web-designers and teachers. NairoBits was in charge of adapting the pilot program developed in Uganda into Kenya urban areas.

---

15   As it may be seen in Document 4 in Annex A, section 'Objectives'.
16   *The World Starts With Me* submission, 2004.
17   *The World Starts With Me* submission, 2004.

In addition to these, other mediators emerge when considering how WSWM worked on field. First, the WSWM software environment itself was a mediator: on one hand, 'by promoting self-esteem and gender equality and by empowering young people with information and skills regarding their (sexual and reproductive) rights, the curriculum *supports* young people and in particular young women in helping them to safeguard and enjoy their own sexual and reproductive health'.[18] On the other hand, the software was an adjutant for teachers, too, as it helped them to connect to their students: 'for teachers in schools it is new approach to education, that gives them the chance to actually reach their students and talk about important life issues'.[19]

Second, teachers were also mobilized as professionals evaluating the project. In the submission, quotations by teachers that run the program in their classes were reported:

> quotes: Alex Okwaput (teacher Bishops Senior, Mukono District and teacher co-ordinator of WSWM): "Using WSWM changed my whole teaching and style in my other classes". Alandi Marion (teacher at Moroto SS): "Do you know what? Guess, during our presentation today one of our students was so excited that he laughed and opened his mouth so widely that his jaws could not close back to normal. Can you imagine that?".[20]

Third, students that had finished their course acted as facilitators for the new students. Some of the trainers were themselves young from the slums that had become web-designers. In the submission, this organizational model was labelled 'experiential learning' and was intended to transform former learners into mediators playing 'an active role in expanding the program to as many others as possible'. This form of knowledge transfer based on the proliferation of mediators is very similar to that of hackers' communities. As in FLOSS development communities, it is peers and not hierarchical figures that translate knowledge in an informal way.[21]

What is striking in this project is exactly the number and assortment of the mediators mobilized to reach the goal of 'giving young people self confidence and control over their own lives'.[22] Public schools, foundations, clinics, NGOs, counselling services are assembled with software, students, artists, peer facilitators, people from the slums in an aggregate that blends formal institutions with informal ties.

---

18   *The World Starts With Me* submission, 2004.
19   *The World Starts With Me* submission, 2004.
20   *The World Starts With Me* submission, 2004.
21   See discussion about FSF below. Even if I cannot account here for the vast literature dealing with ICT and pedagogy, it should be noticed that the WSWM's approach to teaching sounds close to pedagogical theories underpinning the so called 'blended-learning' model. The 'socio-cultural constructivism' paradigm, in fact, extends the insights of constructivism into 'digital pedagogy' and focuses on the situated, interactive and informal components of the learning process. See J. S. Bruner, *Acts of Meaning*, Cambridge, Mass.: Harvard University Press, 1990; , H. Gardner, *Frames of Mind: the Theory of Multiple Intelligences*, New York: Basic Books, 1983;
      S. Papert, *Mindstorms: children, computers, and powerful ideas,* New York: Basic Books, 1980; *The children's machine: rethinking school in the age of the computer,* New York: Basic Books, 1993.
22   *The World Starts With Me* submission, 2004.

The last case is *canal*ACCESSIBLE*, a project dealing with the creation of geo-referenced cartographies of urban places presenting obstacles for the disabled.[23] The project – which was awarded the Golden Nica in 2006 – allowed movement-impaired people to send real time pictures of inaccessible locations to a website, by means of mobile phones equipped with cameras. Every multimedia item was geo-referenced, so that it could be included into a map of the city, available online.

The system was not only aimed at disabled people, but also at other discriminated groups that lacked possibilities of self-expression (e.g., taxi drivers in Mexico City; young gipsies in Lleida y León; prostitutes in Madrid). According to the project's submission, indeed having the possibility to achieve a means for self-expression would allow minorities to by-pass mainstream media representations about them:

> The project is based on the possibility of giving voice and presence on the Internet to groups that suffer discrimination. It is about providing mobile communication technology to these groups so that they can express themselves on the Internet, without having to wait for the representaion that the mainstream means of communication give of them. It is the affected people themselves who explain who they are and what their expectations are. [24]

Mainstream media are thus (anti-)mediators that translate the discriminated groups into their representations. On the contrary, mobile devices cannot be said to be mediators in their own right. They do not affect the output in any way, but are seen as mere channels transporting images from the urban space to the internet website.

More multifaceted considerations are required when it comes to internet and the web. Throughout the application internet is seen as the final platform where maps are published. Under this perspective, it acts as an intermediary, whose presence does not trigger further actions. However, things change in the 'Lessons learned' section:

> when a discriminated group, that is not accustomed to being listened to, obtains the possibility of expressing itself on the Internet through mobile phones, the first thing that happens is that it does not find what contents to communicate. However, gradually each group has found the topics that most affect it and has also organized itself into sub-groups dedicated to each channel of communication, with contents agreed on in the regular meetings. In the end, they have always managed to articulate and publish specific thematic channels of the group.[25]

---

23   The submission in reported in Annex A, Document 5.
24   *canal*ACCESSIBLE* submission, 2006. Author's translation.
25   *canal*ACCESSIBLE* submission, 2006. Author's translation.

	Tonga. Online	Akshaya	Proyecto Cyberela – Radio Tel.	The World Starts with Me	canal*AC-CESSI-BLE
Source of boundaries	Cultural heritage and traditions (Tonga people)	Geopolitical/ administrative (local communi-ties in Kerala)	Statistics (gender)	Statistic (age and, partially, gender)	Social discrimi-nation
Role of digital ICT	Mediators (Alpha Smart triggers 'msg and digital reflections' creating associations with dispersed actants)	ICT-skills and data repository as goals. Wireless net, computers, scanners, etc. as intermedi-aries	ICT-skills are goals. Technical facilities as intermediaries	PC as interme-diary (may be substituted). But ICT-skills as a competence. WSWM is a mediator	Mobile phones and digital pho-tos as interme-di-aries; Internet alternatively as mediator or intermediary
Role of other tech-nologies	Music as mediator that translates the cultural heritage into the digital age	/	Radio as mediator	Low-tech objects (i.e. paper&pencil, local materials) as intermedi-aries	Broadcast media as (anti-) mediators
Mediators/inter-mediaries	Many mediators, agency chain extends in many directions	One mediator, some interme-di-aries. Very short agency chain	Few human mediators, some non-hu-man intermedi-aries	Many mediators	Three mediators, some interme-diaries
Professionals	Journalist	/	/	Teachers	/
Relationship Addresser/ Addressee	No distinction	Clearly distinct (Service delivery business)	Fairly distinct after the advent of digital media	Only during course: stu-dents who finish it become facilitators	Fairly distinct: 'disadvantaged groups' and project promot-ers do not blur

Table 12: Summary of the theories of action associated with 'empowerment'.

Here, it is the possibility of self-expression on the internet that enacts groups by stimulating not only the production of contents, but also the acknowledgement of the most pressing concerns and the organization of the editorial staff. It should be noticed that this theory of action – it is the possibility to access a medium as producers that triggers enacts new actors – is based on a mass-media pattern of interaction where 'self-expression' is usually hampered by the broadcasting form of transmission.

All in all, this project shows a rather short chain of action. Although it recognized the transformative potentials of mass-media, it conceives of ICT, and mobile phones in particular, mainly as intermediaries.

Summing up the results of the four analyses, there emerge two macro-types of digital communities aiming at empowering disadvantaged populations.

This comparison shows that the source of boundaries is a crucial element. It is correlated to the theory of action that underpins the development of a community. Projects addressing disadvantaged groups whose existence appeals to administrative or statistical boundaries tend to display specific narratives of empowerment. According to these narratives, target groups are pushed to acquire ICT skills in order to enter the information age, and ICT skills and digital access are conceived of as a goal in itself. The relationship between digital technologies and social ties is often one of cause-and-effect: access to technical facilities (and occasionally literacy courses) is supposed to immediately lead to better living conditions. As a consequence, the chain that transports agency is rather short, with few mediators and some intermediaries. In these accounts, ICT are conceived of as 'technological facilities' that act as intermediaries.

Furthermore, in similar accounts the roles of Addresser and Addressee are easily distinguishable: there is one entity – the project designer – that acts as sender in a communication process (classes, service provisioning, etc.), and a group which is supposed to be the receiver of this process. In *Akshaya*, for instance, entrepreneurs implement the e-centres and the local communities are the target group which benefits from the activity of the entrepreneurs. Similarly, in *Proyecto Cyberela – Radio Telecentros*, after the advent of digital technologies the role of Cemina as core team got distinguished from that of the radio-makers, who stopped to act as local leaders and became addressees of Cemina's classes. In both cases, group identities pre-exist the course of action and boundaries are stabilized: the community has been black-boxed.

The other model is exemplified by *Tonga.Online*. This project does not deal with statistical boundaries, but rather borrows its source of identity from the cultural heritage. Here, ICT are seen as one of the many types of mediators participating in the course of action. Mediators are not only human beings, but also digital devices and traditional music. Every mediator introduces a bifurcation in the course of action and triggers new participants. The chain that transports agency extends in many directions and includes also a journalist mobilized in order to make the group exist. The empowered community that results is enacted through

this concatenation of action. In this dynamic techno-social assemblage, distinguishing the project designer from the target becomes meaningless.

Lastly, *The World Starts With Me* locates among these two types of digital community. Like the first type, it appeals to statistics in order to legitimize the focus on disadvantaged youth and conceives of computers and technical facilities as intermediaries that may be replaced by paper and pencil. On the other hand, many mediators – both human and machinic, institutional and informal – are involved and the acquisition of ICT skills is not seen only as a goal, but as a competence that triggers other courses of action. In addition, actors' enactment is explicit: through the experiential learning model, former students may become peer facilitators, that is, mediators in their own right.

6.3 'Free' as in 'Freedom': When Digital Communities Become Movements

Distinguishing different typologies of digital communities is less clear-cut when it comes to communities that appeal to freedom as the source of their action. This is the case of projects like the *Electronic Frontier Foundation,* the *Free Software Foundation* and *Telestreet-New Global Vision (NGV)*, which appeal to *freedom* as the source of their boundaries, and entail a political dimension of their action. Looking carefully at their submissions, one could nevertheless notice some minor differences that are expected to lead to different communitarian typologies.

For the *Electronic Frontier Foundation* (EFF)[26] – champion of the independence of cyberspace from the brick-and-mortar world, as seen in section 1.1 – 'freedom in the networked world' acts as the main principle for action. The Foundation's objective is 'to defend freedom of expression, innovation and privacy on the electronic frontier', in the name of the 'public interest in digital rights on a global level'.[27]

Freedom is crucial also for the *Free Software Foundation* (FSF),[28] whose objective is 'to achieve software freedom to cooperate' (*Free Software Foundation* submission). However, a difference may be noticed in FSF's and EFF's accounts. For FSF, the appeal to freedom alone does not justify action. FSF does not address freedom as an abstract concept, but as the practical 'computer users rights to use, copy, study, modify and redistribute computer programs'. In other words, freedom is not so much valuable in itself, but because it is a condition for cooperation and community making:

FSF's founder, Richard Stallman, had participated in the cooperating community of the 70s while working at MIT. When this community collapsed under pressure for commercialization, he decided to build a new community of cooperation. However, with the proprietary software that had become the norm in the 80s, cooperation was illegal or impossible. To redistribute the software verbatim is illegal; to improve it without a

---

26 The Electronic Frontier Foundation won an Award of Distinction in 2007. Its submission form is reported in Annex A, Document 6.
27 *Electronic Frontier Foundation* submission, 2007.
28 Richard Stallman's Free Software Foundation won an Award of Distinction in 2005. Its entry form is reported as Document 7 in Annex A.

copy of the source code is impossible. To have a community would require replacing that proprietary software with "free software"-software that users are free to change and redistribute (and run).[29]

Community and cooperation are thus the actual values that trigger FSF's agency, and around which its identity is built.

The *Telestreet* submission[30] conceives of 'freedom to produce communication' as the 'necessary condition for the development of an active, critic and conscious way of being citizen' (*Telestreet* submission). Its goal is 'creating relational networks and active citizenship through an integrated use of communication means': the principles around which the community takes shape are constituted by appeals to active citizenship, not to freedom alone.

This differentiation between an understanding of freedom for freedom's sake vs. freedom as a condition for cooperation or active citizenship could look like hair-splitting. Nonetheless, it entails further differences. For instance, a further distinction concerns the anti-groups mentioned in the accounts. While for EFF the opponent that limits freedom is the United States Secret Service,[31] Stallman's early community 'collapsed under pressure for commercialization', and Telestreet tend to identify the anti-group with mainstream broadcasting networks.[32] That is, EFF re-enacts early cyberculture's opposition to the nation-state, while FSF and Telestreet attribute the reduction of freedom to market logics.

These differences correspond to different types of artefacts involved by each of the three communities. EFF shows a fairly deterministic theory of action of technology and society: 'ICT

---

29   *Free Software Foundation* submission, 2005.
30   Telestreet was the Italian network of independent micro TV stations air-broadcasting on a neighbourhood scale. Telestreet used to integrate low- and high-tech artefacts in media making, analogue air-broadcasting (at the local level) and digital networking (for organization, footage distribution and decision-making at the national scale). Telestreet won an Award of Distinction in 2005 together with *New Global Vision*, a video archive platform initiated in 2001 during the G8 in Geneva, which used to distribute independent footage via peer-to-peer networks. Telestreet's and NGV's submissions are reported in Annex A (Documents 8 and 9).
31   'The Electronic Frontier Foundation was founded in July of 1990 in response to a basic threat to free expression. As part of an investigation into "hackers," the United States Secret Service seized all electronic equipment and copies of an upcoming book from a games book publisher named Steve Jackson Games, even though the business had no connection to the "hacking." When the computers were finally returned, employees noticed that all of the electronic mail that had been stored on the company's electronic bulletin board computer had been individually accessed and deleted.' *EFF* submission, 2007.
32   'The Italian community of media-activists immediately felt the need to create a new tool to publish and share all the video materials that has been produced after those terrible days, video and images which tells other stories from mainstream media, as well as documentaries which has been censored by official TV broadcasts.' *NGV* submission, 2005. 'Over 60% of Italians access information exclusively through two mainstream broadcasting networks (Rai and Mediaset), which, as a consequence, have the power to mould people's imaginary. [...] Thus, within such flattening of the General Intellect, mainstream television rules unchallenged.' *Telestreet* submission, 2005.

are transforming society and empowering us as speakers, citizens, creators and consumers'.[33] In reproposing the opposition between the digital domain and formal politics ('the power of the Net can trump the power of vested politics'), EFF invokes informational resources as agents of change. However, it is not clear how blog posts, podcasts, online videos, and the newsletter are expected to trigger change: 'EFF works through our website, blog posts,and podcasts, online video projects, "action alerts" that encourage personal political involvement, our email newsletter, the promotion of debates and other interactive events, and online guides and other information for writers and artists who want to express themselves digitally'.[34]

With the exception of action alerts that endow users with a will to act ('encourage personal political involvement'), information resources participate in the course of action as interme-diaries. Even when it is pointed out that 'the website remains the home base for coordinating and disseminating information to our community', it is not clear how the website is supposed to transform the input. Also YouTube, MySpace and social networking sites are seen as inter-mediaries to make EFF's message available to a wider audience.

EFF itself appears as a stabilized institution. There are different levels of participation: EFF core staff (made of coordinators, activists, 'techies', artists, policy analysts, attorneys), EFF members, newsletter subscribers, users of the 'Action Center'. While being open to subscrib-ers, a similar structure quite easily allows to mark the boundaries of the EFF assemblage, so that external Addressees are clearly defined as 'those who create and communicate in the electronic world, [...] those who are interested in technology policy covering free expression, innovation and privacy'.[35]

Compared to EFF's, FSF's submission shows a greater heterogeneity of mediators and does not mention intermediaries. What strikes in this submission is the equivalence of social and technical actors. The GNU operative system, for instance, was developed in order to react to the monopoly of proprietary software that – making cooperation illegal or impossible – used to hamper community making efforts: 'GNU is the only operating system ever developed specifically for the sake of giving computer users the freedom to cooperate.' [36]

While GNU is a mediator, it also activates other mediators, like the FSF itself. The FSF was founded in 1985 'to raise funds for GNU development, and for promoting users' freedom to share and change software'. In turn, FSF acts as a trusted copyright holder supporting a wider global community of developers, a 'legal enforcer of the freedoms individuals in the community want protected as their work is distributed'.[37]

Another crucial actor is the kernel Linux that since 1992 has been co-developed with GNU, thus initiating the first completely free operating system. If Linux could be integrated into

---

33   EFF submission, 2007.
34   EFF submission, 2007.
35   EFF submission, 2007.
36   FSF submission, 2005.
37   FSF submission, 2005.

GNU, it is because it was released under the GNU General Public License. As a consequence, the number of mediators includes also those licenses (GNU GPL, GNU LGPL, GNU GFDL) that 'guarantee the freedom to copy, modify, and distribute the software and the manuals released under them'.[38]

Furthermore, the GNU project owes much of its existence to the 'thousands of volunteer developers around the globe'. The peculiar characteristic of this community is that every software user is a potential mediator, since she can write code or documentation, improve it, engage in political activism or simply diffuse knowledge about free software:

Any free software user can contribute to a project, regardless of that user's educational background, socioeconomic status, or geographical location. All that matters is the ability to write code or documentation and the willingness to share the result and what was learned in its creation. Volunteers who don't write code or documentation help by engaging in political activism and telling other people about free software, using the structures and campaigns run by the FSF as their focus.[39]

In the FSF's submission, the boundaries of the community blur to the point that it is difficult to distinguish an outside. The proliferation of mediators is potentially infinite, as infinite is the number of potential users/developers of free software. This point is explicitly addressed in the 'statement of reasons' section of the submission:

The GNU Project, through developing a free software operating system and the GNU General Public License, built the free software community as we know it today. Just think about all of the various communities on the Web-most, if not all, were made possible by the ethical and practical idea of free software and the freedom to cooperate. Wikipedia, last year's winner of this prize, is licensed under the GFDL. MediaWiki, the software it runs on, is released under the GPL. These projects, like many others, draw their contributors to a large extent from the free software community. We cannot claim credit for all of the projects out there and all of the work that went into them, but our role in intentionally building this community, in writing the licenses that these projects predominantly use, and in providing the space for this amazing growth to continue, made it possible to do them.[40]

With the Free Software Foundation, the digital community becomes a movement. With this, I do not mean that it is no longer an assemblage, but rather that it is the quintessence of a techno-social assemblage that strives to remain fluid, to not be black-boxed. This is possible because the 'ethical and practical ideas' did not remain abstract, but got embodied into software and cooperation procedures that may be unceasingly modified.

---

38   *FSF* submission, 2005.
39   *FSF* submission, 2005.
40   *FSF* submission, 2005.

With Telestreet, the online community as a movement is enacted through low- and high-resolution technologies. Here it is not so much the distinction between developer and user that must be overcome, but that between sender and receiver of pre-digital broadcast media.

> Telestreet tactically partakes reality, and by so doing every citizen reaches the opportunity to turn from passive viewer into an active subject of an utterance. Actually, Telestreet's approach to communication induces non-professional people to experiment and create new spaces of community, in the neighbourhood as on the Web. Indeed, it is the precondition that the relevant technologies are widely accessible that allows the *do-it-yourself* concept to spread and hundreds of micro TVs to raise up.[41]

As for FSF, by providing an 'approach to communication' Telestreet itself is a mediator that 'induces' someone to do something, supported by the new accessibility of media technologies. Since everyone may set up her own TV broadcaster adapting the Telestreet model, the boundaries between senders and receivers tend to blur. Given the reusability of the know-how and the low-cost of the technologies needed, the quantity and quality of potential mediators is infinite. For instance, local authorities 'implemented the Telestreet project by involving their community members'.

Since broadcasting without governmental licenses is illegal, Telestreet activates mediators borrowed from legislative ranks, as well. Telestreet invokes Article 21 of Italian Constitution on freedom of expression to claim the constitutionality of an initiative that aims to assert media access rights. Also members of Parliament are involved, with the role of introducing the issue of public access to media-making to the Parliament's agenda.

Further actors come from the range of technology. At first sight, Telestreet's theory of action may recall technologically deterministic positions conceiving access to media as an empowering factor per se: 'the result is the birth of a citizenship that becomes active as soon as it takes over the most passive-making communicative tool [television], the one where political and symbolic strategies of Power are greatly at stake in Italy'.[42] When taken as single entities, media are black-boxed, seen as mere channels to transport information. Satellite television and the web, for instance, are conceived of as intermediaries to merely 'transmit' Telestreet's video productions, without affecting the final product. Similarly, the website is described in technical and functional terms, but no considerations are made on *how* it shapes relationships.[43]

---

41   *Telestreet* submission, 2005.
42   *Telestreet* submission, 2005.
43   'At the moment, Telestreet's web site presents some sections: news (where everyone can publish information regarding the mediascape, the Telestreet network, '), forum (where users can discuss about legal, technical, political, creative and organisational issues), events calendar, street TVs' database, legal and technical schedules, FAQ, Telestreet open mailing list. Moreover, some new utilities are being implemented: self-moderated discussion area and web site for every street TV (blog), integrated system for video files upload and sharing, video play list for the TVs programming, xml-developed syndication with other news portals on media-activism (Italian and international, as well), convergence between forum and mailing list, creation of local mailing lists, database for collecting and sharing videos coming

Nonetheless, things get more complex when media are combined with other media, or when disassembled into their components. For instance, internet is seen as a mediator that enables social networks when its decentralized nature is combined with the socializing power of the DIY television: 'it is just combining these two means that it is possible to create social networks'.[44] Similarly, once it has been reverse-engineered by turning the receiver into a transmitter, broadcast television stops to be 'a tool for exclusion' and is conceived of as a powerful mediator. It 'stimulates creativity of people coming from widely different social classes', 'enables people to take advantage of their rights', 'gives the chance' to passive users to turn into 'active subjects of communication', 'bridges the Digital Divide regarding age as well as gender'.[45]

In summary, if the black box *par excellence* may act as an agent of transformation, it is because it gets decomposed into its elements: transmitter, modulator, amplifier, 'shadow cones', cameras, VHS player, mixer, etc.[46] If having access to media is sufficient for citizens to become active, it is not because ICT deterministically 'empowers' them, but because they acquire competences through the practice of manipulating, hacking and reverse-engineering media technology. In other words, the DIY ethics itself acts as a mediator that embeds concepts into artefacts in a course of action whose ultimate goal is transforming audience into citizenship. Table 13 (see Annex C) summarizes the above analyses.

In all the three cases analyzed, the digital community participating in the competition is part of a wider global community pursuing respectively freedom in the digital realm, free cooperation in software development, and freedom of expression as a condition to promote active citizenship. Nevertheless, it should be noticed that for EFF freedom is something to be defended, for FSF a value to be achieved, for Telestreet a right to struggle for. That is, according to the EFF's account freedom is something achieved in the past that is to be preserved. According to FSF and Telestreet submissions, conversely, freedom is a process associated with the proliferation of mediators, that is, users that adopt the DIY approach and modify technology according to their needs.

Furthermore, while EFF addresses audiences that are external to its multi-level organization, by including users as mediators FSF and Telestreet bring openness to its extreme consequences, to the point that the boundaries of the community liquefy into a movement. This is possible because ideas are embedded into artefacts that can be modified by users themselves: code and licenses in the case of FSF, broadcasting and web technology for Telestreet.

---

from independent areas.' *Telestreet* submission, 2005.

44   *Telestreet* submission, 2005.
45   *Telestreet* submission, 2005.
46   'The project consists of a very simple and cheap transmitter-modulator-air signal amplifier transmitting images by means of an antenna. It takes only 0,07 watts and covers a 300 meters-wide area. We have looked for a very simple technology because we want it to be accessible for as many people and groups as possible. Therefore, it is possible to set up a street television with common instruments anyone may have at home – a digital video camera, a PC, a video recorder. [...] Telestreet does not occupy other television's channels, but uses what we call 'shadow cones', frequencies granted to commercial networks but unusable because of territorial obstacles.' *Telestreet* submission, 2005.

In this regard, FSF and Telestreet re-enact net art's critique of the author Vs. spectator distinction (section 1.3), as well as mediactivism's attempts of techno-social organization through web platforms (section 1.4).

6.4 The Web as Mediator. Web 2.0 Tools and User-generated-Contents

The novelty introduced by communities like FSF and Telestreet concerns the fact that users and technologies' enter the course of action as mediators in their own right. Another project that goes in this direction is *Overmundo*, a Web 2.0 platform that won the Golden Nica in 2007. It's goal is 'to promote the emergence of the Brazilian culture, in all its complexity and geographical diversity'.[47] [48] This need comes from the lack of adequate coverage of local cultural scenes by mainstream media, which tend to focus on the two largest Brazilian cities. Artists, journalists, bloggers and cultural groups from throughout Brazil are expected to post articles, pictures, movies, music on this Web 2.0 platform, thus getting over isolation and achieving national visibility.

Figure 17 summarizes the actors identified in the analysis of the submission (green labels indicate proper names). What characterizes this project's submission is the attentive account of how the *Overmundo* community has been constituted as the result of a long chain of actions mainly embedded in software.

---

47   *Overmundo*'s submission is available as Document 10 in Annex A.
48   *Overmundo* submission, 2007.

Figure 17: Visualization of the Overmundo network of mediators.

Initially, twenty-seven contributors (one in each of the Brazilian states) were hired by the designer group to regularly post about cultural developments in their states. As proper mediators, 'Overminas' and 'Overmanos' were also in charge of activating other users in their states to start contributing to the website. Furthermore, this initial group set the 'rules of the game', the quality standards to which the subsequent contributions had to adapt.

The Overmundo web platform was tasked with shaping the workflow whereby users could post, decide the priority of items on the homepage, evaluate contributions, determine the duration of a post. It was charged with the task of mediating between the main goal (i.e., achieve 100% of users-produced contents) and the need for a quality control system:

> What types of technological tools should be used to achieve this goal? Should the content be freely editable such as the Wikipedia? Should it be edited by a centralized editorial board, such as the Korean newspaper OhMyNews? In order to answer these questions, Overmundo had to keep in mind very clearly what was the problem it was trying to solve. The choice of one particular model instead of another had to be made
>
> keeping in sight the specific goals to achieve, and the true possibility of building a comprehensive community pursuing the same goals.[49]

For example, the workflow included an initial 'Editing Line' function, which kept new posts in quarantine before publication, so that authors and other users could modify it. After quarantine, items used to pass to the 'Voting Line', where users could vote the article. The voting system made use of 'Overpoints', points associated to positive votes. The position of an article on the homepage was determined by the amount of Overpoints. Finally, users' votes were weighted on the basis of a reputation system called 'Karma'. Users with more Karma points used to have more Overpoints and thus more editorial power.

This workflow exemplifies Shirky's point that 'social software is political science in executable form'[50], as well as the notion of 'script'.[51] The Overmundo platform assigned tasks and decisional power to some actors, while it limited others. In other words, political decisions about representation and reputation were embedded in code, which established the procedures whereby the community could assemble. Summing up, the Overmundo submission described in details the actions that brought to the emergence of the community. By so doing, it showed how the digital community is the result – and not the condition – of distributed agency.

Two further winning communities focused on user-generated contents: *dotSUB* and *Open Clothes*. dotSUB, which won an Award of Distinction in 2007, is a browser-based facility

---

49   *Overmundo* submission, 2007.
50   See section 3.2.
51   Akrich and Latour, 'A Summary of a Convenient Vocabulary for the Semiotics of Human and Nonhuman Assemblies'.

designed to create video subtitles in any language. It is based on a publicly accessible database of .sub files, while the original video can be stored everywhere online. This project's goal is to facilitate cross-cultural communication by means of visual language. Video is seen as an agent of change: 'video has become the creative medium of choice. It is transformative and unique. It encourages a kind of creative energy that fosters new thought and new creativity and new pathways for identifying and solving problems' [52].[53]

However, in order to allow video to express its universal creative potential on a global scale, the problem of footage availability in multiple languages must be addressed. Here is where dotSUB facilities enter the chain of action by providing 'tools that change language barriers into cultural bridges'. The project's theory of action is explicit: 'by putting seamless video subtitling technology into the hands of individuals, *dotSUB* tools make stories from every culture accessible to every culture, fostering intercultural experience, communication, and connection'.[54] However, *dotSUB*'s functioning is not described in details in the submission, and the tool is described more as an intermediary that translates stories from one culture into another, than as a mediator which triggers new action. As a matter of fact, there is no reference to how the platform actually works as a means whereby the community is kept assembled.

Lastly, *Open Clothes* aims to create a network of producers, users and contractors in the garment industry.[55] Echoing the discussion in chapters 2 and 3, this project is characterized by its decoupling of the notion of 'community' from any communalistic intent. Indeed, it defines its community in non-essentialist terms, as a 'clothes production system' involving tailors ('those who make' clothes), users ('those who wear') and professional contractors who economically support the system and extract value from it. To explain the project's idea of community, the submission uses the metaphor of a tree: tailors constitute the trunk, users are the branches and contractors the roots:

"Open-Clothes.com" community is compared to a tree. First, wooden "trunk" is the making-clothes network of "those who make." The function of community is substantial from information exchange to work sale as if annual rings may be piled up. The network which supports activity from beginners to experts in connection with making dress as an individual is formed. Then, it is a "branch" bears (sic) fruits, the works born from the network of "those who make". "Those who wears" gathers in quest of "clothes with stories." [...] Moreover, a "root" is required to suck up nutrition and send to a trunk. The cooperation with the professional contractor who become (sic) a foundation supporting activity of "those who make" is indispensable to making clothes. Then, in Open-Clothes. com, the common production system of "those who make", and "the contractors who make" is built.[56]

---

52   Available as Document 11 in Annex A.
53   *dotSUB* submission, 2007.
54   *dotSUB* submission, 2007.
55   Submission available as Document 12 in Annex A.
56   *Open Clothes* submission, 2004.

The boundaries of this community are constituted by a common interest in clothes. Creating an assemblage to make and buy personalized clothes is the main goal of this project, that relies on 'technology to make the clothes environment' open. Despite its emphasis on technology, the account mentions technology only in terms of cause-and-effect, as one of ICT inducing the aggregation of individuals. Therefore, while showing how human actors can contribute to the making of the community, no space is left to explain how technological artefacts work, nor to describe how this assemblage is made durable.

Summing up, this chapter has focused on the role attributed to artefacts whereby groups are kept together. By so doing, it has tried to describe the theories of action underpinning the rationale of techno-social assemblages labelled as digital/online communities. It is evident that those theories of action constitute a multi-faceted landscape, and no univocal relationship between technological and social elements can be singled out. From time to time information technologies, knowledge and infrastructures can be conceived of as tools, goals, supporters. They can empower established social actors in rather deterministic accounts, they can become almost invisible tools, or they can trigger new actors themselves.

Despite this heterogeneity, the analysis suggests it is possible to identify two main types of communities. On one hand, narratives of empowerment which tend to address the relationship between digital technologies and social ties as one of cause-and-effect show a short chain of action, with few mediators and more intermediaries. Paradoxically, in these accounts ICT themselves are conceived of as 'technological facilities' that act as intermediaries. Such communities tend to be stabilized and appeal to administrative or statistical boundaries. The roles of Addresser and Addressee are clearly separated, and identities pre-exist to the course of action.

The other model does not deal with statistical boundaries, but rather borrows its source of identity from cultural heritage or other qualitatively defined origins. Here, both humans and artefacts can be full-blown mediators participating in the course of action. The chain that transports agency is long and extends in many directions. For similar unstable techno-social assemblages, distinguishing designers from users becomes very difficult, if not meaningless. Community boundaries blur to the point that it is difficult to distinguish an outside. At one extreme of this *continuum*, community boundaries liquefy into movements.

All in all, similar accounts show that online sociability, engagement, and eventually communal ties are only possible because of situated material entanglements. In the case of *Overmundo*, for example, human interaction is allowed by a voting platform that establishes roles, criteria, and procedures for participation. This evidence further questions sociological theory postulating the responsibility of modern artefacts in the demise of sociability and communitarian bounds (see section 4.3). More than marking the end of social and political engagement, digital artefacts mediate different types of sociability. If deterministic explanations can be found, they depend not on artefacts *per sé*, but on how their role is accounted for: either as intermediaries, or as mediators.

Finally, one limit of the previous analysis is its focus on textual accounts. Indeed, story-telling provides one possible lens to capture fleeting assemblages.[57] At the same time, I agree that there can be other lenses, that make use of different materials. The next chapter therefore tries to make sense of techno-social assemblages by addressing different types of accounts.

---

57   Haraway, *Primate Visions*.

7. FROM DEFINITIONS TO MAPS[1]

7.1 Limits of Criteria to Make Sense of Techno-social Assemblages

Cases analyzed so far show considerable differences as far as their goals, source of boundaries, and theories of action are concerned. The features indicated by early sociological literature to identify online communities are not any more helpful.[2] Not all projects, for example, are non-profit initiatives: Akshaya, dotSUB, and Open Clothes are business-oriented projects. Furthermore, many of the projects analysed do not limit themselves to online interaction, but rely also on face-to-face interaction. While the Free Software Foundation and the Electronic Frontier Foundation carry on their activities mainly online, Tonga.Online – smart X tension, The World Starts With Me, and Proyecto Cyberela – Radio Telecentros blend offline interaction with online learning activities. Likewise, as to the focus of interest,[3] while some of the cases analysed (i.e., Open Clothes, dotSUB, The World Starts With Me) address a well-defined issue, in other cases the focus of interest cannot be easily profiled. Telestreet, for example, aims to create the conditions for grassroots universal access to media-making, and Overmundo aims to provide Brazilian culture at large with tools for self-expression. Concerning the type of technology used, while some communities are enabled by peer-to-peer software (e.g., Telestreet and the Free Software Foundation),[4] projects like Overmundo and The World Starts With Me use centralized platforms.

How can we make sense of this heterogeneity? This evidence questions the criteria used to identify online assemblages as 'communities' (Table 14) and eventually suggests abandoning the attempt to single out any ecumenical definition of digital communites.

---

1   A revised version of this chapter was presented at the 6th Wikisym Conference in Dansk in 2010 and published as Pelizza, 'Openness as an Asset: A classification system for online communities based on Actor-Network Theory', *Proceedings of WikiSym 2010, 6th International Symposium on Wikis and Open Collaboration*, New York: ACM Press, 2010. DOI:10.1145/1832772.1832784, http://dl.acm.org/citation.ctm?id=1832784&preflayout=tabs.

2   Jones *Cybersociety; Cybersociety 2.0*; Smith, *Voices from the WELL*; Smith and Kollock, *Communities in Cyberspace*.

3   As discussed in section 3.1, leading internet scholars like Castells and Wellman highlight the switch from territorial community to networks oriented towards specific interests as a major change in the contemporary structure of community.

4   As recalled in section 2.3, according to L. Lessig, *The Future of Ideas: The Fate of the Commons in a Connected World*, New York: Random House, 2001; it is the end-to-end architecture of digital networks that assures the openness of the internet and the creation of digital commons. As seen in chapter 1, the focus on the decentralized character of internet networks is inherited from the hacker culture's attempts to avoid control and, ultimately, from cybernetics.

	Profit/ Non-profit	Only online/ Also offline interaction	Specific focus of interest	Centralized/ decentralized technology <?>
Tonga.Online – smart X tension	Non-profit	Also offline	No	Centralized
Akshaya	Profit	Also offline	No	Centralized
Projecto Cyberela â Radio Telecentros	Non-profit	Also offline	Yes	Centralized
The World Starts With Me	Non-profit	Also offline	Yes	Centralized
canal*ACCESSIBLE	Non-profit	Mainly online	No	Centralized
Electronic Frontier Foundation	Non-profit	Mainly online	Yes	Centralized
Free Software Foundation	Non-profit	Mainly online	Yes	Decentralized
Telestreet	Non-profit	Also offline	No	Decentralized
Overmundo	Non-profit	Mainly online	No	Centralized
Open Clothes	Profit	Mainly online	Yes	Centralized
dotSUB	Profit	Mainly online	Yes	Centralized

Table 14: Classification of winning projects according to orientation to business, relationship between online and offline interaction, focus of interest, centralized/distributed technology used. No correlation emerges among these variables.

It is by now evident that communitarian relationships cannot be conceived in ontological terms, looking for an ideal 'essence' of online sociability. Rather, a more profitable direction of analysis proceeds by replacing identification practices with mapping practices, an essentialist approach with a relational one. Instead of looking for what online assemblages *are*, we should try to map their *diversity*.

7.2 First Criterion: Open Accounts

As for any mapping exercise, criteria are necessary to map the diversity of online assemblages. However, which criteria might be suitable ones? Those identified by sociological literature are not helpful, as they are ambiguous. They phenomenologically register a state of the world, without considering how that state has crystallized. For instance, the online/offline criterion does not take into consideration the face-to-face interactions taking place among developing teams. With *Overmundo*, face-to-face interactions have been fundamental for the establishment of the community. Likewise, the profit/non-profit nature is not easily distinguishable. Non-profit projects like *Proyecto Cyberela – Radio Telecentros* and *Overmundo* depend upon multinational corporations for their sustainability, and provide them returns in terms of image, while for-profit initiatives like *dotSUB* can only rely on their users. Also the degree of specificity of the focus of interest is difficult to be set.

In chapter 6, a criterion has proved to be relevant in distinguishing two types of communities based on their spokespersons' accounts. It was related to the length of the chain of actions leading to the materialization[5] of the digital community. The criterion distinguished between accounts in which the chain of action is short, there are more intermediaries than mediators and the boundaries of the community tend to be stable and taken for granted, and accounts in which the chain of action is long, there are more mediators than intermediaries and the boundaries of the community are not traceable because of the ceaseless proliferation of mediators. *Open Clothes*, the *Electronic Frontier Foundation, Akshaya, canal*ACCESSIBLE, Proyecto Cyberela – Radio Telecentros* and are *dotSUB* classified in the first category; *Tonga. Online – smart X tension, The World Starts With Me*, the *Free Software Foundation, Telestreet, Overmundo* fall in the second category.

In the first category of accounts, information artefacts are conceived of either as mere intermediaries that transport elements without interfering with the output, or as goals to achieve. Paradoxically, to those same technologies that are seen as causes of paradigmatic changes no more interesting role is attributed than that of silently transporting information that has been produced elsewhere. Projects that conceive of ICT as intermediaries are also those where it is possible to distinguish a sender that starts the process of communication and a receiver to which that process is addressed. For instance, the *Electronic Frontier Foundation* acts as an Addresser providing information to a vast audience of people interested in digital freedoms. In similar cases, the inside/outside dichotomy maintains its relevance: even if they are layered into concentric levels of participation (from simple members to the core team), group boundaries tend to be stable and taken for granted.

Differently, in the second type of accounts, community is shown as materializing from a con-

---

5   We could not find a better word than 'materialization' or 'emergence' in order to mean the process whereby community condenses into a shape, starting from the associations of heterogeneous elements. The use of this word does not want to imply a 'natural', 'biologically inevitable' aspect of the existence of online communities, as Rheingold as the digital libertarians postulated (see section 1.1). Quite the contrary, here the term 'emergence' indicates the artificial process whereby certain elements aggregate in a situated, unrepeatable way.

catenation of mediators, the chain of action is well-deployed and each participant activates other participants. These are projects where the digital community is 'what is made to act by a large star-shaped web of mediators flowing in and out of it. It is made to exist by its many ties.'[6] Crucially, ties among heterogeneous elements are not made of 'solidarity', 'harmony' or 'team spirit'. With the *Free Software Foundation*, for instance, GNU OS, licenses, and the Linux kernel are not assembled together by means of 'harmony'.[7] Rather, communality can be the a posteriori, transient recognition of their 'cold' association.

In other words, these are the cases where community is accounted for as an actor-network. As Michel Callon has pointed out,

the actor network is reducible neither to an actor alone nor to a network. Like networks it is composed of a series of heterogeneous elements, animate and inanimate, that have been linked to one another for a certain period of time... But the actor network should not, on the other hand, be confused with a network linking in some predictable fashion elements that are perfectly well defined and stable, for the entities it is composed of, whether natural or social, could at any moment redefine their identity and mutual relationships in some new way and bring new elements into the network.[8]

This quotation explains why in this type of account the dichotomy Addresser/Addressee loses relevance: the elements that the community is composed of can at any moment redefine their mutual relationship and boundaries have not been black-boxed.

The second type of account corresponds to a 'good text'. Indeed, texts are not less objective than experiments or statistics. If a textual account is part of what makes an assemblage exist, this does not mean that it is just a 'fictional narrative'.[9] Its accuracy, objectivity and truthfulness can still be measured. As Latour has pointed out,

textual accounts are the social scientist's laboratory and if laboratory practice is any guide, it's because of the artificial nature of the place that objectivity must be achieved on conditions that artifacts be detected by a continuous and obsessive attention. [...] If the social is something that circulates in a certain way [...], then it may be passed along by many devices adapted to the task – including texts, reports, accounts, and tracers. It may or it may not. Textual accounts can fail like experiments often do' (Emphasis in the text).[10]

6   Latour, *Reassembling the Social*, p. 217.
7   Rather the contrary, if one should pay attention to the well-known controversy between Richard Stallman and Eric Raymond. Actually, in origin, the Linux kernel was developed as a sort of provocation towards GNU's organizing logic. See DiBona *et al*, *Open Sources*.
8   Callon, 'Performativity, Misfires and Politics', p. 93.
9   Haraway, *Primate Visions*.
10   Latour, *Reassembling the Social*, p. 127.

Latour does not only argue for the objectivity of texts, but suggests a criterion for assessing the quality and objectivity of textual accounts. He defines a good account as 'one that *traces a network*, [that is] a string of actions where each participant is treated as a full-blown mediator', where the social is passed along.[11] If we stick to this criterion, the projects analysed in the previous chapter can be distinguished between those which 'pass along the social' – that is, those that numbered more mediators than intermediaries, and those which do not. This is a relevant distinction for our goal to map online sociability – as a sort of meta-principle measuring the objectivity and accuracy of accounts that bring communities into existence, and thus we propose to use it as a mapping criterion.

7.3 Second Criterion: Regimes of Access and Visibility

While applications as texts are performative accounts by which a community and its spokespersons are brought into existence, the social may be passed along by many, also not textual, devices. Textual accounts of how information artefacts aggregate communities are one device through which the social circulates. In the case of online sociability, actual software plays a crucial role, along with texts. As Shirky's understanding of social software as 'political science in executable form' recalls, the social is embedded in specific patterns of communication enabled by software.[12] Software articulates the possibilities and constraints whereby a techno-social assemblage is gathered. How are digital communities brought into existence by actual software?

One way to look at these possibilities and constraints is to consider how they 'configure' different types of users.[13] Akrich and Latour introduced the notion of 'script' to indicate the instruction, possibilities for action and behaviours suggested by artefacts, and consequently the types of users implicitly 'inscribed' or presupposed by software.[14] The standard car seat belt, for example, unfolds over the abdomen and thus presupposes either male users, or non-pregnant women. Actual users can then 'subscribe' to the script, and thus follow the instructions, or not (i.e., they 'disinscribe').

In the case of software architectures, possibilities and constraints are strictly dependable on regimes of access and visibility. Such regimes make some functions accessible and visible to members only, others also to non-members or to different degrees of membership. By focusing on these regimes of access and visibility, I suggest that we can follow how software articulates the processes whereby a digital assembly is gathered and different actors are enacted.

---

11 Latour, *Reassembling the Social*, p. 128 (emphasis in the text).
12 Shirky, 'Social Software and the Politics of Groups'.
13 S. Woolgar, 'Configuring the User: The Case of Usability Trials,' in J. Law (ed.) *A Sociology of Monsters: Essays on Power, Technology and Domination*, London: Routledge, 1991, pp. 57-99.
14 Akrich and Latour, 'A Summary of a Convenient Vocabulary for the Semiotics of Human and Nonhuman Assemblies'.

Literature in the sociology of media and media theory sustains me in this effort. Boyd and Ellison, for example, have argued that structural variations around visibility and access constitute one of the primary ways whereby social network sites (SNSs) differentiate themselves, and constitute their own field of the political.[15] The public display of connections is a crucial component of SNSs: 'what makes social network sites unique is not that they allow individuals to meet strangers, but rather that they enable users to articulate and *make visible* their social networks'.[16] The visibility of users' profiles varies by site and allows different procedures of inclusion/exclusion: profiles on *Friendster* and *Tribe.net*, for example, used to be visible to anyone, including non-subscribers. Conversely, *LinkedIn* filters what a viewer may see based on whether she has a paid account or not; again differently, *MySpace* allows users to choose whether they want their profile to be public or restricted to friends only.

Masanès offers a similar example of articulation of the regimes of access and visibility when referring to the '*fabrique* of the networked environment'.[17] He too argues that web platforms differentiate by the potentiality to access a number of functions as non-members. For instance, while the reading function is open in *Wikipedia* and *Delicious*, it is closed in *Slashdot*. Differently, the submission function is open in *Wikipedia*, but partially closed in *Delicious* (since it requires to log in). Again, while the discussion function is open in *Slashdot*, it is conversely closed in *Wikipedia*. That is, Masanès adds to boyd and Ellison's insight a distinction among multiple functions. Visibility is thus one function among others, to which access can or cannot be granted to guests.

An attention to the regimes of visibility and access characterizes Lovink and Rossiter's analysis of weblogs, as well.[18] They argue that the logic of the blog is that of the link. Links enhance visibility through a ranking system and delimit the club of 'Friends',[19] the cultural enclave. Such a delimitation does not arise out of technical scarcity: virtually there is no reason why one can not include all the existing links. Rather, limits are motivated by affinity: the blogger creates links to those other bloggers whose culture and taste she shares. This is why blogs are said to be characterized by a politics of enclosure: they are 'zones of affinity with their own protectionist policies. If you're high-up in the blog scale of desirable association, the political is articulated by the endless request for linkage. These cannot all be met, however, and resentment if not enemies are born'.[20]

One of the consequences of this articulation is the fact that the non-Friend, the Other, the Outside remains invisible: 'the fact that I do NOT link to you remains invisible. The unan-

15   boyd and Ellison, 'Social network sites'.
16   boyd and Ellison, 'Social network sites', p. 2.
17   J. Masanès, (2007), 'Context in a Networked Environment. Some considerations before starting thinking about contextualisation of online contents'. Proceedings of the *Online Archives of Media Art* conference. *re:place 2007. On the Histories of Media, Art, Science and Technology* conference, Berlin, 14-18 November 2007.
18   Lovink and Rossiter, 'Dawn of the Organized Networks'.
19   We use the term with the capital F in order to distinguish the use that of this mundane world is made on social networking sites and alike.
20   Lovink and Rossiter, 'Dawn of the Organized Networks', p. 7.

swered email is the most significant one. So while the blog has some characteristics of the network, it is not open, it cannot change, because it closes itself to the potential for change and intervention'.[21] Blog software rejects the possibility of involving otherness.[22]

This closure places blogs – seen as a kind of social aggregate *and* as a type of software allowing that aggregate – on one hand of a continuum whose other end is occupied by software which shows the potentiality to involve new entities in the course of action. Similar software would enable assemblages in which 'the entities [they are] composed of, whether natural or social, could at any moment redefine their identity and mutual relationships in some new way *and bring new elements into the network*'.[23]

What would such software look like? As textual accounts can or cannot trace a network where new elements are triggered by mediators, in a similar vein software can or cannot plan in its design the potentiality for the Outside to have access and be visible. As in some textual accounts the dichotomy Addresser/Addressee loses relevance and 'the definition of the "outside" has been dissolved and replaced by the circulation of plug-ins' so some software architectures can help to get over the distinction between 'membership' vs. 'otherness', 'inside' vs. 'outside', while other architectures cannot.[24] A similar software architecture would establish the potentiality for the Outside, the Guest, the Non-member to 'speak', 'be publicly heard' and leave a public trace of the interaction. Examples are non-moderated forums and mailing lists, to which everyone can subscribe online and post a message that will be publicly readable. On the contrary, 'contact us' forms that generate private flows of communication to the website manager do not leave a publicly visible trace of the interaction, even if non-members can submit a message. Yet between closed web forms and open forums there are many intermediate positions and forms of actorial enactment. This second mapping criterion should thus be seen as a continuous, non-binary variable, rather than as a dichotomic distinction.

In order to operationalize this criterion, I navigated through the projects' websites.[25] In so doing, I took note of the functionalities accessible online[26] (see second column in Table 15,

---

21   Lovink and Rossiter, 'Dawn of the Organized Networks', p. 8.
22   It is true that blogs allow the Outside to participate through comments. However, recall that comments have a very different relevance than posts and may be taken down. Furthermore, I would add, many blogs – run especially by institutional personalities – do not even offer the commenting function.
23   Callon, 'Performativity, Misfires and Politics, p. 93. *Author's emphasis*.
24   Latour, *Reassembling the Social*, p. 214.
25   It should be noted that a temporal gap occurs between the moment when accounts were written for competition purposes (from 2004 to 2007) and the moment when the websites underwent my observation (in 2007-8). It is likely that some variations occurred on the software side since when the accounts were elaborated. Still, since this chapter does not aim to find correlations, but to map online communities, this gap is not going to relevantly affect the results. If some correlation between the two criteria emerge, that could suggest a coherence between the subsequent developments in the projects' websites and the initial textual accounts. If no correlation emerge, the results won't be less valid.
26   Observation took into account non-web technologies like mailing lists and ftp upload that were accessible through the projects' websites, but not those that were not accessible through the website, like, for instance, *Tonga.Online*'s *Alpha Smart* mobile devices, about which no reference could be found on the website.

Annex C). Among these, I then sorted out those that allow users to interact with the community and to leave visible traces of their interaction (third column in Table 15). To identify this subset of technologies, I myself acted like a guest on the websites: I posted, commented, subscribed to mailing lists, signed petitions, each time exploring the boundaries embedded into the software architecture. Some websites allow only members to interact, others allow also guests, still others allow guests to register online and become members, either without asking for specific requirements or by anchoring the registration to certified personal data (e.g., passport, ID card, health insurance number).

Each peculiar set of interactive tools can be seen as establishing specific regimes of access and visibility. These regimes enact diverse types of users (see column four in Table 15), and allow different degrees of visibility of the contributions submitted by the tester-researcher acting as a guest (see 'degree of visibility of the Outside': fifth column in Table 15).

Despite being qualitative, this analysis is not less accountable. On one hand, while being subjective, the experience of the researcher is replicable by any other internet user. The researcher's website browsing is comparable to that of an abstract 'Other': the visibility of the contributions posted by the researcher is comparable to the visibility that contributions by any other non-member could achieve. On the other hand, the analysis of the degree of guest visibility allowed by each regime cannot be quantitatively measured without denying the peculiar regimes set by each project. While I tried to obtain a measurement from the ratio of number of interactive technologies to overall number of technologies used, such a value did not distinguish between the different regimes of access for members and guests, nor did it account for the diverse entrance barriers for guests to register as members. I thus had to stick to descriptions, rather than using measurements. Results are reported in Table 15.

7.3.1 Configuring Users through Regimes of Access and Visibility

Results summarized in Table 15 identify various regimes of access and visibility, which inscribe different types of users. In two of the websites analysed, the possibility for either members or guests to interact online is not provided by the software architecture. *Akshaya's* and *Proyecto Cyberela – Radio Telecentros'* websites, in fact, make use of broadcast technologies like textual web pages, video and radio streaming or download, textual documents publishing. Even when some kind of interactive toll is provided, either it does not work (the guestbook in *Akshaya*), or its output remains invisible (the contact form in *Proyecto Cyberela – Radio Telecentros*). In these cases, software inscribes an invisibile type of users – be they guests or members – who are not supposed to interact, at least not publicly.

The case of *The World Starts With Me* is slightly different. Here too, most technologies are one-to-many, but contents are restricted to members. Registered members can interact on the students' discussion forum. Since online registration is not allowed, non-members are not foreseen. Here, software enacts only members, who are allowed minimal interaction.

A similar regime is adopted by *Tonga.Online – smart X tension* and *dotSUB,* with the remarkable difference that here online registration is allowed. *Tonga.Online* adopts some broadcast, non-interactive technologies: *read-only web pages, news feed,* newsletter, audio-video *streaming and download. In addition, the contact form allows a form of interactivity, but it is not accessible from the website. The only interactive tool that enables users to leave visible traces of their passage is the discussion forum. As in the previous case, the forum is accessible only to members. However, here online registration is allowed and the process of registration requires ID and password.* In this case, software inscribes an invisibile Other, but *the entrance barrier for guests to register and become members is very low: they only need to create an ID with password.*

As a decentralized video subtitling platform, *dotSUB* openly publishes videos stored in its database. To upload and subtitle videos, online registration is however required. Such registration allows identifying members and enacts them as translation experts. It is thus noticeable that registration only requires ID and password, and no skill test.

Canal*ACCESSIBLE enacts a different regime of access and visibility. It publishes a database of pictures, city maps and videos reporting cases of *incivismo* at the expenses of disabled people. The database is searchable by date, name of submitter, city area and type of obstacle. In addition to the database, a discussion forum is open for comments: posting does not need registration and posts are immediately visible on the website. In this case, software allows visibility of contents produced by both members and guests.

On the contrary, a politics of access that fosters a rather low degree of visibility of the Outside is shown by the *Electronic Frontier Foundation*'s website. The EFF follows communication strategies used by pre-digital activists. The website is first and foremost a one-to-many source of information and documentation: textual guides, a newsletter, RSS feeds, podcasts and a blog (no comments allowed) contribute to the construction of informed internet users, who nonetheless remain invisible. Users are also asked to take action in favour of digital liberties by spreading awareness to friends (e.g., through the 'Send a postcard' form), by contributing to the EFF's knowledge (e.g., through the 'Submit prior Art' form) and by lobbying decision makers (e.g., through the 'Send your message to decision makers' form, restricted to U.S. citizens). Contacts between users and EFF core team can be established only by means of e-mail addresses provided on the 'contact us' page.

In this broadcasting communication model where an editorial staff produces information that users will consume and propagate throughout, only software development allows a visible interaction among (registered) users and between users and the core team. The EFF software projects subsection makes use of wikis in order to coordinate developers and of mailing lists and *Sourceforge*'s tracker in order to collaboratively develop software. In summary, in the EFF case software enacts three types of users: passive readers, engaged (U.S.) citizens, and developers.

The *Free Software Foundation* further develops this regime, with one noticeable difference. Broadcast technologies like a newsletter, a read-only newsreel, a blog (which does not allow comments) and RSS feeds foster a traditional mass-media communication model. On top of that, some interactive tools generate private, invisible flows of communication, mainly through e-mail. Moreover, in the 'campaigns center' section, 'take action' tools hosted by partner organization like EFF allow members and guests to send appeals to decision makers. Technologies allowing both members and guests to leave publicly visible traces of their communication are implemented to support free software development and distribution. Notably, the 'Free Software Directory' – a database indexing all existing free software – allows both members and guests to download and rate software, submit a level, subscribe to technical mailing lists and IRC channels, view the VCS repository. Furthermore, a wiki aimed at facilitating the organization of regional groups concerned on free software issues is open to guests too. Some other mailing lists focused on specific campaigns are restricted to members. Similarly, code contribution on the *Savannah* platform is open to members only. However, online registration requires only ID and password.

Summing up, in the FSF's website architecture, access to software development and group organization facilities – the core activities of FSF – is open also to non-members. The degree of visibility of the Outside is thus rather high. In this case, software enacts four types of users: passive supporters, engaged citizens, guest developers, and member developers.

The *Telestreet*'s website is rather open to contributions by guest users. In the news section, run by the editorial staff, anonymous guests' comments are allowed. Subscription to the mailing list is open and moderation is exerted only on outrageous posts. The discussion forum requires only ID and password registration. Peer-to-peer video distribution (supported by *NGVision* and using *Bit Torrent*) and ftp video uploading are accessible to both members and guests. As such, two types of users are inscribed in software: an interactive, visible Other intended as video-maker, and members thanks to online, light registration.A regime apart is implemented by *Overmundo*. The website is made of a blog where video, music and texts are openly published, while commenting on posts, writing articles, revising drafts and voting functions are restricted to members.[27] However, software articulates different forms of membership. Members have different voting weights and can access different functions according to the length of their participation in the community. Commenting is open to all members, while revision is restricted to senior members. It should also be noticed that registration requires not only ID and password, but government ID or passport copy for strangers.

All in all, *Overmundo* includes the Outside by transforming it. Membership is not seen as a status, but as a process, and interactive possibilities depend on length of commitment. Since they cannot access any tool, non-members remain invisible, but they are provided with the potentiality to integrate and be transformed into members. Guests are admitted to undertake a process of accumulation of good reputation by registering to the website, providing official data and proving to be active contributors to the community. As a consequence, four types of users are inscribed in software: the invisible Other, members (with heavy registration) who can only comment and vote (although with low weigths), members who can comment, vote (with higher weight) and write, members who can comment, vote (with highest weight), write and revise.

---

27   The peculiar editing process devised by *Overmundo* is described in section 6.4.

Finally, *Open Clothes* follows a similar pattern of communication. The website shows a vast array of participatory tools: from a bulletin board to a selling platform, from members' show-case to a newsmagazine open to contributions. However, these interactive features are restrict-ed to members, who are differently profiled according to their degree of engagement. Like in *Overmundo*, light authentication is not sufficient and registration requires personal data. In summary, in *Open Clothes* software enacts several types of intended members corresponding to different degrees of membership.

7.4 Mapping Online Sociability by Meta-Criteria

This last analysis shows how software can articulate the processes whereby a digital assembly is gathered, and different actors are enacted. As text does, software too contributes to upkeep communities that would otherwise fade. This is a basic insight of this book. As a consequence, any essentialist understanding of digital communities becomes unattainable. However, one should not renounce to make sense of techno-social assemblages that self-declare as 'digital communities' by mapping them.

Two meta-criteria for a similar mapping exercise have been identified in this chapter, indicating the degree of permeability of the distinction between Addresser and Addressees, Members and Outside entailed by self accounts (section 7.2) and software (section 7.3). Table 16 visualizes the two criteria and maps communities accordingly.

Application/ Software	Invisible Other	High barriers to membership	Low barriers to membership	Visible Other
More mediators than intermediaries	The World Starts With Me	Overmundo	Tonga.Online-smart X tension	Free Software Foun-dation Telestreet
More intermediaries than mediators	Akshaya Proyecto Cyberela-Ra-dio Telecentros Electronic Frontier Foundation	Open Clothes	dotSUB	Canal*ACCESSIBLE

Table 16: Map of communities according to degree of permeability entailed by applications (rows) and software (columns).

The last cell in the first row includes cases where the number of mediators in the textual account is higher than the number of intermediaries and where guests' online contributions are visible. The *Free Software Foundation* and *Telestreet* communities are accounted for as concatenations of mediators made to exist by their many ties, and their software architecture enables a high degree of visibility of the Outside. In the *Free Software Foundation*'s appli-cation the boundaries of the community blur to the point that it is difficult to distinguish an outside and mediators emerge at the intersection of social and technical concerns. Similarly, the *Telestreet* account deploys its ties rather accurately. Although there are references to a cause-and-effect relationship, in particular when media, taken as 'channels', are depicted as intermediaries, yet disassembled or combined media are conceived of as mediators. Further-more, since every DIY-television client is also a sender, the dichotomy Addresser/Addressee loses relevance. On the other hand, *FSF*'s website leaves access to software development and group organization facilities open to non-members, as well. *Telestreet* allow guests to interact on their websites in multiple ways, almost without control. In summary, in these cases both textual application and software contribute to shape communities whose boundaries are permeable enough to allow new actors to take part in the course of action.

The other cells in the first row include cases where mediators are more numerous than intermediaries, and software provides few or null opportunities of access and visibility for non-members. *Tonga.Online – smart X tension, Overmundo* and *The World Starts With Me* deploy a high number of mediators and no or few intermediaries. In the *Tonga.Online – smart X tension*'s application, elements from both the ICT domain and the cultural tradition of the Tonga people act as mediators that ferry the geographical community across the Zambezi River, as well as across the Information Age. In *The World Starts With Me*'s account, public schools, clinics, NGOs, counselling services are assembled with software, students, artists, peer facilitators, people from the slums in blending formal institutions with informal ties. As to *Overmundo*, by deploying many and variegated mediators, its application describes in details all the actions that brought to the emergence of the digital community.

On the other hand, their software architecture leaves few or null room for guest contributions, albeit different degrees of permeability of the inside Vs. outside distinction can be devised. *The World Starts With Me* does not only impede any visibility to guests, but its contents are restrict-ed to members. Online registration is not allowed, and therefore no possibility is foreseen for the Other to engage in a process of admission, nor to interact with the community. Here, software shapes community as a closed group whose boundaries are black-boxed. In this, the textual application and software enact two different types of community, and it might be expected that such difference reveals further tensions in the development of the community.

Differently, the *Tonga.Online – smart X tension*'s website allows light registration requiring only online ID and password. Here, the boundary between inside and outside is easily bypassable and does not pose other requirements than creating an online identity. Higher entrance requirements are posed by *Overmundo*. In this case, the distinction is not simply between members and guests, but between different degrees of membership. The *Overmundo* com-munity is shaped on an understanding of membership as a process of assimilation. Software architecture admits non-members to undertake a process of accumulation of good reputation by registering to the website, providing personal data certified by administrative authorities and proving to be active and long-term contributors.

The second row in Table 16 includes cases whose applications number more intermediar-ies than mediators, the chain of action is short, identities are stabilized, and the traditional mass-media distinction between Addresser and Addressee maintains some relevance. In the second cell, those projects whose software architecture does not provide visibility to guests are included: *Akshaya, Proyecto Cyberela – Radio Telecentros* and the *Electronic Frontier Foundation.*

Akshaya's application depicts a very short chain and a deterministic theory of action, mentioning only one mediator (i.e., the e-literacy programmes). Furthermore, its software shapes a closed community, closed not only to external contributions, but also to its members. It indeed resorts mainly to broadcast technologies and the only section likely to allow some degree of interactivity is restricted to members with login credentials acquired offline. Similarly, *Proyecto Cyberela – Radio Telecentros*'s application conceives of communication technologies as intermediaries that transport women into the digital age. Its website displays textual, video and radio information, without any tools allowing some degree of interactivity, neither for members nor for guests. The *EFF*'s application numbers informational resources and in particular the 'action alert' system as the only mediator. In this application, blog posts, podcasts, online videos, and the newsletter are seen as intermediaries transporting information from a central editorial staff to a wider audience. Its software regime of access and visibility is similarly articulated. Mainly broadcast technologies are implemented: the website is first of all a one-to-many source of information and documentation. Some visibility of registered users' contributions is allowed when it comes to software development: the 'EFF software projects' subsection makes use of wikis in order to coordinate developers and of mailing lists in order to collaboratively develop software. All in all, in these three projects both text and software contribute to shape black-boxed communities whose boundaries are impermeable to the constitutive potential of the outside.

Open Clothes shows a consistent relationship between text and software, as well. Here, the application does not mention the role of artefacts as mediators, nor how the assemblage made of tailors, users, contractors and clothes is made durable. Community is thus textually shaped as a stabilized black box whose inner relationships are explained in terms of cause-and-effect. At the same time, software articulates different forms of membership, requiring personal data certified by other authorities, and activite participation through desing sharing. In other words, entrance barriers for guests are rather high.

Barriers are lower for *dotSUB*, which – while recording a rather deterministic textual application – only requires online registration for guests to acquire membership status. Lastly, *canal*-ACCESSIBLE* is the only case whose account numbers more intermediaries than mediators, and whose website affords a rather high degree of visibility of non-members. On one hand, its application mentions broadcast media, a political institution (the Municipality of Barcelona) and the internet as mediators. However, the account tends to consider technological objects as intermediaries, having the sole function of transporting information. On the other hand, the discussion forum is completely open for guests, and software enacts interactive, visible guest users.

In summary, no strong correlation between the two meta-criteria – length of the chain of action and degree of visibility of the Outside – can be noticed. None of the cells in Table 16 is empty. However, it should be noticed that – while cases whose applications follow deterministic explanations tend to be associated with software regimes of invisibility – projects whose accounts number many mediators can develop either visible or invisible software regimes. In other words, cases in whose textual accounts action proliferates in many directions do not assure for this sole reason a high degree of visibility of the Outside. Therefore, it could be hypothesized that it is more feasible for techno-social assemblages to be enacted as fleeting online communities when it comes to textual accounts, rather than when it comes to software. The field of the political constituted through software architecture seems to exert more resistance than text to new elements that strive to enter the network, to the potential for change and innovation.

To conclude, this map shows three main advantages over essentialist definitions. First, being based on two meta-criteria, it brings some order in a variegated panorama without the need to rely on ambiguous criteria like focus of interest, level of participation or type of technology used. As such, it is applicable to a wider range of cases, and does not require to define the object of study in advance. Second, by analysing different materialities through which 'communities' are brought into existence and upkept (i.e., textual, software, but others can be taken into account), it allows tracing the variegated, incoherent, and multi-faceted processes through which online sociability is shaped. Third, as it assesses the degree of permeability of the distinction between Addresser and Addressees, Members, and Outside, this map can turn out useful in evaluating the most innovative and progressive digital assemblages. If we stick to Latour's definition of a good textual account as one in which community is accounted for as an assemblage 'made to act by a large star-shaped web of mediators flowing in and out of it' the first criterion is explicitly normative.[28] The second criterion could similarly suggest a normative approach, in which progressive software architectures would be those that remain open to the potential for change, those that maintain as porous the procedures whereby the community is assembled. Nonetheless, it should be kept in mind that the second criterion focuses on cases in which the Outside is *digitally* visible or invisible. For projects whose websites are closed to guests, there are of course other non-digital ways to include the Other in the course of action, as *The World Starts With Me*'s blended learning model demonstrates.

---

28   Latour, *Reassembling the Social*, p. 217.

8. CONCLUSIONS: DROPPING FOUNDATIONAL DISTINCTIONS

At the end of this book, let me recall the question we started with: 'under what conditions is it possible to conceptualize online sociability in the first decade of the 21st century?'. After the fade of the 'golden age' of online communities, in mid 2000s, many of the seeding possibilities for online sociability of techno-libertarian culture's utopias have come to a cross-roads. Myths about the internet as an intrinsically ungovernable machine, about the creative coalition between knowledge workers and internet companies, and about the spontaneous online interactions of millions of individuals worldwide producing diffuse wealth, stronger participation in political processes, reduction in social inequalities, and empowerment, are facing counter- evidence.

Despite this, instead of claiming the ontological demise of online communalism, this book has suggested an empirical, anti-essentialist approach to techno-social digital assemblages. Such an empirical research has asked actors positioning themselves as community spokespersons what they mean by 'online community'. By analysing the whole data set of submissions to the oldest competition for art, society, and digital technology, *Ars Electronica*, I have analysed how actors speaking for digital communities describe the theories of actions underpinning techno-social collaboration.

From this analysis, three conditions can be highlighted: in the first decade of the 21st century it is still possible to conceptualize online sociability, provided that, first, we abandon the techno-libertarian communalist rhetoric; second, we recognize the role of social theory's foundational distinctions in the online communalist rhetoric, and move beyond it by adopting a material semiotic approach; third, we are willing to give up the effort to devise definitions of online/digital communities, and rather engage in a more encompassing mapping exercise.

As to the first condition, we should realize that if many - although not all - of the 'memes' that characterized digital communalism were rooted in the U.S. cyberculture paradigm, this was not by chance. Rheingold's virtual communitarian framework was not only rooted in, but also contributed to *perform* the U.S. cybercultural, libertarian paradigm. His early book can be conceived of as a rhetorical effort to merge multiple cultural traits and experiences in a coherent account of online sociability, along the lines of the dominant U.S. libertarian paradigm. The virtual communitarian framework was crafted as pliable enough to allow this converging effort.

Despite this, two elements mark the limits of this effort. On one hand, not all forms of online sociability can be traced directly back to New Communalism and the North-American lib-ertarian tradition. Critical internet culture, new media art practices running on mailing lists, political movements commonly subsumed under the umbrella term 'No/New Global', and media activist movements imbibed by hacker ethics have been suspicious of the idea of harmony, consensus, and order entailed by the term 'community'. The notion of 'organized networks', for example, has acknowledged that instability, conflict, heterogeneity, passivity are the norm, and collaboration, unity and cooperation are exceptions. On the other hand, when it comes to explain how digital communities are upkept and reproduced, the virtual communitarian paradigm falls short of convincing explanations, and materialist perspectives have to be mobilized.

I will come back later to the need to consider digital communities' material-semiotic character, in order to understand what they have become. For the time being, it is important to stress the black-boxing nature of discourses *on* online communities. Indeed, the analysis of Ars Eletronica's Digital Communities' data set has returned a definition of digital/online communities considerably overlapping with digital communalism á la Rheingold.[1] In chapter 4, we have seen that when 'digital community' or 'online community' is sown, the data set returns topics like the distinction between real world and virtual life, communitarian localism, focus on individuals as agents of change, suspicion towards institutions and hierarchical forms of reputation. Few paths were abandoned in the 2004-2007 data set with respect to early original cyberculture. However, among these the absence of any reference to the cybernetic discourse and its reliance on technology, together with any explicit reference to the role of technology, are revealing. In discourses *on* online communities (i.e., the seeded analysis), the role of technology appears black-boxed, and artefacts are conceived as mere tools.

Differently, outside the online community discourse there seems to be more room for artefacts to be unpacked. The analyses conducted in chapter 5 and 6 have shown that once the hegemonic cyberculture is set apart, and the rhetoric about 'online communities' is abandoned (i.e., when 'digital community' or 'online community' is *not* sown for analysis), richer accounts of the role of software artefacts emerge. Networked individualism and the physical/virtual separation, for example, are part of the discourse *on* digital communities, but they are not part of current accounts *by* online assemblages. In other words, it is only when the rhetoric about online communities is dropped, that new relations can be accounted for, and artefacts can appear in their role as mediators keeping human relations going. Historical continuities can even be traced between specific software architectures and spatial communitarian arrangements. The neighbourhood-based spatiality entailed by *Telestreet*'s integrated broadcasting technologies since 2002, for example, recalls early experiments with mainframe clients like *Community Memory* (see section 1.2.1).

Moreover, in discourses *by* online communities, early narratives survive in more articulated ways. Indeed, in the tricky task of identifying relevant topics and narratives in the data set without postulating 'online community', we have come to understand what distinguishes narratives associated with 'free software' from those with 'social software', narratives associated with 'local information through ICT' from those with 'locative media', those associated to 'work as an economic activity' from those with 'work as a voluntary act', those associated with 'public space-based art' from those with 'engaged art' and 'political art'. By so doing, we have

witnessed how issues that are central to the digital communitarian heritage (see chapter 1)

---

1   This might not be surprising, if one considers that Howard Rheingold was involved in the design of the competition since the beginning, and part of the first jury board.

hit the ground in a much more multi-faceted way in our data set.

The second condition required conceptualizing online sociability and asks to recognize the role of social theory's distinction between *gemeinschaft* and *gesellschaft* in online communalist rhetoric. As anticipated in the Introduction, this distinction was foundational to modern social theory. Social and political theorists like Durkheim, Tönnies, Adorno - together with more recent ones like Beck, Putnam, Giddens - legitimated the new sociological discipline by rising concerns about the industrial, technological society being responsible for the demise of traditional forms of sociability. Modern, technology-driven society was conceived by the 'fathers'[2] of social thought as suffering from a scarcity of commitment and solidarity.[3]

It is not difficult to find the echo of this dystopic understanding of modern relations in contemporary theorizations of online sociability. By coining the expression 'networked individualism', Castells has questioned even the possibility of identifying communitarian ties. While for Rheingold communitarian ties are a specific kind of social relationship characterized by sense of belonging, structuralist approaches like Castells' connect them to the decentralized form of network organization, which fosters individualism and entrepreneurship as characterizing features of sociability. Wellman has further extended this distinction to computer-mediated communication supporting the spread of individualized networks as the dominant form of sociability. While face-to-face interaction characterized 'groups', in contemporary 'networks' geographical vicinity has been replaced by interest-centric forms of interaction (see section 3.1).

In contrast to such binary theorizations, my analysis of 920 applications to Ars Electronica revealed that loose networks are not the exclusive form of sociability when it comes to communal ties online. Rather, they co-exist with other models of sociability that actors label as 'groups'. 'Network' and 'group' are not even seen as mutually exclusive by actors speaking for techno-social communities. From these results it looks like the relationship between information technology and social forms is definitely much more variegated than expected, and social change cannot be linearly inferred from technological evolution. Rather than a situation where dominant forms of sociability (i.e. loose networks) progressively replace older ones (i.e. bounded groups), the results draw a scenario where co-existence has the better of exclusive binary distinctions. For what above discussed, these results question not only the ontological character of 'online communities', but also the foundations of 21st century social theory on the demise of social engagement and sense of community prompted by technological societies.

With this acknowledgment, I suggest that it is possible to undertake the *pars construens,* and focus on the artefacts whereby communities are enacted and kept assembled. Ars Electronica's accounts show that empowerment, engagement, and eventually communal ties are only

---

2   Although, the fact that they were only 'fathers', without any recognized 'mother', might well work as a
     self-sufficient explanation of the scarcity argument.
3   Note to the 2018 Edition. Three years after the completion of this book, a similar argument was raised
     by Marres (2012), who argued for an 'object turn' in understanding contemporary forms of social and
     political engagement.

possible through situated material-semiotic entanglements, of which those same accounts are part. This evidence further questions social theorizations postulating the demise of sociability and communitarian bounds. More than marking the end of social and political commitment, information artefacts, and digital platforms mediate different types of relationships and enact different types of communities. From case to case, information technologies, knowledge, and infrastructures can be conceived of as tools, goals, supporters. They can empower established social actors in rather deterministic ways, become almost invisible tools, or trigger new actors.

I have read the differences among discursive roles attributed to artefacts by recovering the distinction between mediators and intermediaries. This step has allowed me to include spokespersons' accounts in the chain of translation that brings communities into existence, and upkeeps them.[4] The resulting and unexpected correlation between type of community (expressed by source of boundaries, role attributed to artefacts in upkeeping groups and degree of black-boxing of community's roles and boundaries), and type of account (expressed by length of the chain of action and ratio mediators/intermediaries) shows how powerful 'fiction' can be in enacting social actors.[5]

The third condition in conceptualizing current online communalism requires abandoning the goal of devising univocal definitions, and rather undertakes a more inclusive mapping exercise. A similar insight was already developed by Patrice Flichy who - bypassing both Rheingold's converging account and Castells' dismissive perspective - had proposed not a univocal understanding of online sociability, but a taxonomy of early virtual communities (see section 1.2.1). Results reported in chapter 6 show that theories of action constitute a multi-faceted landscape, and no univocal definition, nor relationship between technological and social elements, can be singled out. Despite this heterogeneity, one should not renounce to make sense of techno-social assemblages that self-declare as 'digital communities', for example by mapping them. I have thus proposed 'length of the chain of action' and 'degree of visibility of the Outside' as two meta-criteria for a similar mapping exercise. They indicate the degree of permeability of the distinction between Addresser and Addressees, Members and Outside, and have allowed distinguishing several types of digital communities according to the porosity of their textual and software boundaries.

Indeed, not only accounts, but especially software enacts and upkeeps communities that would otherwise fade. The way it does so is conducive to different kinds of techno-social assemblages. Notably, software embodies regimes of access and visibility which enact specific community boundaries and roles. Software architectures can help to dilute the distinction between 'membership' vs. 'otherness', 'inside' vs. 'outside', or they cannot. Software can locate the 'constitutive outside' by allowing the 'Other' to be visible and present, or it cannot.

---

4   Sometimes literally, in the case of winning communities who received financial support as part of their award.

5   Haraway, *Primate Visions*.

The different types of digital communities mapped by those two meta-criteria could be recon-nected to Paul Ricœur's distinction between utopia and ideology. According to Ricœur, utopia and ideology constitute the two extreme poles of the social imaginary.[6] While ideology tends to preserve the identity of a given social group, utopia aims at exploring new possibilities. Therefore, ideology and utopia are involved in a continuous tension between stability and change. A similar tension affects the techno-social aggregates mapped in chapter 7 (see Table 16). Communities included in the second cell on the third row could be considered as having reached the stage of ideologies. Their goal is to assure their same preservation: few mediators appear in their accounts and software establishes impermeable boundaries. On the contrary, communities included in the fifth cell on the second row might be seen as lingering at the stage of utopias. They keep including external elements as mediators and have not yet closed their digital boundaries to the Outside. If we consider Latour's definition of innovation as a process in which elements move from one aggregate to another, we may conclude that these projects are those more likely to innovate.[7] They are those that not only remain open to welcome new elements, but that also face the risk of losing some of their existing elements. Of course, both ideological and utopian projects correspond to two extremes, and communities in the other cells participate in the tension, as well.

All in all, the classification system here proposed may help trace innovation. Innovation, in fact, is hardly traceable through traditional categorizations like those based on focus of interest, online vs. offline interaction, weak vs. strong ties, profit vs. non-profit business model. As they require to postulate well-defined classes before starting empirical research, those categoriza-tions are intrinsically unable to trace innovation. Indeed, innovation is about contaminating existing classes by adding, subtracting or mixing elements. The argument that conceives of weak ties and unbounded networks as the dominant form of contemporary sociability, for instance, hinders the observer from noticing the innovative potential of those aggregates wherein weak and strong ties coexist and fulfil different but complementary functions.

To conclude, let me return to the first condition and suggest that putting in perspective the foundational distinction between *gemeinschaft* and *gesellschaft* allows to conceptualize not only online sociability, but contemporary techno-social relationships *tout court*. If indeed there is no specific substance that characterizes solidarity ties online, then digital communities are not distinct from other technologically mediated forms of sociability. They are specific only insofar as software plays a role in bringing them into existence - along with other artefacts contributing to the chain of action (like, for example, accounts submitted to a competition). In this light, it is not clear why concerns about the demise of sociability should be imputed to modern technologies, nor why digital technologies should constitute from time to time the cause or the therapy of the individualistic pathology. As we have seen in the previous chapters, software artefacts can contribute to enacting multiple, different types of techno-social aggre-gates, actors and communities, and their influence is not exerted along a univocal direction.

---

6   P. Ricœur, *Lectures on Ideology and Utopia*, New York: Columbia University Press, 1986.
7   Latour, *Reassembling the Social*.

While anti-determinism is a long-standing achievement in Technology Studies, it has been more ambiguously adopted in digital media studies, which sometimes still propose either the causal or the therapeutical argument. I suggest that here is where digital media studies and Technology Studies can face each other: in questioning the foundations of 21st century's social theory starting from the material semiotics of technologically-mediated sociability. To prompt this encounter, let me finally juxtapose Latour's use of the puppets metaphor to overcome deterministic explanations and media theorist Tetsuo Kogawa's use of the lines metaphor to distinguish interactive media from broadcasting ones:

> Given what [sociologists of the social, as opposed to sociologists of associations. NoA] meant by 'outside', namely the constraining power of context or the causal determi- nation of nature, there was not the slightest chance for plug-ins to deposit anything positive inside the actor. Structural forces had to do most of the work - give or take a few small marginal adjustments by the individuals. In their fanciful theory of action, this was the only way sociologists [of the social] had imagined that the string of the puppet- eer's hand could activate the puppet. But [...] the relationship between puppeteers and their puppets is much more interesting than that. [...] Something happens along the strings that allow the marionettes to move. [...] What was wrong with the metaphor of the marionettes was not their activation by the many strings firmly held in the hands of their puppeteers, but the implausible argument that domination was simply transported through them without translation. [...] The puppeteer still holds many strings in her hands, but each of her fingers is itching to move in a way the marionette indicates.[8]

> The Internet and cable media depend on lines. Lines relate to binding, weaving, and streaming. They can bind audience up into a tightly integrated "network", a mario- nette-like circuit. However, lines are not always tight but loose. Loose lines weave webs. In the weaving-weaved web, the signal does not cast itself but streams by itself. Casting is an one-way process while streaming is interactive: streaming in and back.[9]

Despite the differences in language, both authors aim at overcoming approaches according to which action is transported from one point to another along 'strings' or 'lines' where nothing happens. Conversely, by affirming that 'something happens along the strings' or that 'lines are not always tight but loose', the two authors argue for the necessity to think of action as a 'chain of encounters'.

---

8   Latour, *Reassembling the Social*, pp. 214-216.
9   T. Kogawa, 'Minima Memoranda: a note on streaming media', in Waag Society for Old and New Media (ed.) *Next Five Minutes 3 Workbook*, Amsterdam: De Waag, 1999, p.104. Author's emphasis

ANNEXES

Annex A – List of Documents

Document 1 – Model of entry form for the participation in the Prix Ars Electronica's Digital Communities competition

COMMUNITY PROJECT

Name of Project

Web Address of the Project

Project Details

- Objectives

- Language and Context

- Project History

- People involved in the project

- Lessons learned

Technical Information

- Technological basis

- Solutions

- Implementations

- Users

- Licence

Statement of reasons

Planned use of the prize money

Personal Information of Representative of the Project

- Name

COMMUNITY PROJECT

- Address

- Organization

- Experiences

Document 2 – Akshaya submission (http://www.akshaya.net)

*URL of the work: * www.akshaya.net

Project Details

*Objectives: * I. Universal ICT Access

As a first step, a network of Akshaya e-centers is being set up across Kerala. Run by entrepreneurs, each centre will be a self-sustaining unit with the e-literacy programme assuring baseline revenue. Akshaya centres are being set up within 2 km of every household. 4500-6000 Akshaya Centers will be developed in the State with the objective of one centre for 1000 families. The Centres are being connected through broadband wireless technology. Development of these centres provide direct sustained employment to at least 25,000 people in the IT Sector. Each centre is equipped with 5-10 computers, printers, scanners, Webcam, other peripherals and necessary softwares to carry out various ICT based services. In addition, IP phones are also being made available in these centres.

II. E-Literacy

Akshaya e-centres provide training that not only familiarise people with the basics and scope of IT, but also ensures hands-on skill in operating a computer, using the internet and so on. Aimed at creating a 100% literate state, the programme aims at providing E-literacy to one person in each of the 64 lakh families in the State. A carefully designed content module designed in local language is for 15 hrs. for each person is a major highlights of the programme. The process of providing the skill sets shall lead to the creation of a long lasting relation between the Akshaya centres and the families in the catchment, which on a macrom level will generate a state wide data warehouse and repository; of relevant content for the families.

III. Creation of Micro ICT Enterprises.

The Akshaya e-centers are being set up under the sole initiatives of selected entrepreneurs, who have come forward from among the local community. These centres are set up as pure entrepreneurial ventures, with an investment of Rs. 3-4 lakhs per centre. The entrepreneur spirit has been fully utilised for developing the Micro entrerprise in the ICT sector. As in the case of any conventional enterprise, these entrepreneurs display their skills and resources in

ICT enabled sectors, content creation, fulfilling the communication needs of the community, e-enabling farmers, scholars, medical practitioners, in the community for total development. These entrepreneurs are fulfilling their social commitment to impart e-literacy to his community members.

IV. Creation of ICT Service Delivery Points

The Akshaya ICT access points are envisaged to provide G2C, G2G, C2C and G2B information interchange and dissemination. Akshaya centers shall function as decentralized information access hubs that cater to a range of citizen needs that has an inbuilt integrated front-end. Collection of utility bills and taxes now done through Friends centres is being integrated with Akshaya centres, thereby minimizing the transaction cost to the citizens

*Language and context: * Malayalam.Kerala,India,Asia country

*Project History: * Akshaya begins to bridge the Digital Divide. It inagurated on 18th November 2002,by president of India. The akshaya centres set up by May 2003 and literacy campaign completed by January 2004. Board band connection provided by August 2004 and E-payments statred

*People: * Chief Minister, Secretary-Information Technolgy, Director, Kerala State IT Mission,District Collector-Malappuram, Mission coordinator and Assistant Mission coordinator

*Lessons learned: * At present, the number of Akshaya centres per Panchayat is 5- and each centre has 1000-1500 families. The lesson learnt from the pilot is that the number of Akshaya centres can be limited to 2-4 per Panchayat and the number of families in the catchment can be thus 2000-2500 per centre. This would raise the sustainability of the centres.

Technical Information

*Technological Basis: *

infrastructure at Center-5 pc and periperhals, Wireless Radio

NOC- full fledged NOC

OS-various- Linux at NoC and some centers, Windows

Connectivity- WiFi-802.11 b

Solutions: E-payment software

rural e-commerce through net banking

Implementations: Kerala

*Users: * Citizen of Kerala

*License: *

*Statement of Reasons: * Akshaya wis the most ambitious ICT programs ever attempted in a developing society. The project is expected to generate a network of 6000 information centres in the state, generate about 50,000 employment opportunities and throw up investment opportunities to the tune of Rs.500 Crores, all within a time span of 3 years.

*Planned use of prize money: * For creating more content service delivery platforms in Agriculture, Health and Education

Document 3 – Proyecto Cyberela – Radio Telecentros submission (http://www.cemina.org.br)

*URL of the work: * www.cemina.org.br

Project Details

*Objectives: * La meta del proyecto es promocionar la sustentabilidad social y economica de los radio telecentros que fueron creados y ampliar el proyecto creando nuevos radio telecentros en otras comunidades para poder capacitar a cada vez mas mujeres en las TIC y beneficiar a toda la comunidad involucrada.

*Language and context: * El surgimiento de las tecnologias de

comunicaciòn y informaciòn(TIC) ha transformado las relaciones sociales, la educaciòn, el trabajo, la economia y hasta el comportamiento. Lo mas interesante es que mismo las mujeres siendo la mayoria de la poblaciòn en el mundo (y tambien en la populaciòn brasilena) el perfil del usuàrio de Internet ahùn es prioritariamente del hombre blanco que habla el idioma ingles, tiene cerca de 35 anos, es de nìvel universitàrio y de classe A e B. En Brasil, 72% de las mujeres nunca utilizo una computadora, 86% nunca tuvieron contato com Internet y 30% no sabe lo que es. Esos datos son para demostrar que, asi como se pasa con derechos y oportunidades (como educaciòn, condiciones de trabajo, entre outras) – que las mujeres tambien en relaciòn a las TIC necesitan buscar condiciones de igualdad.

Vale decir que hasta las Naciones Unidas ya reconocieron como

estratégico el aceso de las mujeres a las TIC, y ese dato aparece en tercer lugar en orden de prioridade, después de la pobreza y la violencia.

Fue pensando en esa estratégia que el Proyecto Cyberela investio en capacitaciòn para mujeres en el uso de las TIC y en los

ràdios-telecentros. La distancia de los grandes centros urbanos acentua la dificulad de aceso a recursos técnicos como la manutenciòn de las màquinas y la reposiciòn de los equipamentos.

La baja escolaridad entre mujeres y jovenes de eses municìpios es alta, 30% de las mujeres son consideradas analfabetas funcionales. A causa del poco incentivo y de la poca oportunidad, los empleos son cada vez mas escasos. En ese sentido también la mejor calidad de los programas de radio es mui importante, ya que permite un desempeno activo de las personas que no son capazes de utilizar las herramientas digitales en corto y médio plazo.

Otra necesidade importante que el proyecto contempla es la capacitaciòn para proyectos de generacion de ingresos, fomentando el emprendedorismo.

En 2000, el ìndice de empreendedorismo feminino en el paìs era de 29%; em 2003, ese nùmero subio para 46%. En el Nordeste, region mas pobre, existe una ampla diversidad de actividades artesanaless desarolladas por mujeres que pueden ser potencializadas por la geraciòn de emprego e renda utilizando ferramentas digitais.

Las acciones propuestas em ese proyecto dirigense especificamente a mujeres, que de acuerdo con todos los indicadores de desarollo humano, son los segmentos que mas sufren los efectos de la pobreza y de la desigualdad y ademàs enfrentan el desafio de vencer un prejuicio històrico de las mujeres que no fueron educadas para lidar con màquinas.

*Project History: * Fundado en 1990, Cemina apuesta en el desarollo de liderazgos comunitàrios femininos como agentes de transformaciòn social. El medio ràdio fue escojido para esa finalidad por ser el medio de comunicaciòn mas simples e barato, y que atinge 98% de la populaciòn, siendo que las mujeres son las mayores oyentes. CEMINA elabora programas especiales e campanas que son distribuìdas para emisoras de todo el paìs. Desde 1992, realizo mas de 300 capacitaciones para comunicadoras populares y liderazgos de mujeres que querian aprofundar el contenido de género de sus actividades radiofònicas. La Red de Mujeres de Ràdio (RMR) nascio del deseo de las participantes de los cursos de Cemina de fortalecer sus actividades y cambiar experiencias. Son cerca de 400 comunicadoras de todas las regiones del paìs que atuan en las ràdios comunitàrias, educativas y comerciales. Después de diez anos promoviendo los derechos de las mujeres a traves de la ràdio, el cenàrio impuesto por las nuevas tecnologias de informaciòn y comunicaciòn (TIC) presento un grand desafio para Cemina: o las mujeres hacen parte de ese proceso o serian una vez mas excluìdas de la participaciòn igualitària de la sociedad. Incluir las mujeres en el universo de la informàtica y de la Internet, sin dejar de utilizar el medio radio, passo a ser prioridad para la instituiciòn. En 2002, el Programa Habla Mujer gano status de ràdio en internet. A www. radiofalamulher.com ayudo a intensificar la estratégia de traer las mujeres para ese universo con la disponibilizaciòn de contenidos de radio con foco de género y derechos humanos en Internet. La estrategia seguiente fue la apertura de un concurso direcionado a la Red de Mujeres de Ràdio con el objetivo de facilitar el aceso de las comunicadoras de ràdio a las TIC. Vinte y nueve comunicadoras fueron selecionadas a partir de su capacidad de mobilizaciòn y servicios prestados a la comunidad a traves de la actividad en las ràdios, pero la ausencia de provedores de aceso de internet en muchas ciudades impidio el suceso de todas.

Esas comunicadoras recibieron computadores con programas de ediciòn de àudio, fueron capacitadas para utilizarlos, ganaron conexiòn de banda ancha y asistencia técnica por seis meses con el objectivo de mejorar la calidad de la produciòn de los programas de radio y facilitar el intercambio de àudios via internet, promoviendo asi la creaciòn de una nueva red, la Red Cyberela. Esa iniciativa conto con el apoyo del Programa Infodev del Banco Mundial, de la Fundaciòn Kellogg y de Unesco.

A seguir, Cemina empezo a expandir la conexiòn de banda hancha para toda la comunidad a traves los ràdio-telecentros, que visan promover la capacitaciòn para que todas las mulheres esten incluìdas digitalmente, ademàs de proporcionar aceso a recursos educativos y de generaciòn de ingresos por Internet a la populacion de esas comunidades. Esas ràdio-telecentros creadas por Cemina tambien proporcionaron la mejora de la produciòn de radio, principalmente a nìvel de investigaciòn y de ediciòn de los programas y campanas.

 *People: * El equipo principal creador del proyecto:

.Thais Corral, coordinadora general de Cemina

.Madalena Guilhon, coordinadora de comunicaciòn

.Silvana Lemos, coordinadora ejecutiva del Proyecto Cyberela

.Denise Viola, editora del site www.radiofalamulher.com y capacitadora

[...]

 *Lessons learned: * A partir de la experiencia con los radio-telecentros que fueron creados por el proyecto, la sustentabilidad social es impactante devido a que las comunidades se aproprian del nuevo conocimiento para su proprio desarollo.

La mayor dificultad encontrada hasta ahora es la sustentabilidad economica que depende de la situaciòn economica de cada lugar y es la etapa en la cual estamos invistiendo.

 Technical Information

 *Technological Basis: * Todos los radio-telecentros que ya estan funcionando tienen 10 computadores usados, un servidor, una impresora multiuso, conexion a una antena banda ancha, softwares para edicion de audio y toda la infraestrutura necesaria para su funcionamiento.

 * Solutions: *

 * Implementations:*

 *Users: *

*License: *

*Statement of Reasons: * Dentre todos los proyectos conocidos de

inclusion digital, el Proyecto Cyberela – Radio Telecentros, de Cemina es el unico que inclue la perspectiva de gÈnero y el apoyo de òrganos publicos y privados en su implementaciòn asocidos a una ONG. Tiene como objectivo no solo la inclusion digital pero también el forta-lecimiento no solo el movimiento de las mujeres como de la comunidad local, Ademàs, se preocupa con la capacitaciòn tecnica y la sustentabilidad de los radio-telecentros a largo plazo.

*Planned use of prize money: * El dinero del premio sera usado para proporcionar mas capacitacion tecnica y de contenido a las mujeres comunicadoras que ya estan involucradas en el proyecto Cyberelas – Radio Telecentros.

Document 4 – The World Starts With Me submission (extracts) (http://the-worldstarts.org)

URL of the work: www.theworldstarts.org

Project Details

Objectives: Objectives are: – increase knowledge on the whole spectrum of sexual / repro-ductive health, – systematically promote positive attitudes, – coping with negative social and cultural norms and skills regarding a range of relevant sexual health topics By promoting self-esteem and gender equality and by empowering young people with information and skills regarding their (sexual and reproductive) rights the curriculum supports young people and in particular young women in helping them to safeguard and enjoy their own sexual and reproductive health. – learning basic computer skills Butterfly Works experienced that learn-ing the computer is not only sexy to young people, it also is a necessity to be able to get any place in the formal economy and most of all it gives them an ego-boost. Especially designing on the computer stimulates curiosity to learn more. 'Working with the content' really helps to internalise information and stimulates young people to have a positive approach towards sexuality as a starting point in developing technical and social competencies (eg, negotiation skills, contraceptive use, the right to refuse sex). Common goal The common goal of WSWM is to improve the sexual health of young people in East Africa while providing skills relevant to the job market. To show the need: – the prevalence of HIV/AIDS in Uganda is extremely high – young people are disproportionably infected and affected by HIV – teenage pregnancy is high (over 50% of girls become mother before the age of 18) – abortion is practiced (although its illegal), often in unsafe conditions (a significant part by young people) – sexual activity starts at a young age, between 10 – 14 years old and is often forced – contraception and condom use is low and adequate sexual health knowledge and – skills are often missing – poverty leads often to offering sex in exchange for goods or money – sexual intimidation by teachers is common (the 2nd largest number of forced sex situations) Although Uganda started early in the AIDS epidemic with education, current education is mainly restricted to AIDS preven-tion and is information based. This not only led to an information fatigue, also other sexual health problems hardly get attention. Discussion and talking about sexuality are still taboo. Community interest Many people in African communities want access to relevant, detailed information on SRH issues and look for ways to deal with the SRH problems. Schools and teachers see their former students becoming infected with HIV and current students having problems and wish to reach as many students as possible with programs they feel comfortable with while taking into consideration that they are generally overworked and underpaid. Young people want relevant information, to be taken seriously, some badly want help, they are keen to be involved in new developments such as computers.

Language and context: Context of Uganda WSWM is developed for Uganda but with the idea of implementing the program in the whole of English speaking East Africa. During a test workshop (May ë03), 2 Kenyan peer educators estimated the adaptability of the program for urban Kenya. In April 2004 the Ugandan version will be piloted in NairoBits in Kenya, observed by local SRH experts. After the pilot further adjustment- and implementation plans for Kenya will be made. Tanzanian pilot partners are being looked into. Important for the context of Uganda and the whole of East Africa is the educational system: – methods used and lesson materials are old – groups are large (60/100 students in 1 class is common) – self-expression and own initiative is not encouraged The WSWM aims at behaviour change, which needs a more participatory and experiential learning approach (using experience and activities). Context of technology use The integration of ICTís in urban East-Africa is a fact. For most formal jobs, basic ICT skills are a necessity and the computer has even entered the informal job-market. Missing out on basic ICT-skills is not an option for talented and motivated youth. Providing relevant and youth friendly ICT training that attracts youth to experiment more with computers is therefore also a necessity. Schools and Telecenters with computers (see map of the current Telecenters in Uganda) provide computer training, which are mostly international basic courses with little match to the relevant context of the Ugandan youth. Besides, integrated computer training is rare. That leads to inefficient use of computers. The computers are often few, old and lack of good maintenance, the connection is unreliable. They are however available in schools and Telecenters. WSWM is developed in full awareness of the technical possibilities: – web based: cheap to spread and to update, light to download, burnable on cd-roms, flash player provided – non-computerised alternatives: exercises have a computerized and non-computerised version, can even be done using pencil/paper or natural available material (a methods manual based on locally available material is provided). – soft-copy/hardcopy: if the group is larger than 4 times the number of pcís available, a hardcopy backup is provided to make sure a large number of students can participate

[...]

People: Core team There are five main groups involved in the project, they are; – The WSWM development and program teams; Butterfly Works and WPF, Netherlands – The individual schools, teachers and students who use / run the program in Uganda co-ordinated by School-Net Uganda – The SRH partners for knowledge and counselling back up; WIDE and FPA, Uganda – The SRH partner for online counselling; Straight Talk, Uganda – The NairoBits project, who run the pilot in Nairobi, Kenya Butterfly Works www.butterfly-works.org is the group who developed the progam together with various parties (see appendix for bio). BW develops and produces concepts which create opportunities and insight for young people in challenging circumstances, using multimedia. WPF ñ World Population Foundation www. wpf.org is a Dutch foundation which supports programs regarding sexual and reproductive health and rights in developing countries. School Net Uganda www.schoolnet.co.ug links and supports 52 schools and telecenters in Uganda with computers. WIDE is a small sexual and reproductive health and training office of young trainers in Uganda. FPA, Family Planning Association has offices and clinics all over Uganda supporting people in sexual and repro- ductieve health issues. NairoBits project Kenya www.nairobits.com is a digital design school for young people from slum areas in Nairobi. (This school was founded by Butterfly Works in 2000). Users The users of the program are potentially all English speaking African youth. The current users are young people 12-19 yrs mainly in Uganda and secondly in Kenya. They are facilitated by their co-users of the program, school teachers and youth workers. Uganda The schools in Uganda are all part of the Schoolnet Uganda network. Each school has a computer lab with 10+ average to old pcís and a medium to fast internet connection. The teachers are highly motivated and youth friendly. Students are aged from 12-19 and selected by their peers to take part. They agree to inform their peers on what they learn as a pre-condition. Students from the pilot program assist the teacherís with new students. Schools are from all over Uganda (see map). They are a mix of day, boarding, all girls, all boys, mixed, poorer, richer, urban and rural. Kenya The users in Kenya are members of slum area youth organisations in Nairobi co-ordinated by Nairobits. They are both in and out of school youth ages 14 to 16. The trainers of the program at Nairobits are themselves youth from the slums who have become web designers and teachers. They also have a history of peer education activities. The trainers in Kenya took part in the preparatory training in Uganda and due to their relatively advanced ICT skills will be involed after more SRH training in adapting the program for Kenya. In this way not only the program users but the making of the progam will migrate to East Africa. Characteristics of users The users are young people and of course not a homogenous group. On the computer front they have mostly no previous computer experience. They can read and write and have followed at least some formal education. They speak English as a second language, schooling is in English. The education style followed in East Africa is denoted as 'Chalk and Talk' with the teachers as holder of knowledge which the students must copy exactly for good results. Thus students are happily surprised by the active role they get to play in the program. Young people are interested in youth culture such as reggae music, hip hop and gospel and current clothing fashions. Many users are Christians or Muslims and find their faith an important element in their lives. Young East Africans are often dogged by poverty and lack of opportunities either to get educated or work. In urban areas they have to work hard to avoid crime. In rural areas lack of information and sadly even food is a problem. The teachers and youth workers in the program are generally those who are interested in supporting the young people around them in difficult decisions and issues in their lives, getting to know young people better and interested in new and ICT teaching styles. See also the section on common goal on SRH issues. Resticted use Due to the sen- sitive nature of the topic and the embedded nature of the program, access is not so much restricted as supported. 'live' support is given to teachers and students who do the program. The teachers who run the program get a week long training in sexual and reproductive health and counseling issues and using e-learning in the classroom. They have regular on and offline contact with a local coordinator teacher who is also running the program in his school.

They are backed up by WIDE trainers who are professional sexual and reproductive health trainers who they can call to or email for advice . The students are supported in that when they come forward with issues related to the course such as sexual abuse or the need for a HIV test they can be referred to the counselling services or medical centers of FPA (Family Planning Association). In Kenya where the program is being piloted the program is similarily supported. As the program grows the support procedures are being developed.

Document 5 – canal*ACCESSIBLE submission (http://www.zexe.net/barcelona)

*URL of the work: * http://www.zexe.net/barcelona

Project Details

*Objectives: * El objetivo del canal*ACCESSIBLE consiste en trazar en Internet la cartografía de los puntos inaccesibles de la ciudad, a partir de las fotografías que 40 personas con distintas discapacidades físicas envían desde teléfonos móviles a la Web del proyecto.

Barcelona es una ciudad orgullosa de su urbanismo y arquitectura pero un grupo de personas discapacitadas provistas de teléfonos móviles, nos demuestran que no todo es tan radiante como la ciudad nos quiere hacer creer.

Desde finales de diciembre 2005 los emisores han documentado y publicado en Internet 3.336 barreras arquitectónicas y otros casos de inaccesibilidad agrupados en las distintas categorías: escalones, escaleras, aceras, transporte, wc, incivismo y casos de mala adaptación. Cada caso enviado a la Web es geo-referenciado de manera que aparece la imagen junto al respectivo mapa local y su correspondiente comentario de audio o texto.

Los emisores se reúnen semanalmente en consejos de redacción asamblearios en los que se deciden las zonas de la ciudad a documentar, se analiza la evolución de los canales existentes y se votan las propuestas para la creación de nuevos canales. Un ejemplo de canal en emisión aceptado en una de estas reuniones es el canal*SI, donde los emisores publican casos de buena accesibilidad.

El proyecto canal*ACCESSIBLE se inició a finales de diciembre 2005 y las emisiones siguen hasta el fin de marzo. La asamblea de emisores ha decidido crear una asociación para la continuidad del proyecto después de esa fecha.

El proyecto ha conseguido movilizar a la comunidad de personas con discapacidad física y también sensibilizar a la opinión pública, gracias a la amplia difusión que ha tenido en los medios de comunicación tradicionales y en Internet. El ayuntamiento de Barcelona cuenta con información directa de los usuarios afectados para tomar las medidas necesarias para corregir los desajustes de accesibilidad de la ciudad.

*Language and context: * El proyecto canal*ACCESSIBLE se realiza en la ciudad de Barcelona y es bilingüe: catalán y castellano. El contexto específico es el de la problemática de accesibilidad con la que a diario se enfrentan las personas discapacitadas que habitan en Barcelona.

Hay 117.745 personas que sufren discapacidades físicas en Cataluña y 8.000.000 en la comunidad europea. A partir de la misma problemática, el contexto puede llegar a ser mucho más amplio.

*Project History: * El proyecto se basa en la posibilidad de dar voz y presencia en Internet a colectivos que sufren discriminación. Se trata de facilitar tecnología móvil de comunicación a estos grupos para que puedan expresarse en Internet, sin tener que esperar la visión que de ellos nos dan de los medios de comunicación preponderantes. Son los propios afectados quienes nos explican quienes son y cuales son sus expectativas.

Con un historial de investigación que arranca en 2003, se han realizado proyectos en http://www.zexe.net con los siguientes colectivos:

2004 Taxistas de la ciudad de México

2005 Jóvenes gitanos de Leída y León, España

2005 Prostitutas de Madrid

2006 Personas discapacitadas de Barcelona

En la actualidad se preparan proyectos con otros colectivos de Manila(Filipinas) y Sao Paulo (Brasil)

*People: * Concepto y dirección del proyecto: Antoni Abad

Programación: Eugenio Tisselli

Coordinación: Mery Cuesta

Asistente de coordinación: Pilar Cruz

El proyecto canal*ACCESSIBLE cuenta con 40 emisores discapacitados que transmiten regularmente en Internet desde teléfonos móviles con cámara integrada.

El acceso como emisor esta restringido a los emisores registrados aunque la convocatoria es abierta a todas las personas con discapacidades físicas. El sitio Web del proyecto es de acceso público.

*Lessons learned: * Por las anteriores experiencias con taxistas mexicanos, jóvenes gitanos españoles y prostitutas de Madrid, cuando un colectivo discriminado que no esta acostumbrado a ser escuchado, obtiene la posibilidad de expresarse en Internet mediante teléfonos móviles, lo primero que sucede es que no encuentra que contenidos comunicar. Pero paulatinamente cada colectivo ha ido encontrando los temas que mas le afectan y también se ha organizado en grupos emisores dedicados a cada canal consensuado en las reuniones periódicas. Al final siempre han conseguido articular y publicar canales temáticos específicos del colectivo y a menudo constituir un reflejo de la sociedad que les envuelve.

A menudo ha habido que programar especialmente para adaptar el dispositivo a las necesidades comunicativas especificas de cada colectivo, como es el caso del canal*ACCESSIBLE, que incluye los planos locales de cada caso de inaccesibilidad publicado.

Technical Information

*Technological Basis: * La base tecnológica del dispositivo consiste en el envío desde teléfonos móviles con cámara integrada, de mensajes multimedia a direcciones específicas de email, que corresponden cada una a un determinado canal temático de los publicados en la página Web del canal*ACCESSIBLE.

El dispositivo en el servidor Linux consiste en una base de datos mSQL-php que gestiona los contenidos enviados a cada uno de los canales publicados.

* Solutions: * El dispositivo del canal*ACCESSIBLE utiliza el software de envío de mensajes multimedia (mms) presente en los teléfonos con cámara integrada.

La interpretación de estos envíos en la base de datos del servidor consigue ordenar los contenidos en canales temáticos públicos en Internet.

El dispositivo cuenta también con la posibilidad de edición en línea de los contenidos publicados: eliminación de mensajes, cambio de posición de mensajes y edición de texto.

* Implementations:* El dispositivo ha sido utilizado por los siguientes colectivos:

2004 Taxistas de México DF

2005 Jóvenes gitanos de Leída y de León (España)

2005 Prostitutas de Madrid

En la actualidad esta siendo utilizado por 40 personas discapacitadas de la ciudad de Barcelona.

Se preparan nuevos proyectos en Manila (Filipinas) y en Sao Paulo (Brasil)

*Users: * Los usuarios potenciales del dispositivo son colectivos o comunidades victimas de discriminación que de esta manera consiguen expresarse en total libertad, sin tener que esperar las opiniones que de ellos vierten los medios de comunicación preponderantes.

*License: * Se planea realizar una distribución pública del dispositivo cuando esté más desarrollado.

*Statement of Reasons: * Porque a partir de tecnología móvil e Internet abre la posibilidad de que colectivos o comunidades discriminados puedan expresarse por si mismos y en total libertad.

*Planned use of prize money: * 1/3 Investigación de necesidades de comunicación distintos colectivos y diseño de las interfaces resultantes. 1/3 Programación de base de datos e implementación de nuevas funcionalidades. 1/3 Gastos de viaje y estancia para la preparación de nuevos proyectos en Manila (Filipinas) y en Sao Paulo (Brasil).

Document 6 – Electronic Frontier Foundation submission (http://www.eff. org/)

*Description of project: * The Electronic Frontier Foundation digital community – begun in 1990 and growing until the present day – champions freedom in our networked world. EFF works through our website, blog posts and podcasts, online video projects, "action alerts" that encourage personal political involvement, our email newsletter, the promotion of debates and other interactive events, and online guides and other information for writers and artists who want to express themselves digitally.

The people involved in this project include EFF staff, more than 13,000 EFF members around the globe, more than 46,000 subscribers to our newsletter, and more than 68,000 users of our Action Center.

We address those who create and communicate in the electronic world – through digital art, blogs and other online composition, computer code, or other means – as well as those who are interested in technology policy covering free expression, innovation, and privacy.

*URL of the work: * http://www.eff.org/

Project Details

^Objectives: * From the Internet to the iPod, technologies are transforming our society and empowering us as speakers, citizens, creators and consumers. When freedoms in this vibrant new electronic environment come under attack, the Electronic Frontier Foundation is the first line of defense for the public interest – getting people informed and involved in protecting expression and innovation on the electronic frontier. Our website and other resources are used to identify, discuss, and then act on the critical digital freedom issues as they develop in cyberspace.

*Language and context: * EFF's communications are primary in English, with parts of our website translated into Spanish. Our multi-national staff has assisted groups from Peru to Russia, and regularly tour and speak internationally. Our headquarters and legal arm are in San Francisco, with additional offices in Brussels, Toronto, and Washington, D.C. EFF staff also attends meetings of the World Intellectual Property Organization in Geneva in order to fight for the public interest in digital rights on a global level. EFF has inspired companion organizations in Finland (Electronic Frontier Finland), Australia (Electronic Frontiers Australia), Canada (Electronic Frontier Canada); our Blue Ribbon Internet Freedom campaign inspired sister campaigns in Australia, Belgium, Canada, France, Portugal, the United Kingdom and South Korea.

*Project History: * The Electronic Frontier Foundation was founded in July of 1990 in response to a basic threat to free expression. As part of an investigation into "hackers," the United States Secret Service seized all electronic equipment and copies of an upcoming book from a games book publisher named Steve Jackson Games, even though the business had no connection to the "hacking." When the computers were finally returned, employees noticed that all of the electronic mail that had been stored on the company's electronic bulletin board computer had been individually accessed and deleted.

In an electronic community called the Whole Earth 'Lectronic Link (now WELL.com) several informed technologists understood exactly what freedom of expression issues were involved. Mitch Kapor, former president of Lotus Development Corporation, John Perry Barlow, Wyoming cattle rancher and lyricist for the Grateful Dead, and John Gilmore, an early employee of Sun Microsystems, decided to do something about it. They formed an organization to work on digital freedom issues raised by new technologies.

As EFF's lawyers began to work through the U.S. courts, other staffers began building an international community. In October of 1990, EFF opened a forum on CompuServe, an early online computer service. In 1991, EFF began publishing its online newsletter EFFector. Also in 1991, we sent out our first "Action Alert," asking U.S. citizens to contact their senators to oppose new restrictions on encryption. In 1994, EFF took its electronic community to the World Wide Web, creating a website which became the hub of our activism and education work. A year later, EFF started creating off-line educational forums and organizing opportunities for supporters. EFF was the first organization to hire an "online activist", and pioneered many of the techniques that political and civic society groups use on the Net today. EFF continues to spearhead new projects in both the physical and digital world, but the website remains the home base for coordinating and disseminating information to our community.

*People: * EFF's staff of 27 is the core team – including activists, technologists, artists, policy analysts, attorneys, and event coordinators. EFF has more than 13,000 members around the globe, as well as more than 46,000 subscribers to our newsletter, and more than 68,000 users of our Action Center. All sorts of people participate in our community: artists and writers concerned about freedom of expression in their digital work, innovators creating new ways to communicate and connect through technology, activists who want to work with their local or national governments to change policy, journalists looking for insight into important developments in the digital world, and dissidents concerned with the role of technology in oppressive regimes. While the EFF staff creates or edits most of the content on the public EFF website, we are constantly soliciting input and advice from the community, and web posts are as likely to point outward to others' work as they are to point inward to EFF's projects. Everyone is encouraged to use the work on EFF.org as part of their own activism and art, and the site is published under a Creative Commons license.

*Lessons learned: * We have learned that a community of educated people can help influence technology policy on the electronic frontier and make the digital world safe for free expression and innovation. For example, in 1996, thousands of websites turned their sites black and linked back to EFF to protest a U.S. Internet censorship law. Later that same year, EFF launched the Blue Ribbon Campaign so web users could signal their opposition to online censorship. Much of the U.S. law was overturned, and the Blue Ribbon Campaign is still running strong. In 2004, EFF supported the development of Tor, technology that facilitates anonymous communication. Tor now has hundreds of thousands of users who are making the system more robust, and protecting whistleblowers, dissidents, and other activists who need to communicate electronically in a safe and private way. This year, we have also learned the power of using YouTube, MySpace, and other social networking sites to increase the reach of our community. Last summer, we posted an animated video we created about restrictive intellectual property proposals to YouTube, and so far it has had more than 1 million views.

We've also learned that the power of the Net can trump the power of vested politics. For a short period of time, EFF attempted to lobby the American Congress to take digital freedom seriously. Our experience of the restrictions of traditional engagement with established powers – and the political possibilities of empowering an online community free from those compromises – brought us back to online activism and the virtual world.

Technical Information

*Technological Basis: * The Electronic Frontier Foundation tries wherever possible to use open source (libre) software. We have been firm advocates of the free software approach to development, and have supported open source projects such as Tor (http://tor.eff.org/) and MythTV/GNU Radio (we represented them in deliberations at the European DVB organization).

*Statement of Reasons: * For more than 16 years, the Electronic Frontier Foundation online community has been building and evolving to serve our ever-changing electronic environment and to protect our digital rights. The stakes have grown higher every year, as more people around the world depend on digital communication for artistic and personal expression, companionship, activism, and political change. EFF has served – and will continue to serve – as a supporter and enabler of this global digital community.

*Planned use of prize money: * EFF would use the prize money to continue our activism and education work on our website and around the world.

Document 7 – Free Software Foundation submission (http://www.fsf.org)

*Description of project: *

*URL of the work: * http://www.fsf.org, http://www.gnu.org

Project Details

*Objectives: * Our main objective is to achieve software freedom for everyone. The FSF is dedicated to promoting computer users' rights to use, copy, study, modify, and redistribute computer programs. We promote the development and use of free software, particularly the GNU operating system, used widely today in its GNU/Linux variant; and free documentation. FSF and GNU Web sites and discussion mailing lists are places where people can come to coordinate their efforts toward these goals. All of these efforts improve the ability of people to share knowledge with each other and build communities around that knowledge.

*Language and context: * The FSF itself is based in the United States, but the free software movement we organize is truly international. FSF President and founder Richard Stallman speaks all over the world on behalf of the cause, and delivers his speeches in English, French and Spanish. As of this writing in March 2005, he has visited Belgium, Bolivia, Chile, Colombia, Iceland, India, Italy, Norway, and Syria – since the beginning of the year. Around 30% of FSF donating associate members live outside the United States.

Free software development today is global; the version of GNU/Linux that we recommend is developed in Argentina. Free software usage today is also global. GNU/Linux is used in cluster supercomputers and in cheap computers for the masses, used to run much of the Internet, used for advanced research, used by the World Social Forum and by large brokerage companies, and used in the Telecenters of Sao Paulo that provide computer access to poor neighborhoods. It has been adopted for state schools in parts of Spain and India.

*Project History: * FSF's founder, Richard Stallman, had participated in the cooperating community of the 70s while working at MIT. When this community collapsed under pressure for commercialization, he decided to build a new community of cooperation.

However, with the proprietary software that had become the norm in the 80s, cooperation was illegal or impossible. To redistribute the software verbatim is illegal; to improve it without a copy of the source code is impossible. To have a community would require replacing that proprietary software with "free software"-software that users are free to change and redistribute (and run). So Stallman set out to develop a free software operating system, called GNU. Most operating systems are developed for technical or commercial reasons; GNU is the only operating system ever developed specifically for the sake of giving computer users the freedom to cooperate.

Development of GNU started in January 1984. The FSF was founded inOctober 1985 to raise funds for GNU development, and for promoting users' freedom to share and change software.

Over the years, thousands of developers on several continents have joined in developing GNU. As part of developing GNU, we also developed the concept of "copyleft", a way of using copyright law to defend everyone's freedom instead of to take it away. This is implemented in the GNU General Public License (GNU GPL), whose first version was released in January 1989.

In 1992, the kernel Linux was released as free software under the GNU GPL. As GNU was then missing only a kernel, GNU and Linux together made a complete operating system, which now has tens of millions of users. This was an early example of a new form of growth: other projects developing software and releasing it as free software, inspired by the community that we built.

*People: * Richard Stallman, the founder of the FSF and free software in general, remains the head of the Foundation and the conscience and soul of the movement. There are now hundreds of GNU programs, each with its own core team of developers. Thousands of volunteers around the globe contribute. Any free software user can contribute to a project, regardless of that user's educational background, socioeconomic status, or geographical location. All that matters is the ability to write code or documentation and the willingness to share the result and what was learned in its creation. Volunteers who don't write code or documentation help by engaging in political activism and telling other people about free software, using the structures and campaigns run by the FSF as their focus.

*Lessons learned: * We have realized how hard people are willing to work for a cause they believe in. We have learned that, when given a chance and something to study, many different kinds of people can and will become programmers and make useful contributions to the free software knowledge base. What has been difficult, once free software reached the point of being functionally superior to proprietary software, and began to attract users and developers who sought practical benefits alone, is keeping attention focused on the importance of freedom to cooperate. That is currently our highest priority.

Technical Information

*Technological Basis: * The GNU/Linux operating system consists of the GNU system plus the Linux kernel. Of the many programs we developed for GNU (called "GNU programs"), the most commonly used are Emacs, gcc, gdb, make, and mailman. Other free software programs that have grown in response to the GNU Project include Apache, Perl, Python, MySQL, and PHP.

* Solutions: * Proprietary software is a social problem: it is distributed in a scheme to keep users divided and helpless. Users of proprietary software must take what is handed to them, and pay license fees for that privilege. The source code that would tell them how the software works is usually a secret; sometimes they get a copy it for a large payment, but they are not allowed to tell anyone else what they have learned from it.

Free software solves this problem by giving users the freedom to redistribute the software, to study the source code, to change it, and to publish their changes. They are also free to use and pass on all that they have learned from reading the source code. Users of free software pay no license fees, and can modify the software to suit their needs. With the source code they are better equipped to handle problems that may arise. In handling them, they create and share knowledge that will help other people as well.

 * Implementations:* The GNU Project developer tools (the Emacs text editor, the gcc C compiler, the debugging tool gdb, and the build tools make and autoconf, among many others) are used worldwide among software developers. GNU Project packages, as well as much other free software, are widely used in academia in general and academic research in particular. The Internet runs largely on free software: the Apache server, the MySQL database, and the Perl, Python, and PHP scripting languages run a huge number of Web sites. The vast majority of free software is licensed under the GNU General Public License. Many of the technological projects nominated for this award have surely used our licenses or been inspired by the community we built.

 *Users: * Software developers benefit by improving their software, through feedback and contributions from user/developers all over the word.

Schools and non-profits that are hard-pressed financially can get quality software that they can customize to fit their needs exactly without paying licensing fees.

Talented youth with access to a PC running GNU/Linux can learn the art of software development in the most effective way: by reading large programs, and making improvements in them. In the past, only the best universities offered the opportunity to learn this way.

Commercial users that value support and are ready to pay for it can get better support for their money with free software. This is because support for proprietary software is usually a monopoly, but support for free software is a free market. Programmers in all regions can benefit from the opportunity to provide support for free software, since that is not monopolized by a rich foreign corporation.

End users benefit by being able to use software that has been vetted and improved by users around the world, not just the team of one company. They also benefit from the fact that free software develops under the control of its users, rather than under the control of one developer. Of course, only programmers know how to write changes, but everyone can then use them, and all participate in choosing which directions of development are generally adopted. Because free software rejects the "priesthood of technology" by inviting everyone to read the program's "sacred text"-its source code-users are encouraged rather than forbidden to learn whatever amount of programming knowledge they might wish to acquire.

Society as a whole benefits by eliminating the power of software developers over the users of that software, and by avoiding the concentration of wealth that proprietary software brings.

The precedent for knowledge-sharing set by the free software movement is now inspiring sharing and cooperation in other areas, such as reference works, academic publishing, music, and the arts. Wikipedia is one example.

*License: * The FSF developed the two major licenses that free software is released under: the GNU General Public License (GNU GPL) and the GNU Lesser General Public License (GNU LGPL). Thousands of programs have been released under these licenses. Both of these licenses guarantee the freedom to copy, modify, and distribute the software released under them. As a measure of how widely it is has been adopted, roughly 90% of the almost 4,000 packages in the FSF's Directory of free software (which includes programs licensed under a number of free software licenses) are under the GPL or LGPL. The FSF also wrote the GNU Free Documentation License (GFDL) for free manuals and reference works. For many GNU programs, contributors also assign copyright for their work to the FSF. This means that the FSF serves not only as author of the licenses under which most free software is distributed, but also as trusted holder of the copyrights on many community-generated works. This role is vital, as it empowers the FSF to use its resources to act as legal enforcer of the freedoms individuals in the community want protected as their work is distributed.

It is hard to know how many users there are, since everyone can redistribute free software and with no obligation to inform us. Estimates of the number of computers running GNU/Linux range up to 100 million.

*Statement of Reasons: * The GNU Project, through developing a free software operating system and the GNU General Public License, built the free software community as we know it today. Just think about all of the various communities on the Web-most, if not all, were made possible by the ethical and practical idea of free software and the freedom to cooperate. Wikipedia, last year's winner of this prize, is licensed under the GFDL. MediaWiki, the software it runs on, is released under the GPL.

These projects, like many others, draw their contributors to a large extent from the free software community. We cannot claim credit for all of the projects out there and all of the work that went into them, but our role in intentionally building this community, in writing the licenses that these projects predominantly use, and in providing the space for this amazing growth to continue, made it possible to do them.

*Planned use of prize money: * Our newest project is a organizing a community database on the fsf.org Web site recording which models of hardware devices fully support free software. This will pressure hardware manufacturers to cooperate with free software by directing users to manufacturers that do.

We will continue all of our work in organizing the efforts of the international free software community. Specific plans in this area include maintaining our Free Software Directory, which indexes thousands of free software programs so people can locate software appropriate for their needs; creating a comprehensive list of innovations made by free software programmers; and organizing a collection of testimonials from individuals and organizations who have used free software for their work.

Another important project in our future is releasing version 3 of the GNU GPL. The new version will improve the ability of free software to spread in a context that has changed technologically a great deal since version 2 of the license was written in 1991. Finishing the new version will entail organizing a process for obtaining community feedback. We will also continue enhancing our Web site as a focal point for community discussions, protecting the integrity of the licenses and meeting the infrastructure requirements of the free software community as it continues its astounding growth.

Document 8 – Telestreet submission (www.telestreet.it)

*Description of project: *

*URL of the work: * www.telestreet.it

Project Details

*Objectives: * Since its birth, the Orfeotv-Telestreet project has aimed at sharing knowledge and technology, giving everyone the means to practice freedom of expression by setting up citizens open editorial staffs around the street televisions or enabling people to create their own street TV. In particular, the project considers the right to access communication channels a fundamental issue for every citizen as much as the right to health care and instruction. Indeed, open access to communication channels is an expression of such freedom of information, enabling people to take advantage of their rights. The community finds its common ground above all in the discovery of multiple points of view to portray the reality surrounding it, but also in the sharing of the produced video material through the web and the broadcasting. Telestreet is a bottom-up convergence project where neighbourhood-based micro-antennas are connected each other by the broadband to share knowledge. The ultimate aim is creating relational networks and active citizenship through an integrated use of communication means, from the most traditional and common-people oriented ones to digital technology. Everyone can easily set up his own street TV and every street TV can rely on consociated-televisions collaboration. Thus, what matters is not how many people watch television but how many people communicate and speak out. Making television is the opposite of suffering it. This is what a bottom-up convergence is about: i.e. when communication re-establishes its relationship with reality. By thinking globally and acting locally, Telestreet tactically partakes reality, and by so doing every citizen reaches the opportunity to turn from passive viewer into active subject of an utterance.

Actually, Telestreet's approach to communication induces non-professional people to experiment and create new spaces of community, in the neighbourhood as on the web. Indeed, it is the precondition that the relevant technologies are widely accessible that allows the do-it-yourself concept spread and hundreds micro TVs raise up.

*Language and context: * At the moment the project is being developed in Italy, Argentina, Spain. The choice of a *traditional* broadcasting channel such as air * although in combination with broadband web and satellite television * was influenced by Italy's peculiar context for communication. As a matter of fact, over 60% of Italians access information exclusively through two mainstream broadcasting networks (Rai and Mediaset), which, as a consequence, have the power to mould people's imaginary. At the same time, reading rates for newspapers and books reaches among the lowest in Europe. Thus, within such flattening of the General Intellect, mainstream television rules unchallenged.

The Telestreet circuit de-structures and re-sematicises exactly the popular means par excellence, so that whoever has so far been passive has the chance to overcome such condition by turning into an active subject of communication. The result is the birth of a citizenship that becomes active as soon as it takes over the most passive-making communicative tool, the one where political and symbolic strategies of Power are greatly at stake in Italy.

 *Project History: * A group of eight (intellectuals, students, filmmakers, workers) got the project going because they felt disillusioned with the Italian mediascape because of the current monopoly over television communication. Orfeotv was born on June 21st 2002, and on February 20th 2003 ' after a d-day with over 20 street televisions ' the Telestreet network was initiated.

Nowadays, there are more than 250 street TVs in Italy. Some of them are communitarian televisions, born out of some public administrators' will to implement the Telestreet project by involving their community members. Every street TV can rely on consociated-televisions collaboration as far as its legal position, technical issues, artistic and linguistic matters are concerned.

Orfeotv and Telestreet have gained great attention from people and from mainstream communication, not only in Italy. Tiny Orfeotv stimulated creativity of people coming from widely different social classes all around Italy: they have the possibility to experiment how to produce a television, rather than being overwhelmed by it.

Besides, Telestreet is acting from a 'glocal' point of view. It was part of the No War Tv project, a satellite television born during the Iraqi war and made by Italian independent journalists and media-activists. A lot of Telestreet productions on rallies were transmitted during the war by this television in order to produce different and Europe-visible information.

Moreover, it is necessary to mention that the Orfeotv-Telestreet project is illegal according to Italian laws. However, it is constitutional according to article 21 of the Italian Constitution. In October 2003 some MPs placed an item on the Italian parliament's agenda in order to allow the Telestreets some freedom at least until the phenomenon has been properly regulated.

Finally, Dutch project Next Five Minutes has recently announced the will to realise the Telestreet experience in the Netherlands. Reproducing the hybrid air/web-broadcasting model, it is going to start with the Proxivision experience.

 *People: * Orfeotv's editorial staff members are 15, though a larger number of people gravitating around it. There are students willing to learn how to use new digital technologies, independent videomakers, people from the neighbourhood who recur to Orfeotv to denounce problems or to have their interviews broadcasted. Italy harbours about 250 street televisions with 10 to 15 people working around each one. Participation in the street television project takes place under the fulfilment of only three principles: anti-racism, anti-sexism and anti-fascism. Everyone is welcome to participate, without any limitation and technology is placed into everyone's hands. But above all, everyone can set up a street television, as happened with the existing ones. Orfeotv offers theoretical and technical free advice via web site as well as 'face to face'.

*Lessons learned: * One of the main achievements is the creation of an editorial staff that infused the project with new energy and a plurality of points of view. Orfeotv editorial staff produces documentaries, videos and interviews strictly linked to the area, to life in theneighbourhood and to the city (Bologna). At the same time, it is constantly connected with the other members of the Telestreet network with whom it shares video works, information and digital technology know-how. The network also organises various events (demonstrations, audio-visual productions, meetings) of which live air broadcasting and streaming is often co-realised.

Still, there came a time when the need to belong to Orfeotv's editorial staff was felt by all participants, since, due to a generation gap, the younger had problems squaring up to the elders, as well as women to men. The issue has been solved by giving everyone the opportunity to access the technology to realise videos and to broadcast, so that everyone may transmit auto-produced material (especially young video makers), shoot and edit videos, invent formats and so on. Actually, technology ' far from being a tool for exclusion ' has become a mean to bridge the Digital Divide regarding age as well as gender.

Technical Information

*Technological Basis: * – Video. The project consists of a very simple and cheap transmitter-modulator-air signal amplifier transmitting images by means of an antenna. It takes only 0,07 watts and covers a 300 meters-wide area. We have looked for a very simple technology because we want it to be accessible for as many people and groups as possible. Therefore, it is possible to set up a street television with common instruments anyone may have at home – a digital video camera, a PC, a video recorder. Furthermore, it is also possible to use a small mixer for live directing.

– Web. The Telestreet network is setting up an Internet database, developed in xml, for all street televisions' productions, where anyone can upload their works and download the ones made by the others. The archive is a very important tool for achieving video material for the programming of each television. Thus, a web site (www.telestreet.it) has been realised using free software. It is developed in php language by means of CMS, in particular MD Pro. The site is an open-access tool for all the people taking part in the Telestreet project and for whoever (individuals, groups, institutions) decides to set up a street television for the first time.

– Satellite. The possibility to set up a satellite channel (or terrestrial digital channel when such technology will be the norm in Italy) is being considered. Every single independent street television will be able to broadcast its productions through this channel. The result would be a nation-wide broadcaster with fully horizontal public and democratic access, where everyone could book his or her daily airing time via the web.

* Solutions: * From a technical point of view, Telestreet does not occupy other television's channels, but uses what we call 'shadow cones', frequencies granted to commercial networks but unusable because of territorial obstacles. This means that – although not having a regular frequency – the circuit doesn't damage other televisions owning regular transmitting concessions. By so doing, Telestreet shows how raising up an antenna and broadcasting whatever you cannot watch on commercial television as well as accessing means of 'emergent democracy', is possible, cheap and easy.

* Implementations:* At the moment, Telestreet's web site presents some sections: news (where everyone can publish information regarding the mediascape, the Telestreet network, '), forum (where users can discuss about legal, technical, political, creative and organisational issues), events calendar, street TVs' database, legal and technical schedules, FAQ, Telestreet open mailing list.

Moreover, some new utilities are being implemented: self-moderated discussion area and web site for every street TV (blog), integrated system for video files upload and sharing, video play list for the TVs programming, xml-developed syndication with other news portals on media-activism (Italian and international, as well), convergence between forum and mailing list, creation of local mailing lists, database for collecting and sharing videos coming from independent areas.

*Users: * Street televisions' users are the neighbourhood's inhabitants, whereas those who use the web site and the video database are the televisions' editorial staffs, citizens, cultural associations, media-activists, people interested in setting up a street television, researchers studying the Telestreet phenomenon.

*License: * gpl, Creative Commons

*Statement of Reasons: * Television experiences transmitting with low costs have already taken place in the last years (in the Netherlands and Germany, for example). However, what is new with Telestreet concerns mainly the fact that it is a grassroots circuit implementing the convergence between a powerful socialising tool like television and a democratic, horizontal channel like the Internet. It is just combining these two means that it is possible to create social networks. We have chosen the 'Digital Communities' category because the project Orfeotv-Telestreet is creating social networks fundamental for the sharing of knowledge and for community communication projects diminishing the Digital Divide and nurturing emergent democracy. Starting with an integrated system for grassroots communication (through an air signal, the web and the broad band) citizens are able to access communication channels and become experienced with ICT. Thus, this newly gained freedom to produce communication is the necessary condition for the development of an active, critic and conscious way of being a citizen. Indeed, our aims concern the possibility to enable people to recognise their rights by means of digital and common technologies. From a theoretical point of view, the questions relates to tactical relationships between old and new media. Although it is clear that Telestreet begins as television, the centrality of social and technical networks in its development makes it a far more interesting hybrid. Television must be considered a new prosthesis and an extension of the net: but to avoid another media alternative "ghetto", the horizontally of the net must meet the "socialising" power of television. It is a truism that in our society power is more likely to exercise itself through exclusion than exploitation. Telestreet has identified the weak points in one of the main institutions that govern the process of exclusion. Tactical media are practices based on the recognition that the most powerful institutions governing exclusion are never just social but socio-technical. Telestreet has positioned itself critically at the interface connecting the social to the technological. All this takes place without any help from public institutions or private enterprises and suffers the limitations imposed on the project by Italian legislation which denies public access to communication means.

For this reason, an award would mean above all the recognition of the merits for an extremely challenging and visionary project, where the burden is born exclusively by common citizens ' since neither the Italian government nor its parliament seem to be interested in creating the right conditions to implement the freedom of expression typical of a democratic society based on ICT. An award would therefore signal a strong support for the extended right to self-expression, knowledge and public access to communication means.

*Planned use of prize money: * improvement of the broadcasting technology and of the web site's functionality. Development of the open satellite channel project (or terrestrial digital). Payment of management expenses (neither Orfeotv nor Telestreet receive any kind of funding and they mainly collect money in order to survive). Initiatives to involve neighbourhood people. Continuity to the productive routine.

Document 9 - New Global Vision submission (http://www.ngvision.org)

*Description of project: *

*URL of the work: * http://www.ngvision.org

Project Details

*Objectives: * To create an historical archive of independent videos -To organize a distribution network through peer-to-peer, ftp servers, RSS/RDF feed – To establish a producer and distributor community which agrees on the use of the Creative Commons licenses and keep track of their activities through ad hoc blogs – To develop a publishing, archiving and distribution set of software which is available for other communities to use: http://devel.ngvision. org/index -To be a useful tools for independent television which need to share and retrieve contents (see the telestreet network)

*Language and context: * NewGlobalVision is rooted in the Italian context and is mostly in Italian but it is increasingly moving toward a European and transcontinental space.

*Project History: * NewGlobalVision was born in 2001 in a very Italian context and strongly connected with global struggles. It was born immediately after the tragic days of the G8 demonstrations in Genoa (July 2001). Those days were characterised by a clear mystification of reality by global power and a shameful censorship of information by official media. The Italian community of media-activists immediately felt the need to create a new tool to publish and share all the video materials that has been produced after those terrible days, video and images which tells other stories from mainstream media, as well as documentaries which has been censored by official TV broadcasts. From July 2001 up to now (march 2004), the project has been increasing the number of videomakers which use it to distribute their own productions. The project developed an awareness of questions connected to independent distribution, especially that of licences, proposing the Creative Commons as a possible solution. The numbers of downloads increase in a very significant way as does the variety of contents. NGV became a tool in the hands of the new born Telestreet network (terrestrial low frequency Italian pirate TVs). NGV opened itself to European and international communities, it develops RSS/RDF feed to be a tool for international video projects in a decentralized way (http://oce-ania.indymedia.org/newsreal.php). It becomes available on different peer-to-peer networks (from edonkey to bittorrent), it increases the number of ftp serves available, it develops an automatic upload system (http://upload.ngvision.org) which is also becoming an useful editorial tools. Last but not least, Ngvision is addressing the importance of Blogs for producers and it releases a monthly newsletter to all the users. NGV created a mailing list for the producers community, to share points of view on creation and techniques. Some data: 2002 -> 6395 visits / 106330 hits; 2003 -> 72709 visits / 1520892 hits; 2004 -> 21590 visits / 404561 hits.

*People: * Together all over Italy using a mailing list as the main mean of discussion together with internet relay chat and physical meetings. About 20 groups are involved as members and users, between them there is the ECN community which technicals resources are used by NewGlobalVision. All the individuals and groups involved have different attitudes and approaches; there are hackers and technicians who take care of the servers and develop the software paying particular attention to accessibility and videomakers and artists that are more interested in promoting the tools and creating a community as an alternative to the official media. All the people involved in the project are strongly driven by a desire for the autonomy and independence of communication, and of sharing knowledges. Because of these reasons access to the project is open and promoted through workshops and laboratories.

*Lessons learned: * The objective was to have space and bandwidth to archive and distribute independent video productions. We also had to address the problems related to downloading: how to have enough bandwidth to let many users download the same video file? The problem was solved setting up a network of ftp servers that are automatically updated. A file is named ngv_place_language_date_name.avi/mov so that it is easy to find on peer-to-peer networks (edonkey, bittorrent). This system is actually working, but not in all its possibilities. The culture of peer to peer is still to be disseminated amongst ngv users.

Technical Information

*Technological Basis: * New Global Vision is based on a set of software developed in a unix system environment and it can be used by any other archiving and distributing project. FTP servers and peer-to-peer technologies (edonkey- bittorrent) are used to distribuite the files. Data mining tools are also used and a distributed database system is to be implemented.

*Users: * The users and beneficiaries of NGV are the coming communities of independent producers, not only Italian but international and European. Amongst its users are also all those who love to download and watch good documentaries or movies from the Internet or to access a good source of direct information. It is important to remember that the beneficiaries are also the media networks such as the Italian Telestreet network and satellite TVs all over the world, as long as they can access NGV as a source for their programs.

*License: * The set of software of Ngvision is released under the GPL licenses, while Creative Commons licenses are applied to all the video inserted in the NGV archive

*Statement of Reasons: * NGV is a young project but in 4 years it has grown really fast with up to 300 videos uploaded?. – NGV is a pioneer in video archiving and distributing communities and up to now is one of the few really functioning systems – NGV is a decentralized tool which works for everyone who wants to create a digital community around video sharing (see oceania newsreal which uses ngv RSS/RDF feed) – Due to actual political situation NGV is a crucial tool for the Italian independent media community – NGV is not static but keeps developing, especially for giving tools to producers to exchange information – NGV helps in the process of transforming the user into the producer – NGV is not only a digital community but reaches into the non-digital as it is a tool to create a common space of information which are broadcasted on terrestrial frequencies or screened in cinemas.

*Planned use of prize money: * The money will be used to pay for hardware implementations, hard disks and a new server which will be used for live streaming and streaming of a cycle of the last five uploaded videos. The streaming will be done in mpeg4 using a Darwin server. The streaming will be automatically broadcast by any independent television who wants to connect.. NGV already experimented with the streaming but we need a dedicated server to do so. The money will be also used to organize series of workshops and laboratories all over Europe to share the necessary skills to be part of the NGV community. To promote sharing of skills is a very important thing that helps the network of independent pirate tv (telestreet) and alternative media to connect to one other. Ngv is also preparing a catalogue with all the available videos. We would like to use the money to print and distribute the catalogue to promote screenings in different venues.

Document 10 – Overmundo submission (extracts) (www.overmundo.com.br)

*Description of project: * Overmundo is at the same time a community and a software tool. Its goal is to promote the emergence of the Brazilian culture, in all its complexity and geographical diversity. Overmundo was created by a group of four people, who coordinated the efforts of other 35 collaborators. Overmundo is open to anyone at large.

Overmundo today consists of the largest community of people in Brazil aimed at promoting a big and neverending conversation about the Brazilian culture. Using "web 2.0" tools, individuals and groups from all over the country write articles, post pictures, films, music, texts, describing their own places and communities, and creating national visibility for cultural events and scenes all over the country. Before Overmundo was created, these possibilities seemed almost unimaginable. A quick glance at one single article at the website demonstrates the diversity and comprehensiveness of the conversations taking place on it. It is easy to perceive the multiple diversities brought together by Overmundo: diversities of age, gender, race, geography, and above all, worldviews.

*URL of the work: * www.overmundo.com.br

[...]

*Project History: * The origin of Overmundo goes back to 2003, when the anthropologist Hermano Vianna was invited by Minister of Culture Gilberto Gil to think of a project that would integrate cultural movements and scenes from all over Brazil. Hermano then created the project Movimento (Movement), that would count with the help of collaborators spread all over Brazil, creating a network of individuals and institutions dealing with cultural production.

The project was then modified by the Ministry of Culture, and eventually became the general framework for the Pontos de Cultura ('Cultural Hotspots') project successfully developed by the Minister.

Nevertheless, the total potential of the Movimento project remained yet unexplored. In 2005, Petrobras, the largest oil company in Latin America, and the most important financer of the arts in Brazil (every year Petrobras invests more than U.S.$120 million in financing cultural projects in Brazil) invited Hermano Vianna to help solving a problem.

The problem was that Petrobras was financing a broad range of cultural productions in Brazil, but the majority of those productions were simply being lost, or quickly becoming unavailable to the public. For instance, Petrobras was financing the recording of CD¥s by numerous artists, music compilations from indigenous communities, documentaries, short-films, books, plays and all sorts of cultural manifestations. These cultural artifacts were in general printed in limited issues (sometimes only a few cds were printed, or a few books). Quickly the cds were distributed, very feel copies were left, and the majority of the public still had permanet point of access to those cultural productions. Accordingly, Petrobras realized that its huge investments in culture, such as recording an album, or restoring a compilation of traditional music, were becoming ineffective. There was virtually no use of digital technology or the Internet as a distribution channing or for archiving.

Hermano Vianna was then invited by Petrobras to develop a project to build a 'digital magazine', a website who would compile and store all the cultural production sponsored by Petrobras. Hermano then invited a team of three other collaborators to discuss the invitation. The team came to the conclusion that they would have no interest in developing this 'digital magazine'.

Accordingly, the team decided to make a counter proposal to Petrobras. They would create a website where Petrobras could include its sponsored cultural products. However, that should not be the focus. Instead, the group said it was interested in trying to solve a bigger problem of the Brazilian cultural context. The group would only accept the invitation if the website was entirely collaborative, and open to any one in the country to contribute with articles, and any other sort of cultural productions. In other words, the group proposed to use the tools of the so-called 'web 2.0', but mxing them up in order to solve the particular goals they had in mind.

After a couple of weeks, Petrobras agreed to give complete and absolute freedom for the group to develop the website.

The strategy proposed by the group (named as 'Group of Ideas Movimento') creating the best possible environment for collaboration and participation. Nevertheless, Movimento had it clear that the challenge was not only technological, but also of community-building. How to build a community in a country with more that 186 million people, and with vast geographical diversity?

The strategy devised for building the community was as follows. Movimento would hire one contributor in each of the Brazilian states (27 in total). These contributors would be responsible for writing periodically to the website for a period of 18 months, about the culture of their own states. The contributors would also be responsible for 'agitating' and 'energizing' other contributors in their own states to start contributing to the website as well. The contributors of this group were called 'Overmanos' and 'Overminas' (meaning 'Overbros' and 'Oversistas').

The assumption of Movimento was that after 18 months Overmundo would have been able to achieve enough content and momentum to continue the task by itself, only with the support of a decentralized community, built with the original help of the Overmanos and Overminas. To achieve that, the budget for the project would cover the payment of all Overmanos and Overminas, 28 in total, one for each state of Brazil and two for the state of Sao Paulo. The total budget of the project, including technological development and sustainability of the community of collaborators for 18 months was of U.S.$1 million.

The technological development of the site started in June 2005. A national meeting with the selected Overmanos and Overminas was made in October 2005 (a weblog reporting the meeting can be found at www.overmundo.blogspot.com.br). After the meeting, the group of 28 overmanos and overminas were hired in November 2005, to start producing the initial content for the website. A temporary website was posted online, based on a wordpress platform. The website would publish 1 single article everyday, until the official launch of the website, programmed to March 2006.

Accordingly, for more than 4 months, one article was published per day at the Overmundo website, at the time, a conventional weblog. That helped calling a little attention to the project, and gave the Movimento Group time to work on the technological tools that would be used in the final website.

On March 2006, the official Overmundo website was launched, with all its collaborative tools, making it possible to receive decentralized contribution of anyone. Also, the editorial board of the website was also collaborative: the community itself was responsible for deciding what to publish or not at the website, and also what should have more visibility and make the headlines of the website.

Three months after the launch, the Overmundo model and strategy proved to be extremely successful. The success was so surprising, that the original group of paid overmanos and overminas proved to be no longer necessary: almost 100% of the content of the website at that time started to be produced by decentralized contributions. Nevertheless, the overmanos and overminas were kept for other additional 3 months, but changing completely their role. Instead of producing content to the website, the overmanos and overminas became exclusively 'agitators', disseminating the idea of collaboration and bringing people interested in creating visibility to their cultural activities to contribute to the website.

The community was then built, and it was a very comprehensive one. Not only there was a huge demand for dissemination of culture (almost as if culture always wanted to emerge, but did not have the means for doing that), but also people started quickly to realize that by posting contributions at Overmundo they were opening a channel for cooperation, for visibility, for building alliances, and for receiving commentary and help from people from all over the country.

As a result, the U.S.$1 million budget predicted to fund the overmanos and overminas was no longer necessary in its totality. Only a portion of it had been used after 6 months of the project, and the project was already clearly successful. Petrobras was so happy with the results that they actually inquired Overmundo whether it would like to receive more funding for the full year of 2007 (since the original budget covered the website activities only until July 2007). Unanimously, the group refused to receive more money, and instead, extended the duration of the project until the current budget allows it to continue.

Finally, the development of Overmundo was divided in three phases:

1) technological development and launch of the website

2) building the community and expanding its outreach and collaboration

among its members

3) finding ways of self-sustainability for Overmundo

Phases (1) and (2) have been successfully completed. The challenge ahead of Overmundo is now how to achieve its own self-sustainability, becoming independent from any external financers. The Movimento Group is currently focused on this task.

[...]

*Solutions: * At Overmundo, the community is king. It produces all the content, and it also decides what content to publish, and what content should gain more visibility.

For achieving this goal, Overmundo incorporated a broad range of 'web 2.0' tools.

As mentioned above, the goal was that 100% of the content was produced by the community and edited by the community. But then, how to achieve a quality control system?

The strategy for that was primarily inspired by the Kuro5hin (www.kuro5hin.org). Every item that is contributed to Overmundo goes first to the 'Editing Line' (Fila de Edição). For 48 hours, the item remains on it 'quarantined'. During this period, any user can make suggestions and comments. The author decides whether the item should be modified or not according to the suggestions. Only the author can modify the item (different from the Wiki model).

After the 48-hour period, the item goes to the 'Voting Line' (Fila de Votação). During this period, users of the website can vote whether they liked the article. The voting system is similar to Digg (www.digg.com). However, there is an important difference. At Digg, the order of the items does not correspond to the order of the votes (if one goes to the Digg page, there will be articles with less votes on top of articles with more votes). The reason for that is that the algorithm used by Digg is not open – only the website knows the true 'points' that an article needs to be on the top. Overmundo adopts a system of 'Overpoints', that is, each vote gives the article a certain number of overpoints. And the position of the article at the website is determined according to the number of Overpoints. Accordingly, the algorithm is clear.

In order to be finally published at the website, the article has to receive a minimum amount of Overpoints. Once the minimum amount of points is achieved, the item is published at an intermediary position. From that position, the article can continue to be voted, moving to the top and eventually achieving the headline of the website. If the item is not voted, time takes its Overpoints away, and the article is brought down.

Overmundo also uses a system of 'karma', by which users can earn reputation points at the website. Users with higher 'karmas' will have more Overpoints than users with smaller karmas, and therefore, more editorial powers. Accordingly, the karma system is helping Overmundo to build a decentralized governance model for the website site. The 30 users with the highest karmas are now being invited to a separate discussion list. Our goal is that in the near future, the whole governance of the website will rely on these 30 users, which will be renewed periodically, according to their karma variations along time.

In order to view all the other websites considered by Overmundo in its design, it is worth checking the credits webpage of the website at the following address:

http://www.overmundo.com.br/estaticas/creditos.php

Document 11 – dotSUB submission (http://dotsub.com)

Type of project: browser based tool enabling any film or video to be subtitled into any language without any downloads or training, in an open source wiki type of way. The final video, with all languages, is viewable and embeddable from any website in all languages.

*Description of project: * VISION

dotSUB provides tools that change language barriers into cultural bridges. By putting seamless video subtitling technology into the hands of individuals, dotSUB tools make stories from every culture accessible to every culture, fostering intercultural experience, communication, and connection.

MISSION

As a result of the Internet?s ability to connect us to our most distant neighbors, we are now able to share our collective creative output as never before. With words, images, music, and video moving across the globe in a matter of seconds, we collectively possess a new innovative power for cross-cultural communication.

The emergence of relatively inexpensive digital video technologies and low cost storage and bandwidth have radically democratized our ability to tell compelling stories. We are limited only by our imaginations and our neighbors' capacity to understand the language that weaves the images together.

We believe that video is a universal language and the world's appetite is increasing as viewing and showcasing technologies continue to evolve. Until now however, the ability to seamlessly subtitle videos in multiple languages has curbed the opportunities for creators and viewers to maximize the potential of the medium.

As educators, governments, NGOs, and corporations increasingly create, utilize and rely on moving images as crucial communication tools, we believe that there is a tremendous opportunity for a new technology tool that increases the potential of digital video. Additionally, as traditional media companies exercise more control over distribution of content, dotSUB provides an alternative approach for new media models to make content available to more people.

RATIONALE

Regardless of whether one is a professional filmmaker, a corporate trainer, a teacher with a new curricular idea, a student with a burning passion, or an organization with a specific message?video has become the creative medium of choice. It is transformative and unique. It encourages a kind of creative energy that fosters new thought and new creativity and new pathways for identifying and solving problems.

Using the dotSUB tools, filmmakers and owners of film content have the ability to see their work subtitled in multiple languages and thus made available to much larger global viewing audiences. Even when distribution agreements are in place, films are not often translated into more than a small handful of languages. Rather, they are made available in languages with easily recognized market audiences.

*URL of the work: * dotsub.com

Project Details

*Objectives: * TO FACILITATE CROSS CULTURAL COMMUNICATION THROUGH VIDEO AND FILM, IN ANY LANGUAGE, USING A RADICAL NEW BROWSER BASED TOOL

*Language and context: * THERE IS NO GEOGRAPHICAL LOCALE FOR THIS PROJECT, AS IT IS LANGUAGE NEUTRAL. IT ENABLES VIDEO OR FILM FROM ANY LANGUAGE TO BE SUBTITLED INTO ANY OTHER LANGUAGE ? ALL GENRES, SUBJECTS, LENGTHS, FORMATS, ETC.

*Project History: * THE PROJECT WAS BORN OUT OF MY FRUSTRATION WITH THE DIRECTION THE WORLD WAS GOING IN THE PAST 5 ? 10 YEARS. AS DIGITAL TECHNOLOGY WAS ENABLING QUICKER, CHEAPER AND FASTER GLOBAL COMMUNICATION, THE WORLD WAS GROWING FURTHER AND FURTHER APART. I WANTED TO CREATE AN ELOQUENTLY SIMPLE TOOL TO ENABLE ANYONE, IN ANY COUNTRY, SPEAKING ANY LANGUAGE, ASSUMING WE HAD THE PERMISSION OF THE RIGHTS HOLDER, TO BE ABLE TO SUBTITLE ANY FILM OR VIDEO FROM ONE LANGUAGE INTO ANY OTHER LANGUAGE WITH OUT ANY DOWNLOADS OR TRAINING.

IT STARTED IN 2004, TOOK 2-1/2 YEARS TO DEVELOP THE TECHNOLOGY, AND WE HAVE BEEN EXPERIMENTING WITH ITS POSSIBLE APPLICATIONS AND USES FOR THE PAST 8 MONTHS.

*People: * 3 PEOPLE ON THE CORE TEAM ? MICHAEL SMOLENS ? CHAIRMAN AND CEO, LAURIE RACINE ? PRESIDENT, AND THOR SIGVALDASON ? CTO. THE PROJECT IS TOTALLY OPEN.

*Lessons learned: * OUR PROJECT IS A DOUBLE PARADIGM SHIFT IN THINKING FOR MOST PEOPLE, AS THE ABILITY TO EASILY, QUICKLY AND INEXPENSIVELY (MOSTLY FREE) ABILITY TO SUBTITLE VIDEO INTO OTHER LANGUAGES HAS NEVER EVEN BEEN A REMOTE DREAM. AS MORE AND MORE ORGANIZATIONS/COMPANIES BEGIN TO UNDERSTAND ITS POTENTIAL, THE VARIETY OF USES FOR OUR TOOL IS INCREASING WEEKLY.

Technical Information

*Technological Basis: * A BROWSER BASED TOOL, REQUIRING NO DOWNLOADS. HUMAN BEINGS ENTER TEXT INTO THEIR BROWER (SEE DEMO AT http://dotsub.com/demo/) – AND THE TEXT IS STORED IN A DATA BASE ON DOTSUB SERVERS. THE VIDEO FILE CAN

RESIDE ANYWHERE, AND THE VIDEO PLAYER AND FUNCTIONALITY ARE EMBEDDABLE. WHEN A SPECIFIC LANGUAGE IS CHOSEN, IT SELECTS THAT TEXT AND RENDERS IT ON TOP OF THE VIDEO AS IT IS PLAYING.

*Solutions: * ALREADY ANSWERED ABOVE

Implementations: VIDEO PODCASTS, NON PROFITS, NGO?S, CORPORATIONS

*Users: * ANYONE WHO USES VIDEO AS A TOOL OF COMMUNICATION, EITHER IN EDU-CATION, HEALTHCARE, MEDIA, ENTERTAINMENT, LAW, POLITICS, ETC.

*License: * IT IS AVAILABLE GENERALLY AS A FREE TO USE, FREE TO EMBED API, AS LONG AS THE CONTENT OWNER HAS NO COMMERCIAL APPLICATIONS FOR THEIR CONTENT. IF THE CONTENT OWNER HAS PLANS TO MONETIZE THEIR CONTENT IN ANY LANGUAGE MADE POSSIBLE USING OUR TOOL, WE WILL WORK EITHER ON A REVENUE SHARE, LICENSE FEE PER STREAM, OR WORK FOR HIRE ? DEPENDING ON THE NEEDS, DESIRES AND BUDGETS OF EACH CLIENT.

*Statement of Reasons: * AS THE WORLD BECOMES MORE WIRED, AND BANDWIDTH COSTS DECREASE, WITH VIDEO ENABLED PCS, MOBILE DEVICES, AND OTHER VIEWING SCREENS BECOME UBIQUITOUS, IT BECOMES MORE AND MORE IMPORTANT TO BE ABLE TO VIEW AND UNDERSTAND THE FEELINGS AND PASSIONS AND FEARS OF PEOPLE IN ALL CULTURES. TRADITIONAL MEDIA, AND EXISTING SUPPLY CHAIN TECHNOLOGIES, ESPECIALLY TOUGHER AND TOUGHER COPYRIGHT RULES MAKE THIS NEARLY IMPOS-SIBLE FOR ALL BUT THE BEST FUNDED FILMS. DOTSUB HOPES TO BE ABLE TO MAKE ANY VIDEO OR FILM AVAILABLE IN ALL LANGUAGES ? AN EFFORT THAT COULD HAVE PROFOUND IMPACT ON THE WORLD.

*Planned use of prize money: * FURTHER ENABLE WORTHY NON PROFITS AND OTHER EFFORTS WHO NEED HELP COMMUNICATING ACROSS CULTURES.

Document 12 – Open Clothes submission (http://www.open-clothes.com/)

Description of project: "Open-Clothes.com" is a community on the Internet for who makes clothes, for who wants clothes, and for everybody who likes clothes.In which community, anyone can participate for free on the theme of "making the clothes of 'I' size". "Those who make" can enjoy making clothes, at their own pace conveniently. "Those who wear" can enjoy making clothes which matched liking and the body exactly. "Open-Clotes.com" community is compared to a tree. First, wooden "trunk" is the making-clothes network of "those who make." The function of community is substantial from information exchange to work sale as if annual rings may be piled up. The network which supports activity from beginners to experts in connection with making dress as an individual is formed. Then, it is a "branch" bears fruits, the works born from the network of "those who make" . "Those who wears" gathers in quest of "clothes with stories." The micro demands of "how it is made", "wanting such dress fits me", etc. which are difficult to respond on a ready-made, are realized, together with "those who make." It is the common manufacture system of "those who wear", and "those who make." Moreover, a "root" is required to suck up nutrition and send to a trunk. The cooperation with the professional contractor who become a foundation supporting activity of "those who make" is indispensable to making clothes. Then, in Open-Clothes.com, the common production system of "those who make", and "the contractors who make" is built. [1] Individuals with the energy of making a thing gather and build "society". [2] The new "culture" is produced, which finds out the value in the produced work which is different from ready-mades. [3] The "industry" will be cherished, which supports making the thing, value added and can respond to a market. Healthy tree may attach rich leaves and rich fruits on a trunk, and returned to the ground as nutritive substance. They may be taken in from the root and may send out to a trunk and the growth may be continued.Like the tree, culture, and industry and a social system cooperation is realize according to the power of the community and the continuation of making dress. We "Open-Clothes.com" think such expansive circulation will be produced.

URL of the work: http://www.open-clothes.com/

Project Details

Objectives: Open-Clothes carries out the help which finds such "making the clothes of 'I' size" out of communication. People who participate "Open-Clothes" can have much possibility. * Who "Wants to make" can – cancel questions and troubles with information exchange. – present her / his works and hear opinions and evaluations about them. – sell works. – perfome manufacture management. – find business partners. – share sale / advertisement channels. – produce with a few lot. – harness her / his knowledge and technology. * Who "Wants to wear" can – buy clothes, looking at the background of manufacture. – make the clothes suitable for size or liking from "JOINT MADE", which means make together with those who make. – study happily and be a person "who makes." We will realize the "clothes" environment opened by knowledge and technology of all people in connection with clothes – that is, – "Open-Clothes." Clothes are the themes in connection with all people. We think optimal "clothes" environment will be required for people with the style which is different in each. Through construction, management of "Open-Clothes.com" which is community computing environment, we will discover and solve subjects in connection with clothes. We aim at the following gradual results. – Offer of a choice called new production / circulation in a fashion field. – Offer of the place where we can find the partner based on a style. – Opportunity creation of a work and a volunteer. – Construction of the knowledge database about clothes. – Edit and offer of teaching materials about clothes. – Construction of a clothes database. – Secondary use as resources of common products, and protection of a right. – One to one production. – Development and improvement in clothes related technology. – Energy curtailment by cooperation of apparel systems. – Realization of the high quality human service on the Internet. – Activation of production. – The proposal of the sustainable and expansive management technique of community energy.

Language and context: From now on we are active only in japan. We are affected by the diversity of japanese fashion. There is no class in japanese fashion. And the passion for fashion is very strong in Japan. There is the student with full of the motivation in "I want to study making dress", the young designer who asks for the place of the further activity with her / his brand, the fashion professional which are engaged in making dress as an occupation, the housewife and "the fine elderly people" as a former pro desires works and volunteers to harness knowledge and technology after retirement, the person who enjoys making dress at their pace as a hobby. Although the production shift to China, consumption depression, etc. pose a serious problem in the apparel industry, such people with full of the energy in Japan are striving for making clothes in quest of the place of activity still more. We perform making the "place" where such people construct a networks and can take various communications through the knowledge and the work. In the Future, We will connect all people who in connection with clothes. For example, you make clothes of 'I' size, designing with American and making pattern of clothes with Italian, using japanese textile which Indians yarned and dyed, sewing or knitting by your partner in your country who you found in "Open-Clothes.com"

Project History: When we, core members, were university students, we studied about fashion industry, and make and sell clothes by ourselves. But it was difficult to circulate making and selling our works. Furthermore, we felt sorry for being unable to meet expectations of friends "Please make my clothes". From the reflection, we worries earnestly about "the good relation" between clothes and the Internet, at last. We heard the episode that the man with six fingers said "My life is happy if it removes that there is no glove fits me." We thought it should be that there is the glove fits him too, and that everybody can get favorite and suited things. What it did not realize was the negligence of those who were engaged in the fashion industry. Then the project started in March, 2000 with 4 friends. The community site started in May, 2001. We managed the community as we bring up our baby. The community expanded little by little, by word of mouth. From early time, we also started real meetings where members of the community can meet and communicate each other. We have held about 30 events, such as exchange meetings, study meetings, factory inspection meetings, the exhibitions of clothes, and so on. Moreover, we started Open-Clothes Expo as compilation of our vision last year. The Expo is held two times a year.

People: 4 core staffs and about 40 volunteers carry the project. The project team takes very open style. Everybody who is interested in the project, can perticipate in it and taste feeling of fullness and contribution. About 4,500 people are the members of the community where everybody can perticipate for free with no regulation. About 50 companies and schools support the community.

Lessons learned: * WORKED (not perfectly) – Human network community – Knowledge database – Indivsual empowerment – Digital archive of works   Common production / cir culation / selling system – Matching of a hobby and taste * NOT WORKED – Tools for design – e-learning – Protection of designs and copyrights – 3-dimensional measurement of a human body – 3-dimensional modeling / pattern making – Wearable computing – Old-clothes recy cling system – Low energy production – Realization of the quality of life

Technical Information

Technological Basis: Web based tools as infrastructure. Tools and platform for communication, design, presentation, business, knowledge and fashion life itself.

Solutions: N/A

Implementations: N/A

Users: Everybody can watch the site [about 400,000 people accessed since 2001/3]. More function for submitted Users [4,500 users till now] for free. From 5 to 10 persons a day submit as users. Composition of submitted members. – The level of 10 years old (30%), 20 (30%), 30 (15%), 40(10%), 50 (10%), over 60 (5%). – Students (30%), professionals (40%), housewives (20%), other (10%). – Japan (Tokyo 70%, other 25%), Other (5%). The number of beneficiaries will be up to "6-billions", every people all over the world.

License: N/A

Statement of Reasons: We offer new way of community and society and industry in fashion. Although limited field, there is the various life activity itself. The members do not only gather and speak, but produce values. They Co-municate, Co-design, Co-laborate, Co-product to make clothes they want. That is to say, "Open-Clothes" is new community mixing virtual and real, and producing values.

Planned use of prize money: We want to start new service to bring up young designers which connect to industries. The service was very difficult to start because of lack of money. We think once the service started, the energy of young people drive not only "Open-Clothes" community but also japanese industry itself to a good direction.

Annex B – List of Figures

Figure 1: Conceptual map for 'digital community'. Bird's eye

Figure 2: Co-occurrence pattern for the 'online community'

Figure 3: Logical intersections between 'online community', 'network', 'group'

Figure 4: Conceptual map without word seeding. Bird's eye

Figure 5: Temporal trend for 'rural'

Figure 6: Temporal trend for 'software'

Figure 7: Co-occurrence between 'software' and 'free'/'open'/'social'

Figure 8: Temporal trend for 'information'

Figure 9: Co-occurrence map for 'information'

Annex C – List of Tables

Table 1 – Resume: from epistemological assumptions to techniques of data collection and analysis

Epistemological assumptions	Choice of the sample	Technique of data collection	Technique of data analysis
Performative classification of digital communities (DC): DC definition is the result of clustering together objects said to be occurrences of the concept. Acknowledgement as distributed enuciative action	Objects of study are the projects participating in Ars Electronica's competition. They are said and acknowledged as DCs by different social actors: the projects authors + Prix Ars Electronica's International Advisory Board + independent jury	Submissions exported from online archive as txt file with ASCII codification	Quali-quantitative (for N cases) and qualitative (for n cases) analysis of submissions

Epistemological assumptions	Choice of the sample	Technique of data collection	Technique of data analysis
Study of controversies 1) Meaning emerges from comparison and/or polemic structures. 2) Controversies and agency are made visible into accounts	1) Prix Ars Electronica competition as a form of controversy, a situation where meaning emerges from comparison between different projects struggling to be defined as successful DC. 2) Use of archived submission forms as accounts: meaning emerges also from distance in time	Navigation of DCs' websites	Profile analysis of websites

Table 2 – Ranked Concept List for 'digital community'

Concept	Absolute Count	Relative Count
community	3446	100%
development	818	23.70%
world	627	18.10%
local	573	16.60%
social	491	14.20%
creating	490	14.20%
members	466	13.50%
support	441	12.70%
digital	436	12.60%
tool	435	12.60%
cultural	370	10.70%

Concept	Absolute Count	Relative Count
training	333	9.60%
sharing	331	9.60%
resources	326	9.40%
rural	288	8.30%
collaborative	283	8.20%
education	279	8%
build	267	7.70%
help	258	7.40%
learning	228	6.60%
youth	219	6.30%
global	198	5.70%
organizations	189	5.40%
groups	183	5.30%
international	163	4.70%
include	161	4.60%
interest	160	4.60%
model	159	4.60%
environment	157	4.50%
real	152	4.40%
networks	149	4.30%

Table 3 – Co-occurrence list for 'online community'

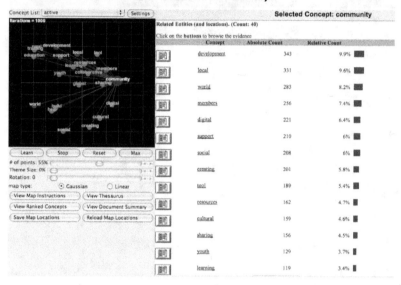

Table 4 – InfoRapid Search & Replace's results for A = DIGCOM&group&!network (Hypothesis A < B)

Searched for	DIGCOM&group&!-network		
In Files	*.txt		
In Directories +	C:and Settings3.3txt TOTALE 920		
Search Options	Pattern matching Match whole words Use internal converters		
Matches found	401	Files found / total	62 / 742

COMMUNITIES AT A CROSSROADS

Table 5 – InfoRapid Search & Replace's results for B= DIGCOM&network&!group (Hypothesis A < B)

Searched for	DIGCOM&network&!group		
In Files	*.txt		
In Directories +	C:and Settings3.3txt TOTALE 920		
Search Options	Pattern matching Match whole words Use internal converters		
Matches found	208	Files found / total	33 / 742

Table 6 – InfoRapid Search & Replace's results for C = group&network (Hypothesis C = 0)

Searched for	group&network		
In Files	*.txt		
In Directories +	C:and Settings3.3txt TOTALE 920		
Search Options	Pattern matching Match whole words Use internal converters		
Matches found	3117	Files found / total	301 / 742

Table 7 – InfoRapid Search & Replace's results for C = group&network&DIG-COM (Hypothesis D = 0)

Searched for	group&net-work&DIGCOM		
In Files	*.txt		
In Directories +	C:and Settings3.3txt TOTALE 920		
Search Options	Pattern matching Match whole words Use internal converters		
Matches found	2144	Files found / total	157 / 742

Table 8 – Leximancer settings for Task 2

Leximancer settings			
Setting	Description	Value	Explanation
Pre-processing Phase			
Stop-word removal (yes/no)	Remove words in the predefined Stop List from the data	yes	
Edit stop-word list	It allows to check the words that were counted as stop-words and remove them from the Stop List	no additional changes in the stop-word list	

Leximancer settings			
Make folder tags (do nothing/make folder tags/ make folder and filename tags)	This parameter is very important when comparing different documents based on their conceptual content. It causes each part of the folder path to a file, and optionally the filename itself, to be inserted as a tag on each sentence in the file. These tags will be included as concepts in the map. Thus, inspecting the links formed with the other concepts can allow the comparison of the content of the various folders	make folder tags (folders named as year of submission from 2004 to 2007)	Since the task is about comparing the textual documents by the year of submission, this selection allows the generation of year-related tags that will appear in the map
Automatic Concept Identification			
Automatically Identify Concepts (yes/no)	Enable/disable the automatic generation of concepts. By disabling this option, only concepts defined by the researcher will be shown on the map	yes	This selection enables the automatic generation of concepts on the basis of frequency. This setting allows the researcher not to set any pre-defined concept in advance
Total concept number (automatic/1-1000)	The number of automatically selected concepts to be included in the map	automatic	
Number of names (automatic/1-1000)	Of the number of concepts chosen, what is the minimum number of concepts that should be forced to be names	automatic	'Automatic' allows a natural mixture by not forcing names into the list

Leximancer settings			
Concept Editing			
TAB Auto Concepts	*It allows to delete, merge and edit automatically extracted concepts	- Merge all plurals and derived morphological forms*	
TAB Auto Tags	*It allows to delete, merge and edit folder tags	year-related tags*	
TAB User Defined Concepts	It allows to create, delete, merge and edit manually defined concepts	none	I do not set concepts in advance
TAB User defined tags	It allows to delete, merge and edit user defined tags	none	
Thesaurus Learning			
Learn Concept Thesaurus (yes/no)	Turning off the thesaurus learning will prevent Leximancer from adding additional items to the concept definitions	yes	Vast data se: need not only for simple keyword search, but also weighted accumulation of evidence
Learning Threshold (1-21)	This setting allows to control the generality of each learned concept. Increasing the level will increase the fuzziness of each concept definition by increasing the number of words that will be included in each concept	14 (normal)	

Leximancer settings			
Sentences per Context Block (1-5)	This option allows to specify the sentences that appear in each learning block	3	value for most circumstances
Break at paragraph (ignore/break at paragraph)	This setting is to prevent context blocks from crossing paragraph boundaries	yes	
Learn Tag Classes (yes/no)	Turning it on will treat Tag classes as normal concepts, learning a thesaurus definition for each	no	
Concept Profiling			
Number to discover (0-1000)	It indicates how many extra concepts should be discovered	0 (feature disabled)	
Themed discovery (Concepts in ALL/ ANY/ EACH)	It selects how the discovered concepts should be related to the pre-defined concept set		
Classification and Indexing			
Entities	Entities are the concepts that are actually shown on the conceptual map, and represent the top-level of classification of the text	Concepts Tag classes	

Leximancer settings			
Properties	Properties, in contrast to entities, are concepts that are checked for co-occurrence with the entities, but are not displayed on the cluster map		
Kill classes	Kill classes are concepts that if found in a classified block of text, cause all other classifications of that block to be suppressed		
Required classes	Required classes are classifications that must be found in blocks of text, or else the blocks are ignored		
Classification Settings			
Sentences per context block (1 – 100)	Specify how many sentences per tagged text block	3 (default)	
Break at paragraph (yes/no)	Prevent tagged context blocks from crossing paragraph boundaries	yes	
Word Classification Threshold (0.1-4.9)	This threshold specifies how much cumulative evidence per sentence is needed for a classification to be assigned to a context block	2.4 (default)	

Leximancer settings			
Name Classification Threshold (2.6-5)	This threshold specifies the minimum strength of the *maximally weighted* piece of evidence to trigger classification	4.5 (default)	
Blocks per Bucket (1-100)	A bucket contains one or more consecutive context blocks. If the sum of the evidence of a particular concept within the bucket is below a threshold, the specific concept tag is removed from all the sentences in the bucket	1	
Mapping and Statistic			
Conceptual Map			
Map Type (Linear/Gaussian)	The Gaussian map has a more circular symmetry and emphasises the similarity between the conceptual context in which the words appear. The linear map is more spread out, emphasising the co-occurrence between items	Linear	
Concept Statistics			
Attribute Variables	It allows to set attribute variables from the Concept List	'art', 'city', 'government', 'group', 'local', 'mobile', 'network', 'open', 'political', 'public', 'web'	

Leximancer settings			
Category Variables	*It allows to set category variables from the Concept List*	*TG_2004_TG TG_2005_ TG TG_2006_TG TG_2007_TG*	

Table 9 – Ranked Concept List for the whole data set without word seed

Concept	Absolute Count	Relative Count
site	720	22.30%
art	608	18.80%
work	537	16.60%
information	457	14.10%
software	451	13.90%
media	375	11.60%
development	298	9.20%
local	277	8.50%
system	259	8%
mobile	237	7.30%
cultural	235	7.20%
social	226	7%
open	218	6.70%
technology	211	6.50%
world	189	5.80%
online	187	5.80%

Concept	Absolute Count	Relative Count
video	173	5.30%
members	172	5.30%
network	149	4.60%
org	144	4.40%
group	133	4.10%
free	133	4.10%
digital	127	3.90%
money	125	3.80%
services	114	3.50%
public	114	3.50%
students	102	3.10%
support	101	3.10%
research	96	2.90%
rural	95	2.90%
web	95	2.90%
health	92	2.80%
learned	87	2.60%
time	80	2.40%
radio	76	2.30%
political	72	2.20%
program	71	2.20%

Concept	Absolute Count	Relative Count
space	68	2.10%
music	64	1.90%
design	63	1.90%
government	63	1.90%
city	62	1.90%
youth	62	1.90%
including	61	1.80%
school	43	1.30%
countries	43	1.30%
team	42	1.30%
server	39	1.20%
text	33	1%
internet	32	0.90%
human	31	0.90%
global	30	0.90%
international	27	0.80%
created	25	0.70%
life	21	0.60%
map	15	0.40%
database	14	0.40%
collaboration	14	0.40%

Concept	Absolute Count	Relative Count
concept	13	0.40%
collective	10	0.30%
environment	10	0.30%

Table 10 - Analysis sheet

Descriptive categories	Operative questions	Index
Project objective(s)		A
Goals	What is the goal(s) that the project aims at achieving?	A1
Source of boundaries	To what element does the application appeal in order to depict the community as a stable, taken for granted assemblage?	A2
Actors involved		B
Addresser	Is there any entity that designed/developed the project?	B1
Addressee	Is there any identifiable target of the action of the Addresser? Are Addresser and Addressee clearly distinguishable?	B2a B2b
Anti-groups/anti-actants	Are there anti-actants that interfere with the course of action in a negative way?	B3
Actants as mediators Vs. intermediaries	Is there any entity that contributes with some competences to the course of action? Does the actant trigger further actions/mediations? Does it activate new participants? Does it introduce a bifurcation in the course of action? Does it 'transport' (shift) or 'translate' (modify) what it is supposed to carry? Is the output predictable starting from the input? Does the actant determines some other event? How long is the chain of action? How many passages can be counted?	B4 B4a B4b B4c B4d B4e B4f B4g
Professional mobilized	Are there professionals (journalists, social scientists, statisticians) quoted as part of what makes possible the durable definition of the community?	B5

Descriptive categories	Operative questions	Index
Spokesperson	Do the spokespersons that speak for the group existence – namely, the author of the application – appear as agents in the account?	B6

Table 11 – Proyecto Cyberela – Radio Telecentros. Variations in the role of radio, ICT and gender concerns following the advent of digital media

	Before the advent of the digital domain	With advent of the digital domain
Radio	(Analogue)	(Internet radio)
	Mediator	Mediator
ICT	(correspond to analogue radio)	(Seen as 'skills')
		Goal to be reached
Gender and human rights commitment	(Attention)	(Becomes 'Contents')
	Result of policies	Intermediary

Table 12 – Summary of the theories of action associated with 'empowerment'

	Tonga. On-line	Akshaya	Proyecto Cyberela – Radio Tel.	The World Starts with Me	canal*AC-CESSI-BLE
Source of boundaries	Cultural heritage and traditions (Tonga people)	Geopolitical/ administrative (local communities in Kerala)	Statistics (gender)	Statistic (age and, partially, gender)	Social discrimination

	Tonga. On-line	Akshaya	Proyecto Cyberela – Radio Tel.	The World Starts with Me	canal*AC-CESSI-BLE
Role of digital ICT	Mediators (Alpha Smart triggers 'msg and digital reflections' creating associations with dispersed actants)	ICT-skills and data repository as goals. Wireless net, computers, scanners, etc. as intermediaries	ICT-skills are goals. Technical facilities as intermediaries	PC as intermediary (may be substituted). But ICT-skills as a competence. WSWM is a mediator	Mobile phones and digital photos as intermediaries; Internet alternatively as mediator or intermediary
Role of other tech-nologies	Music as mediator that translates the cultural heritage into the digital age	/	Radio as mediator	Low-tech objects (i.e. paper&pencil, local materials) as intermediaries	Broadcast media as (anti-) mediators
Mediators/intermediaries	Many mediators, agency chain extends in many directions	One mediator, some intermediaries. Very short agency chain	Few human mediators, some non-human intermediaries	Many mediators	Three mediators, some intermediaries
Professionals	Journalist	/	/	Teachers	/
Relationship Addresser/ Addressee	No distinction	Clearly distinct (Service delivery business)	Fairly distinct after the advent of digital media	Only during course: students who finish it become facilitators	Fairly distinct: 'disadvantaged groups' and project promoters do not blur

Table 13 – Comparison among EFF, FSF, Telestreet/NGV

	EFF	FSF	Telestreet
Objective	'To defend freedom of expression, innovation and privacy on the electronic frontier'	'To achieve sw freedom to cooperate for everyone'	To create relational networks and active citizenship through an integrated use of communication tools
Object of value	Public interest in digital rights on a global level	Computer users rights to use, copy, study, modify and redistribute computer programs	Citizens right to access communication channels
Source of boundaries	Freedom in the networked world	Community and cooperation (software freedom is a condition for this)	Active citizenship (Freedom of expression is a condition for this)
Addresser	Different levels of participation: EFF staff (coordinators, activists, techies, artists, policy analysts, attorneys), EFF members, nl subscribers, users of Action Center	Richard Stallman made it start. Then it proliferated through users and developers (see mediators)	Orfeo TV started it, but everyone can set up a street TV. Participation is open and the aim is to overcome the distinction between sender and receiver
Addressee	'Those who create and communicate in the electronic world', those who are interested in technology policy covering freedom	see mediators (none is only addressee)	see mediators (none is only addressee)
Anti-groups	United States Secret Service	Pressure for commercialization. Proprietary software	Two mainstream broadcasting networks

	EFF	FSF	Telestreet
Additional mediators	'Action alerts', encourage personal political involvement. EFF as supporter and enabler of global digital community.	GNU OS gives computer users the freedom to cooperate. FSF itself raises funds for GNU, promotes users freedom, is trusted copyright holder. Volunteer developers from around the world. Kernel Linux ('inspired by the community that we built'). Licenses guarantee freedom.	Telestreet induces non-professional people to experiment. Users are mediators. Article 21 of Italian Constitution invoked to assert Telestreet constitutionality, deputies mobilized.Media when combined or disassembled: Internet + DIY TV stimulates creativity, gives chance to become active, enables people, bridges gender and age divide. DIY ethics
Inter-mediaries	website, blog posts, podcasts, online video projects, newsletter, online guides. YouTube, MySpace, social network sites	/	Media when taken as single channels (satellite Tv, website)

Table 14 – Classification of winning projects according to orientation to business, relationship between online and offline interaction, focus of interest, centralized/distributed technology used

	Profit/ Non-profit	Only online/ Also offline interaction	Specific focus of interest	Centralized/ decentralized technology <?>
Tonga.Online â smart X tension	Non-profit	Also offline	No	Centralized
Akshaya	Profit	Also offline	No	Centralized
Projecto Cyberela â Radio Telecentros	Non-profit	Also offline	Yes	Centralized

	Profit/ Non-profit	Only online/ Also offline interaction	Specific focus of interest	Centralized/ decentralized technology <?>
The World Starts With Me	Non-profit	Also offline	Yes	Centralized
canal*ACCESSIBLE	Non-profit	Mainly online	No	Centralized
Electronic Frontier Foundation	Non-profit	Mainly online	Yes	Centralized
Free Software Foundation	Non-profit	Mainly online	Yes	Decentralized
Telestreet	Non-profit	Also offline	No	Decentralized
Overmundo	Non-profit	Mainly online	No	Centralized
Open Clothes	Profit	Mainly online	Yes	Centralized
dotSUB	Profit	Mainly online	Yes	Centralized

Table 15 – Analysis of the websites of the winning projects according to the degree of visibility of the Outside allowed by the technologies used

	Technologies used	Interactive technologies that allow users to leave publicly visible traces	Inscribed users	Degree of visibility of the Outside
Akshaya www.akshaya.net	Textual web pages (read only); Guestbook form (does not work); 'Contact us' link: list of phone numbers; Restricted area: it is not possible to register online	None	1. Passive, invisible guest	Invisible, no online registra-tion
Proyecto Cyberela – Radio Telecentros www.cemina.org.br	Textual web pages (read only); Video streaming; PDF documents' publishing; Radio streaming/down-load; Contact form	None	1. Passive, invisible guest	Invisible, no online registra-tion
The World Starts With Me www.the-worldstarts.org	Flash animations accessible only to students and teach-ers; Contact e-mail addresses; Students forum	Students forum accessible only by registered students. Online registration is not allowed	1. Members inter-acting with each other	Invisible, no online registra-tion
Tonga.Online – smart X tension www.mulonga.net	Textual web pages (read only); News feed; Discussion forum; Contact form; Newsletter; A/V streaming and download	Discussion forum: read-only for guests, submission-open for members. Online registration is allowed	1. Members inter-acting with each other; 2. Passive, invisible guest	Invisible, but low barriers to mem-ber-ship

	Technologies used	Interactive technologies that allow users to leave publicly visible traces	Inscribed users	Degree of visibility of the Outside
dotSUB dotsub.com	Video screening is open; To upload one's own videos and subtitle other people's videos registration is required	Video uploading and subtitling is restricted to members. But online registration is allowed	1. Members as experts; 2. Passive, invisible guest	Invisible, but low barriers to membership
Canal*ACCESSIBLE www.zexe.net/ barcelona	Photo, map and video database searchable by date, name of submitter, city area, type of obstacle; Open discussion forum	Open discussion forum: it does not need registration	1. Interactivevisible guest	Visible
Electronic Frontier Foundation www. eff.org	Contact e-mail addresses.; Newsletter; RSS Feeds; 'Send a postcard' form; 'Send your message to decision makers' form: restricted to U.S. citizens; HTML/PDF guides for Internet users; 'Line Noise' Podcast; 'Submit prior Art' form; EFF software projects: wikis, mailing lists and Sourceforge's tracker; 'Deeplinks' blog: no comment facilities	EFF software projects make use of wikis for coordination, mailing lists and Sourceforge's tracker for development	1. Passive, invisible Other 2. Engaged citizens 3. Developers	Invisible

	Technologies used	Interactive technologies that allow users to leave publicly visible traces	Inscribed users	Degree of visibility of the Outside
Free Software Foundation www.fsf. org www.gnu.org	Newsletter; News section (read only); Mailing lists on specific campaigns; 'Contact us' e-mail address; Free Software Directory (db on all existing free sw): users can download and rate sw, submit a level, subscribe to development-focused mailing lists and IRC channels, view VCS repository; Campaigns center: information on campaigns and access to 'take action' tools hosted by partner organization like EFF's action alert; FSF Groups Wiki; FSF Blogs publishes blog entries by 'people in the community', no comments allowed, but it possible to suggest one's own blog; Events section: RSS feed; Code contribution: open to members	Mailing lists on specific campaigns restricted to members, but registration is allowed online; Mailing lists of code development open also to non-members; Free Software Directory: non-members can rate sw, subscribe to development-focused mailing lists and IRC channels; FSF Groups Wiki open to guests too; Code contribution: open to members, but online registration is allowed on Savannah servers	1. Passive, invisible Other 2. Engaged citizens 3. Guest developers 4. Member develop-pers	Guest develop-pers are visible

	Technologies used	Interactive technologies that allow users to leave publicly visible traces	Inscribed users	Degree of visibility of the Outside
Telestreet www. telestreet.it www. ngvision.org	News section run by editorial team, guests' comments allowed; Open a posteriori moderated mailing list (Telestreet); Closed mailing list (NGV); Discussion forum; Video download; Peer-to-peer video distribution; Ftp upload of videos	Open comments on news; Open mailing list; Discussion forum (need registration which is allowed online); Peer-to-peer distribution and ftp upload open to guests	1. Interactivevisible Other 2. Low barriers member-ship	Visible
Overmundo www. overmundo.com.br	Blog: open to read, only members can comment, submit, revise, vote articles; Contact form to contact the core team	Blog: only members can comment, propose, revise and vote articles to be published. Online registration is allowed BUT requires sensitive data. Members have different voting weights according to the length of their participation in the community	1. Invisible Other 2. Entry members 3. Established members 4. Senior members	Invisible, barriers to member-ship posed by time, commit-ment and ID

	Technologies used	Interactive technologies that allow users to leave publicly visible traces	Inscribed users	Degree of visibility of the Outside
Open Clothes www. open-clothes.com	Read-only news section; Bulletin board; 'Recipe' download; Database on members ('Harbour'); B2B and B2C selling platform; Members showcase ('Deji-ma'); Newsmaga-zine; Database of fashion schools; 'Production journal' showcase	Bulletin board: posting requires membership; B2B and B2C selling platform: access requires member-ship; Members showcase requires membership; News-magazine open to contributions by members	1./2./3./4Diverse forms of mem-ber-ship	Invisible, barriers to member-ship posed by time, com-mit-ment and ID

Table 16 – Map of communities according to degree of permeability entailed by self accounts (rows) and software (columns)

Application/ Software	Invisible Other	High barriers to membership	Low barriers to membership	Visible Other
More mediators than intermediaries	The World Starts With Me	Overmundo	Tonga.Online-smart X tension	Free Software Foun-dation Telestreet
More intermediaries than mediators	Akshaya Proyecto Cyberela-Ra-dio Telecentros Electronic Frontier Foundation	Open Clothes	dotSUB	Canal*ACCESSIBLE

BIBLIOGRAPHY

Akrich, M. 'Des réseaux vidéocom aux réseaux électriques: Machines, Gestion, Marchés', Centre de sociologie de l'innovation. *Ces réseaux que la raison ignore*, L'Harmattan, pp.5-30, 1992.

Akrich, M. and Latour, B. 'A Summary of a Convenient Vocabulary for the Semiotics of Human and Nonhuman Assemblies', in Bijker W. E. and Law, J. (eds) *Shaping Technology/Building Society: Studies in sociotechnical change*, Cambridge, MA: The MIT Press, 1992, pp. 259-264.

Amin, A. and Thrift, N. *Cities: Reimagining the urban*, Cambridge: Polity Press, 2001.

Anderson, C. *The Long Tail: Why The Future of Business in Selling Less of More*, New York: Hyperion, 2006.

Aronowitz, S. *Post-Work: Per la fine del lavoro senza fine,* Roma: DeriveApprodi, 2006.

Barad, K. M. *Meeting the Universe Halfway: Quantum Physics and the Entanglement of Matter and Meaning,* Durham and London: Duke University Press, 2007.

Barlow, J. P. 'A Declaration of the Independence of Cyberspace', 1996, http://homes.eff.org/~barlow/Declaration-Final.html.

Barnes, S. 'A privacy paradox: Social networking in the United States', *First Monday,* 11.9, 4 September 2006, http://www.firstmonday.org/ojs/index.php/fm/article/view/1394/1312.

Bartle, P. *The Sociology of Communities*, Victoria, Canada: Camosun Imaging, 2005.

Bazzichelli, T. *Networking: la rete come arte*, Milano: Costa & Nolan, 2006.

—.'Stalder: il Futuro delle Digital Communities', *Digimag*, 14 May 2006, https://digicult.it/it/hacktivism/stalder-the-future-of-digital-communities/

Beck, U. *The Reinvention of Politics: Rethinking Modernity in the Global Social Order*, London: Polity Press, 1996.

D. Bell, 'Communitarianism', in E. N. Zalta (eds.) *The Stanford Encyclopedia of Philosophy*, Stanford CA: Stanford University, 2016, https://plato.stanford.edu/archives/sum2016/entries/communitarianism/.

Benedikt, M. (ed.) *Cyberspace: First Steps*, Cambridge, Mass.: MIT Press, 1991.

Benkler, Y. *The Wealth of Networks: How Social Production Transforms Market and Freedom, New Haven,* CT: Yale University Press, 2006.

Berardi, F. *Il sapiente, il mercante, il guerriero*, Roma: DeriveApprodi, 2004.

Bey, H. *Temporary Autonomous Zones*, Brooklyn: Autonomedia, 1992.

Boorstin, J. 'Facebook's New Ad Play In a Down Economy', *CNBC.com*, http://www.cnbc.com/id/27682302.

Bourdieu, P. *Méditations pascaliennes. Éléments pour une philosophie négative,* Paris: Seuil, 1997.

boyd, D. M. and Ellison, N. B. 'Social network sites: Definition, history, and scholarship', *Journal of Computer-Mediated Communication* 13.1 (2007): 210-230.

Broeckmann, A. 'Towards an Aesthetics of Heterogenesis', *Convergence*, 3.2 (1997): 48--58. DOI: 10.1177/135485659700300207.

—. 'Public Spheres and Network Interfaces', in Graham, S. (ed.) *The Cybercities Reader*, London: Routledge, 2004, pp. 378-383.

Bruner, J. S. *Acts of Meaning*, Cambridge, Mass.: Harvard University Press, 1990.

Butler, J. 'Performative Agency', *Journal of Cultural Economy* 3.2 (2010): 147-161.

Callon, M. 'Society in the Making: The Study of Technology as a Tool for Sociological Analysis', in Bijker, W. E., Hughes, T. P. and Pinch, T. (eds) *The Social Construction of Technological Systems*, Cambridge, Mass.: MIT Press, 1989, pp. 83-103.

Callon, M. 'Performativity, Misfires and Politics', *Journal of Cultural Economy* 3.2 (2010): 163-169.

Caronia, A. 'AHACamping. Le Trappole del Social Networking', *Digimag* 38, October 2008, http://isole.ecn.org/aha/camper/doku.php?id=antonio_caronia_-_ahacamping._le_trappole_del_social_networking.

Carr, N. 'The Amorality of Web 2.0', *Rough Type*, 3 October 2005, http://www.roughtype.com/archives/2005/10/the_amorality_o.php.

—. 'Hypermediation 2.0', *Rough Type*, 28 November 2005, http://www.roughtype.com/archives/2005/11/hypermediation.php.

Castells, M. *The Urban Question*, London: Edward Arnold, 1972.

—. *The Rise of The Network Society, Volume I: The Information Age*, Oxford: Blackwell, 1996.

—. *The Power of Identity, Volume II: The Information Age*, Oxford: Blackwell, 1997.

—. *The End of Millennium, Volume III: The Information Age,* Oxford: Blackwell, 1998.

—. *Internet Galaxy.* Oxford: Oxford University Press, 2001.

—. 'Space of Flows, Space of Places: Materials for a Theory of Urbanism in the Information Age', in Graham, S. (ed.) *The Cybercities Reader.* London: Routledge, 2004, pp. 82-92.

Choi, J. H. 'Living in Cyworld: Contextualising Cy-Ties in South Korea', in Bruns, A. and Jacobs, J. (eds) *Use of Blogs (Digital Formations),* New York: Peter Lang, 2006, pp. 173-186.

Christensen, W. and Suess, R. 'Hobbyist Computerized Bulletin Boards', *Byte,* November issue, 1978: 150-158.

Coquet, J. C. *La quête du sens. Le langage en question,* Paris: PUF, 1997.

Daniels, D. *Kunst als Sendung: Von der Telegrafie zum Internet,* München: Beck Verlag, 2002.

Della Porta, D. et al. 'Searching the Net: An Analysis of the Democratic Use of Internet by 266 Social Movement Organizations. WP 2', in *Democracy in Europe and the Mobilization of Society Research Project,* 2006. http://demos.iue.it/PDFfiles/PressReleaseMay06.pdf.

Deseriis, M. and Marano, G. *Net.Art. L'arte della connessione,* Milano: Shake Edizioni, 2003.

DiBona, C., Ockam, S. and Stone, M. *Open Sources: Voices from the Open Source Revolution,* Sebastopol: O'Reilly Publishing, 1999.

Dick, P. K. *The Simulacra,* New York: Ace Books, 1964.

Donath, J. and boyd, D. M. 'Public displays of connection', *BT Technology Journal* 22.4 (2004): 71-82.

Downes, L. and Mui, C. *Unleashing the Killer App: Digital Strategies for Market Dominance,* Boston, Mass.: Harvard Business School Press, 1998.

Drew, J. 'From the Gulf War to the Battle of Seattle: Building an International Alternative Media Network', in Chandler, A. and Neumark, N. (eds) *At a Distance: Precursors to Art and Activism on the Internet,* Cambridge, Mass: MIT Press, 2005, pp. 210-224.

É. Durkheim, *De la division du travail social,* Paris: PUF, 8th edition 1967. English translation by G. Simpson, *On the Division of Labour in Society,* New York: The MacMillan Company, 1933.

Flichy, P. *L'imaginaire d'Internet,* Paris: La Découverte, 2001.

Florida, R. *The Rise of the Creative Class: And How It's Transforming Work, Leisure, Com-*

munity and Everyday Life, New York: Basic Books, 2002.

Formenti, C. *Mercanti di Futuro,* Torino: Einaudi, 2002.

—. 'Composizione di classe, tecnologie di rete e post-democrazia', in Di Corinto, A. (ed.) *L'innovazione necessaria,* Milano: RGB-Area 51, 2005.

—. *Cybersoviet. Utopie postdemocratiche e nuovi media,* Milano: Raffaello Cortina Editore, 2008.

Fuster i Morell, M. 'The new web communities and political culture', in VV.AA., *Networked Politics: Rethinking political organisation in an age of movements and networks,* Seminar Networked Politics, Berlin, June 2007, https://www.scribd.com/document/118788762/Networked-Politics-Rethinking-political-organization-in-an-age-of-movements-and-networks.

Gardner, H. *Frames of Mind: The Theory of Multiple Intelligences,* New York: Basic Books, 1983.

Gasperoni, G. and Marradi, A. 'Metodo e tecniche nelle scienze sociali', in *Enciclopedia delle Scienze Sociali,* vol. v, Roma: Istituto della Enciclopedia Italiana, 1996, pp. 624-643.

Gibson, J. J. *The Ecological Approach to Visual Perception,* London: Hillsdale, 1986.

Giddens, A. *Modernity and Self-Identity: Self and Society in the Late Modern Age,* London: Polity Press, 1991.

Goldsmith, J. and Wu, T. *Who Controls the Internet? Illusions of a Borderless World,* New York: Oxford University Press, 2006.

Graham, S. 'Introduction: Cities, Warfare, and States of Emergency', in

Graham, S. (eds) *Cities, War and Terrorism. Towards an Urban Geopolitics,* Malden, Mass.: Blackwell Publishing, 2004, pp. 1-25.

—. 'Software-sorted geographies', *Progress in Human Geography* 29.5 (2005): 1-19.

Graham, P. 'Web 2.0', November 2005, http://www.paulgraham.com/web20.html.

Grassmuck, V. 'Copyright Instead of Data Protection', in Stocker, G. and Schöpf, C. (eds) *Goodbye Privacy. Ars Electronica 2007,* Ostfildern: Hatje Cantz Verlag, 2007.

Greimas, A. J. and Courtés, J. *Sémiotique: Dictionnaire raisonné de la théorie du langage,* Paris: Hachette, 1979.

Grossman, L. 'Time's Person of the Year: You', *Time,* 13 December 2006.

Hafner, K. and Lyon, M. *Where Wizards Stay Up Late: The Origins of The Internet*, New York: Simon & Schuster, 1996.

Hagel, J. and Armstrong, A. G. *Net Gain: Expanding Markets Through Virtual Communities*, Boston, Mass.: Harvard Business School Press, 1997.

Halleck, D. D. 'Una tempesta coinvolgente. Il cyber-forum aperto Indymedia', in Pasquinelli, M. (eds) *Media Activism. Strategie e pratiche della comunicazione indipendente*, Roma: DeriveApprodi, 2002.

Haraway, D. 'A Cyborg Manifesto. Science, Technology, and Socialist-Feminism in the 1980s', *Socialist Review*, 80 (1985): 65--108. Reprinted in Haraway, D. (ed.) *Simians, Cyborgs and Women: The Reinvention of Nature,* New York: Routledge, 1991: 149-181.

—. *Primate Visions: Gender, Race, and Nature in the World of Modern Science,* New York: Routledge, 1989.

—. *Modest_witness@Second_Millenium.FemaleMan_meets_Onco_ Mouse™: Feminism and Technoscience,* New York: Routledge, 1997.

Harvey, D. *The Condition of Postmodernity: An Enquiry into the Origins of Cultural Change,* Oxford: Blackwell, 1989.

Hayles, K. *How We Become Posthuman*, Chicago: University of Chicago Press, 1999.

Himanen, P. *The Hacker Ethic and the Spirit of the Information Age,* New York: Random House, 2001.

Hobijn, E. and Broeckmann, A. 'Techno-parasites: bringing the machinic unconscious to life', *Lecture at the 5th Cyberconference, Madrid, 1996,* http://v2.nl/archive/articles/techno-parasites.

Hodgkinson, T. 'With friends like these...', *The Guardian*, 14 January 2008, https://www.theguardian.com/technology/2008/jan/14/facebook.

Hornik, D. 'Where's the Money in the Long Tail?', *Venture Blog*, 13 December 2005, http://www.ventureblog.com/2005/12/wheres-the-money-in-the-long-tail.html.

Ippolita collective. *Luci e ombre di Google*, Milano: Feltrinelli, 2007.

Jacobs, J. *The Death and Life of Great American Cities,* New York: Random House, 1961.

Jenkins, H. *Convergence Culture: Where Old and New Media Collide*, New York-London: New York University Press, 2006.

Jennings, T. 'Fidonet History and Operation', February 1985, http://www.rxn.com/~net282/fidonet.jennings.history.1.txt.

Jones, G. S. *Cybersociety*, Thousand Oaks, Ca.: Sage Publications, 1995.

—. *Cybersociety 2.0: Revisiting Computer-Mediated Communication and Community*, Thousand Oaks, Cal.: Sage Publications, 1998.

Kelly, K. 'The Web Runs on Love, not Greed', *The Wall Street Journal*, 4 January 2002, https://kk.org/wp-content/uploads/2010/06/Kevin-Kelly_-The-Web-Runs-on-Love-Not-Greed.pdf.

Kim, A. J. *Community Building on the Web: Secret Strategies for Successful Online Communities*, London: Addison Wesley, 2000.

Kogawa, T. 'Minima Memoranda: a note on streaming media', in Waag Society for Old and New Media (ed.) *Next Five Minutes 3 Workbook*, Amsterdam: De Waag, 1999, pp. 103-104.

Kopomaa, T. *City in Your Pocket: Birth of the Mobile Information Society*, Helsinki: Gaudeamus, 2000.

Landowski, E. *La société réfléchie*, Paris: Seuil, 1989.

Lanzara, G.F. and Morner, M. 'Artifacts rule! How Organizing Happens in Open Source Software Projects', in Czarniawska, B. and Hernes, T. (eds) *Actor Network Theory and Organizing*, Copenhagen: Liber, 2005, pp. 67-90.

Lash, S. and Urry, J. *The End of Organized Capitalism*, Madison: University of Wisconsin Press, 1987.

Latham, R. and Sassen, S. 'Digital Formations: Constructing an Object of Study', in Latham, R. and Sassen, S. (eds) *Digital Formations: IT and New Architectures in the Global Realm*, Princeton: Princeton University Press, 2005, pp. 1-33.

Latour, B. 'How to Talk About the Body?: The Normative Dimension of Science Studies', in *Body & Society* 10.2--3 (2004): 205-229.

—. *Reassembling the Social. An Introduction to Actor-Network-Theory*, Oxford: Oxford University Press, 2005.

—. 'From Realpolitik to Dingpolitik Or How to Make Things Public', in Latour, B. and Weibel, P. (eds) *Making Things Public: Atmospheres of Democracy*, Cambridge, Mass.: MIT Press, 2005, pp. 14-43.

Latour, B. and Weibel, P. (eds) *Iconoclash. Beyond the Image Wars in Science, Religion, and Art*, Cambridge, Mass.: MIT Press, 2002.

Lessig, L. *Code and Other Laws of Cyberspace*, New York: Basic Books, 1999.

—. *The Future of Ideas: The Fate of the Commons in a Connected World,* New York: Random House, 2001.

Levy, S. *Hackers: Heroes of the Computer Revolution,* New York: Dell Book, 1985.

Lovink, G. *Dark Fiber*, Cambridge, Mass: MIT Press, 2002.

—. My First Recession: Critical Internet Culture in Transition, Rotterdam: V2_NAi Publishers, 2003. Italian edition Internet non è il paradiso: reti sociali e critica della cibercultura, Milano: Apogeo, 2004.

—. *Zero comments*, New York: Routledge, 2007. Italian edition *Zero Comments. Teoria critica di Internet,* Milano: Bruno Mondadori, 2007.

Lovink, G. and Rossiter, N. 'Dawn of the Organised Networks', *Fibreculture Journal* 5(2005), http://journal.fibreculture.org/issue5/lovink_rossiter_print.html.

Lovink, G. and Rossiter, N. *Organization after Social Media*, Colchester / New York / Port Watson: Minor Compositions, 2018.

Lyon, D. *Surveillance as Social Sorting: Privacy, Risk and Automated Discrimination,* London: Routledge, 2002.

Marres, N. *Material Participation: Technology, the Environment and Everyday Publics,* New York: Palgrave MacMillan, 2012.

Masanès, J. 'Context in a Networked Environment: Some considerations before starting thinking about contextualisation of online contents'. *Online Archives of Media Art* conference. *re:place 2007. On the Histories of Media, Art, Science and Technology* conference, Berlin, 14-18 November 2007.

Mascio, L. 'Le comunità virtuali *text-based*', *Versus*, 2003.

Mattelart, A. *Histoire de la société de l'information*, Paris: La Découverte, 2001.

Mauss, M. and Halls, W. D. *The Gift: The Form and Reason for Exchange in Archaic Societies,* New York: Norton, 1990.

McCarty, D. 'Nettime: the legend and the myth', *EduEDA. The Educational Encyclopedia*, 1997, http://www.edueda.net/index.php?title=Nettime:_the_legend_and_the_myth (in Italian).

Meikle, G. *Future Active*, Sydney: Pluto Press Australia, 2002.

Neumark, N. 'Art/Activism', in Chandler, A. and Neumark, N. (eds) *At a Distance: Precursors to Art and Activism on the Internet*, Cambridge, Mass: MIT Press, 2005, pp. 2-24.

Nielsen, J. *Designing Web Usability*, Indianapolis: New Riders, 1999.

—. 'The 90-9-1 Rule for Participation Inequality in Social Media and Online Communities', *Nielsen Norman Group Newsletter*, 9 October 2006, http://www.useit.com/alertbox/participation_inequality.html.

Nissenbaum, H. 'Privacy in Context', in Stocker, G. and Schöpf, C. (eds) *Goodbye Privacy. Ars Electronica 2007*, Ostfildern: Hatje Cantz Verlag, 2007.

Norman, D. A. *The Psychology of Everyday Things*, New York: Basic Books, 1988.

Oldenburg, R. *The Great Good Place: Cafes, Coffee Shops, Community Centers, Beauty Parlors, General Stores, Bars, Hangouts, and How They Get You through the Day*, New York: Paragon House, 1991.

O'Reilly, T. 'What Is Web 2.0. Design Patterns and Business Models for the Next Generation of Software', *O'Reilly*, 30 September 2005, https://www.oreilly.com/pub/a/web2/archive/what-is-web-20.html.

—. 'Web 2.0 Compact Definition: Trying Again', *O'Reilly*, December 10 2006, http://radar.oreilly.com/2006/12/web-20-compact-definition-tryi.html.

Paccagnella, L. *La comunicazione al computer: Sociologia delle reti telematiche*, Bologna: Il Mulino, 2000.

Papert, S. *Mindstorms: children, computers, and powerful ideas*, New York: Basic Books, 1980.

—. *The children's machine: rethinking school in the age of the computer*, New York: Basic Books, 1993.

Pariser, E. *The Filter Bubble: What the internet is hiding from you*, New York: Penguin Press, 2011.

Pasquinelli, M. (eds) *Media Activism. Strategie e pratiche della comunicazione indipendente*, Roma: DeriveApprodi, 2002.

—. *Animal Spirit. A Bestiary of the Commons*, Rotterdam: NAi Publishers, 2008.

Pelizza, A. 'Dall'Auditel al General Intellect. Un modello evolutivo del pubblico televisivo', in Adamoli, P. and Marinelli, M. (eds) *Comunicazione, media e società. Premio Baskerville 'Mauro Wolf' 2004*, Bologna: Baskerville, 2005, pp. 45-78.

—. (2009), *Tracing back Communities: An Analysis of Ars Electronica's Digital Communities archive from an ANT perspective.* Ph.D. thesis, University of Milan-Bicocca.

—. 'Comunicare l'immediatezza. Una televisione dal basso a Rotterdam' [Communicating Immediacy. A grassroots TV broadcaster in Rotterdam], *Inchiesta. Rivista di Studi Politici,* 152. April/June (2006): 12-18.

—. 'Stretching the Line into a Borderland of Potentiality. Communication technologies between security tactics and cultural practices', in Aurigi, A. and De Cindio, F. (eds) *Augmented Urban Spaces. Articulating the Physical and Electronic City,* Aldershot: Ashgate, 2008, pp. 235-254.

—. 'Openness as an Asset: A classification system for online communities based on Actor-Network Theory', *WikiSym 2010. 6th International Symposium on Wikis and Open Collaboration,* New York: ACM Press, 2010. DOI: 10.1145/1832772.1832784, http://dl.acm.org/citation.cfm?id=1832784&preflayout=tabs.

Prix Ars Electronica. 'Call for Digital Communities application' http://www.aec.at/prix_categories_en.php?cat=Digital%20Communities, 2004.

Raymond, E. *The Cathedral and the Bazaar: Musings on Linux and Open Source by an Accidental Revolutionary,* Sebastopol, O'Reilly, 1999.

Rheingold, H. *The Virtual Community: Homesteading on the Electronic Frontier, Reading,* Mass.: Addison-Wesley, 1993/2000.

—. Smart Mobs: the Next Social Revolution, New York: Basic Books, 2002.

Ricoeur, P. *Lectures on Ideology and Utopia,* New York: Columbia University Press, 1986.

Rodotà, S. *Tecnopolitica,* Roma-Bari: Laterza, 1997.

Rossiter, N. 'Creative Industries, Comparative Media Theory, and the Limits of Critique from Within', *Topia: A Canadian Journal of Cultural Studies* 11 (2004): 21-48.

Rössler, B. *The Value of Privacy,* London: Polity Press, 2005.

Rullani, E., 'Lavoro immateriale e società della conoscenza', in Gosetti G. (ed.), *Il lavoro: condizioni, problemi, sfide,* Milan: Franco Angeli, 2011, pp.13-34.

Sassen, S. *Territory, Authority, Rights: from medieval to global assemblages,* Princeton: Princeton University Press, 2006.

Saxenian, A. *Regional Advantage: Culture and Competition in Silicon Valley and Route 128,* Cambridge, Mass.: Harvard University Press, 1994.

Scott, A. J. *Metropolis*, Los Angeles: University of California Press, 1988.

Shannon, C. and Weaver, W. *A Mathematical Theory of Communication*, Urbana-Champaign, Ill.: University of Illinois Press, 1949.

Shirky, C. 'Social Software and the Politics of Groups', posting to Networks, Economics, and Culture mailing list, 2003, http://shirky.com/writings/group_politics.html.

Silver, D. 'Looking Backwards, Looking Forwards: Cyberculture Studies, 1990-2000', in Gaunlett, D. (ed.) *Web.Studies*, London: Arnold Publishers, 2000, pp. 19-30.

Smith, M. *Voices from the WELL: The Logic of the Virtual Commons*, Unpublished dissertation at University California Los Angeles, Los Angeles, 1992, https://dlc.dlib.indiana.edu/dlc/bitstream/handle/10535/4363/Voices_from_the_WELL.pdf?sequence=1&isAllowed=y.

Smith, M. and Kollock, P. *Communities in Cyberspace*, New York: Routledge, 1999.

Stone, A. R. *The War of Desire and Technology, at the Close of the Mechanical Age,* Cambridge, Mass.: MIT Press, 1995.

Storper, M. *The Regional World*, New York: Guilford Press, 1997.

Strangelove, M. 'Free-Nets: community computing systems and the rise of the electronic citizen', *Online Access* 8, (Spring, 2004).

Strum, S. C. 'Un societé complexe sans culture matérérielle: Le cas des babbouins', in Latour, B. and Lemonnier, P (eds) *De la préhistoire aux missiles balistiques*, Paris: La Découverte, 1994, pp. 27-44.

Suchman, L. A. Plans and Situated Actions: The Problem of Human-Machine Communication, New York: Cambridge University Press, 1987.

Swisher, K. 'Chatty Zuckerberg Tells All About Facebook Finances', *All Things Digital*, 31 January 2008, http://kara.allthingsd.com/20080131/chatty-zuckerberg-tells-all-about-facebook-finances/.

Tanz, J. 'How Silicon Valley Utopianism Brought You the Dystopian Trump Presidency', *Wired*, 20 January 2017, https://www.wired.com/2017/01/silicon-valley-utopianism-brought-dystopian-trump-presidency/?mbid=nl_12217_p3&CNDID.

Taylor, M. *The Possibility of Cooperation*, Cambridge: Cambridge University Press, 1987.

Jeffrey I. Cole et al., 'The 2007 Digital Future Report: Surveying the Digital Future. Year Six.' USC Annenberg School Center for the Digital Future. 2007. https://www.digitalcenter.org/wp-content/uploads/2013/02/2007_digital_future_report-year6.pdf

Tönnies, F. *Gemeinschaft und Gesellschaft*, Leipzig: Buske, 8th edition 1935. English translation by C. P. Loomis, *Community and Society*, Mineola, N.Y.: Dover Publications, 2002.

Turner, F. *From Counterculture to Cyberculture: Stewart Brand, the Whole Earth Network, and the Rise of Digital Utopianism*, Chicago and London: The University of Chicago Press, 2006.

Visciola, M. *Usabilità dei siti web*, Milano: Apogeo, 2000.

Wark, M. *A Hacker Manifesto*, Cambridge, Mass.: Harvard University Press, 2004.

Weber, R.P. *Basic Content Analysis*, Newbury Park, CA.: Sage Publications, 1990.

Weber, T. 'YouTubers to get ad money share', *BBC News*, 27 January 2007, http://news.bbc.co.uk/2/hi/business/6305957.stm.

Wellman, B. 'The Community Question: the Intimate Networks of East Yorkers', *American Journal of Sociology*, 84: 1(1979), 201-31.

—. 'Structural analysis: from method and metaphor to theory and substance', in Wellman, B. and Berkowitz, S. D. (eds) *Social Structures: A Network Approach*, Cambridge: Cambridge University Press, 1988, pp. 19-61.

—. 'Physical place and cyberplace: The rise of personalized networking', *International Journal of Urban and Regional Research* 25.2 (2001): 227-252.

Wellman, B., Carrington, P. J. and Hall, A. 'Networks as personal communities', in Wellman B. and Berkowitz S. D. (eds) *Social structures: A network approach*, Cambridge, Mass.: Cambridge University Press, 1988, pp. 130-183.

Wellman, B. and Gulia, M. 'Netsurfers don't ride alone: virtual communities as communities', in Wellman, B. (ed.) *Networks in the Global Village*, Boulder, Col.: Westview Press, 1999, pp. 331-366.

Wellman, B. and Leighton, B. 'Networks, Neighborhoods and Communities. Approaches to the Study of the Community Question', *Urban Affairs Quarterly* 14 (1979): 363-90.

Whitfield, S. J. *The Culture of the Cold War*, Baltimore: John Hopkins University Press, 1996.

Wiener, N. *Cybernetics: Or Control and Communication in the Animal and the Machine*, Paris: Hermann & Cie, 1948.

Wittgenstein, L. *The Blue and Brown Books*, Oxford: Blackwell, 1975.

Woolgar, S. 'Configuring the User: The Case of Usability Trials,' in Law, J. (ed.) *A Sociology of Monsters: Essays on Power, Technology and Domination*, London: Routledge, 1991, pp.

57--99.

Zizek, S. 'Nobody has to be vile', *London Review of Books*, 2006, http://www.lrb.co.uk/v28/n07/zize01_.html.

www.ingramcontent.com/pod-product-compliance
Lightning Source LLC
LaVergne TN
LVHW012329060326
832902LV00011B/1793